Broken for His Glory

What Life is All About

Why God Allows Suffering

*A merry heart maketh a cheerful countenance:
but by sorrow of the heart
the spirit is broken.*

PROVERBS 15:13

LIVED AND WRITTEN BY

ESTHER SUTER

PUBLISHED BY FIDELI PUBLISHING INC.

ISBN: 978-1-962402-22-4

Fideli Publishing, Inc.
119 W. Morgan St.
Martinsville, IN 46151

www.FideliPublishing.com

Contents

Acknowledgements

I first want to thank and praise the Father, Son and the Holy Spirit for being with me and helping me through my whole life. For teaching me the things I have written in this book.

They have helped me become a new and better person, to use them to fight and win many spiritual battles. I hope this book helps many others in the same way.

I want to thank Rhonda Burpo, Paula Deweese, Juanita Edwards and Sheila Green, my good and close friends. Their encouragement motivated me to write this book.

I had wanted to, and believed I should, but I do not type. I tried a few times but it didn't work out and I believe that was because I didn't have all the information I needed, so I believed it just wasn't time to write it yet.

I want to especially thank Paula DeWeese because she unselfishly volunteered to type it for me, which she did.

I also want to especially thank, with much gratitude, Patsy Thacker, who worked on editing and preparing this book to be published. She had some help from her husband, Donald. They worked on it this whole spring and summer. They are wonderful neighbors and friends.

May God grant them many blessings for their generous kindness. May He also bless those who read this book. May He open their understanding that they may learn and grow much in their souls and spirits.

I would also like to thank Aaron Maple. He doesn't know how much he encouraged me to write this book. Thanks, Aaron!

I also give a great big thank you to J. R. Landis and my brother, James McCartney, for the help they gave me.

I also give a great big thank you to J.R. Landis, my wonderful brother James McCartney and my precious daughter Melissa Contrares for the monitary and encouraging help they so freely gave.

I want everyone who helped me in this endeavour to know that I not only thank them, but love them one and all for their kindness, generosity and the work they put into helping me write and publish this book.

Foreword

The more we grow, the more we come to know the power of God in our lives. This book will, with out a doubt, help you grow in your relationship with our amazing Creator. Esther has always inspired me with her words, wisdom and experience. You will be encouraged and challenged as you read the pages of spiritual insight that have come through Esther's life. She has truly fought the good fight and has something great to share with you.

I know that my wife and I, as well as many others, have been impacted by the ministry and example of Esther's life. You will come to know this same ministry as you read this book. As God breaks us of our sin, He then restores us into the image that He destined for us to be. Esther is one whose image has been restored as a beautiful testimony of God's faithfulness and power. You, too, will experience God's faithfulness and power as you journey through the words written by a faithful servant of The Most High. Allow God to open up your heart as you read this heartfelt tapestry of a life rescued, changed and used for the glory of the Lord.

John Barrett,
Author, and associate pastor of Hoosier Harvest Church

Introduction

I repeatedly wrote certain scriptures, phrases and instructions all through this book. I have found that if I repeat something to a person a number of times, they will soon use them in their own conversation.

These are some things the Holy Spirit has repeated to me many times through the years. He wanted me, as I do you, to know they are very important to our understanding why certain things take place in our lives.

They can be used as guideposts as we progress in our spiritual walk.

It is like we were taught the alphabet. Going over and over it until we knew and could use it.

It is my hope that this will be a tool that you will use often as you grow.

A word about the devil and the word satan. In this book satan's name will be written with small "s" to show that he is not worthy that it should be capitalized. He is the monstrous epitome of evil. He will get what he deserves.

CHAPTER 1

Love

What is the meaning of life? What is life all about? Why am I here? What is God's will for me? I asked these questions one day while cleaning my kitchen floor. Instantly the Holy Spirit gave me the scripture Matthew 22:37-39. It tells us to love God with all our heart, soul, mind and strength and to love our neighbor as ourselves. God creates a spirit being and puts it in a physical body. He sent us here to choose Him and His eternal values or satan and his sinful pleasures. God is love. If we seek His eternal values He will create His love in our hearts.

There is a scripture that tells us to store up treasure in Heaven. When I first read this I could not understand how we could take anything to Heaven. I was pretty ignorant and dense when I first turned my life over to Jesus. The Holy Spirit put into my spirit, "Your treasure in Heaven is the Godlike qualities that you acquire while here on earth." My next question was what are Godlike qualities? The answer: They are the fruits of the Holy Spirit, i.e., love, joy, peace, gentleness, tenderness, patience, kindness, goodness, faithfulness, self-control and also mercy, forgiveness and tolerance.

In our nature we want everyone to love us. We buy them things, we work for love, and we even give sex for love. We all want to be loved. If we feel or believe just one person loves us, we do not feel we are all alone in this world. If we believe no one loves us then we feel we are all alone with no one to help or protect us. We will begin trying anything we think that will get someone to love us.

I know a few people who believed as a child that no one loved them but someone felt sorry for them when they were ill or hurt. They were either sick or suffering something all their lives because they had substituted sympathy for love. They reasoned, "No one loves me but I can get them to feel sorry for me." They will always be ready to tell anyone who will listen to what sickness or any other suffering is going on in their lives. They will unconsciously cause these things themselves. They will not eat a healthy diet or take good care of themselves.

The important word is unconsciously. We do many things to get people to love us but we do not realize that is the motive behind our actions. We feel sorry for ourselves and want everyone else to feel sorry for us too. We all want to be loved! However, nowhere in the Bible does it tell us to strive to be loved. The Bible tells us to give love. Give and it shall be given to you. You reap what you sow. It is more blessed to give than to receive. Love God and love your neighbor as yourself.

My parents were angry and violent people. They tried to solve their problems with anger. If that did not work they would start hitting. We learn by the example our parents display. As children we look at the actions of those around us. We do not really know how to become a man or woman when we grow up; therefore, we look at those around us and copy their actions.

It is written in the Bible to raise up a child in the way he should go, and when he is old he will not depart from it. We are all born with a sinful nature. It is our nature to sin and it is the parent's job to train children to control that nature and teach and train them God's ways. Why? Because children will not depart from how they are taught and trained when they get old—good or bad. The training is put into the subconscious mind. What the subconscious believes will make us live that way. If we are told we are dumb, ugly, or not good enough, we will go through life believing and feeling that about ourselves. We will not depart from feeling that when we are old.

If we feel that way we will never like ourselves and we will always believe no one else likes us either. We will always feel lonely because we have isolated ourselves. We never feel a real oneness with others, but we will try to find someone who will love us. We will always feel empty and alone. We will seek someone or something to fill the emptiness and take away the loneliness. The only one who can change that is Jesus. I was living that life. After I turned my life over to Jesus, even though I was married, I still felt empty and alone. I would pray to be able to be in love and feel loved. After my husband died, I began the seeking again.

One night I dreamed I walked up some stairs. Jesus was at the top looking out a window. He looked very sad. I asked Him why and he answered, "My family has gone shopping. They just keep shopping and shopping. I love them and want them to come home so I can show them I love them. They will not come home so that I can. They all have emptiness here." He put his hand over his heart. "They are all trying to fill the emptiness but they never will. It is a spiritual emptiness and I am the only one who can fill it. But they will not come home and let me do that and show them that I love them."

When I awoke, I realized that was what I was doing. The Holy Spirit showed me that I had made falling in love and having someone love me an idol. That was my greatest desire in life. He gave me the scripture Matthew 6:33. "Seek first the Kingdom of God and His righteousness. His righteousness is the fruit of the Holy Spirit." All of my life I had been seeking love and all the time I was doing the opposite of God's will.

It was very difficult for me to give up my idol. I went through a very strong emotional battle with myself but, with the Lord's help, I won the battle. At first I would not show love because I had been very hurt by my mother and others as I grew up. The devil had put into my subconscious mind that if I loved I would suffer. Loving was one of my greatest fears. I had a stony heart. After Jesus gave me the dream, I would still not let myself show love that I did not feel.

One morning as I awoke, the Holy Spirit gave me this poem:

A time to give a crust of bread.
A time to pat a troubled head.
A time to teach a lesson learned.
A time to give a dollar earned
A time for past stories to be told.

A time to loosen a loving hold.
A time to give a loving smile.
A time to go an extra mile.
Oh well, oh well, too bad the feeling.
Alas, alas, another dealing.

The poem told me there were many ways to give love even if I did not feel it. Love is the greatest commandment. I was not to go by my feelings or lack of them. I was to obey God's commandment and give love in actions.

He showed me that even if I hated someone, I was not to let that feeling control my actions. I've had people say (and I have said it myself in earlier times): "You are a hypocrite if you pretend that you like someone you really hate." If you do it just to hide your real feelings, it is hypocritical; however, if you are doing it to be in obedience to God, it is not hypocritical. We will be obeying the Word of God and not letting our sinful self and feelings control us.

When the poem stated, "Too bad the feeling, alas, alas, another dealing," it meant that I had refused (because of fear) to show or express love. I was going to have to go through some more suffering until I would obey. I would be listening to someone tell of suffering they were going through, and I would want to put my arm around them to show them love and comfort; however, something inside seemed to close and prevent me from doing that.

After the poem I began making myself hug people. It was very difficult at first, but it gradually got easier. Now it comes naturally and the feelings are there also. I had been making myself do this for a while when one night I dreamed of a garden. In the dream I was very happy to see the plants that were growing. They were healthy, flourishing plants and I was given the understanding that the seeds of love I had planted were growing. I was beginning to feel and show love without the fear. Not only that, but people were beginning to return that love. I was giving so I was receiving just as God's Word tells us we will. His Word is true!!

So do not worry about people loving you. You show them love and it will naturally come back to you. It probably will not happen the next day. It takes time for seeds planted to grow, but grow they will. Give and it will be given to you. People think that means just money but it does not. It means love, forgiveness, help, mercy, acceptance and so forth.

Try it, you will like it. Life is so much better when we are giving and receiving love rather than trying to control other people's emotions all the time. That is very stressful and frustrating. In God's Word, it tells us to let the love of God be shed abroad in our hearts. That means to let the Holy Spirit create God's love in us. God's love is perfect. Perfect love casts out fear.

I read the scripture that perfect love casts out fear. I could not grasp the real meaning of that scripture. I had been praying about it one day. That night I dreamed a large bear was chasing me. I was running in terror. I came to a garage that had an old-fashioned barrel beside it. I thought if I jumped on the barrel I could get on the garage roof and the bear could not reach me, so I did that.

When I reached the roof I turned and saw that the bear had gotten on the barrel also and was climbing onto the roof. I was terrified and felt helpless. I was sure I was going to die. The bear looked at me with fear in his eyes and pointed at his throat. I knew he had something lodged in his throat that was choking him to death and he was begging me with his eyes to save him!

I thought if I saved him then he would kill me, but I felt sorry for him and wanted to help him. I thought if I stick my hand in his mouth and dislodge the thing choking him, he would then bite off my hand. I was still very afraid but could not just watch him suffer and die, so I stuck my hand in his mouth and dislodged whatever it was that was choking him. He jumped up on the roof, hugged me and said, "Oh, thank you, thank you." As I awoke I heard someone say to me, "Perfect love casts out fear."

I understood that the fear of loving was a self-centered fear and I was thinking only of myself. The Holy Spirit said very forcefully for me to get my mind off of myself and think of others, put others first!

I have heard and read many times someone will say that their Mom or Dad loved their brother or sister more than they loved them. Some of these people saying this were in their 40's and 50's and were still hurt because Mom or Dad did not love them the most. My mother did not love me at all. My dad drank and always had one mistress after another. We lived in a shack and he would give Mom barely enough money to feed us. We went hungry at times.

I had three brothers and I was the only girl. Mom was full of anger, rage and jealousy. She took that out on me. She finally got the courage to get a job in a factory. She would buy my brother's clothes for school but she did not buy me any. She did buy me some underwear and socks. I just wore what others gave me. I thought she loved my older brother more than me because she let him physically, mentally and emotionally abuse me. He was two years older, but she would not punish or correct him. At times I hated him and wanted him to die so I would be free of him. Sometimes I felt sorry for him because adults abused us both.

After I turned my life over to Jesus, He began bringing out the things of my childhood that satan had used to try to destroy me. I had buried most of it in the depths of my subconscious but He began to bring it out for me to acknowledge and deal with. He showed me that as a child Mom told me no one liked girls. I believed no one loved me. They loved my brothers but not me. I prayed for Jesus to give me His thoughts and attitudes about it.

"Let the love of God be shed abroad in your hearts." Matthew 5:43 through 48 tells us God's will. It also tells us what perfect love is: Perfect love means we are willing to suffer and/or die for others. Jesus said, "Love one another as I have loved you." He sacrificed His life for others. We can give our lives in ways other than death. The Bible tells men to give their lives for their wives and to live their lives for the welfare of their wives and not for themselves. Some mothers live their lives for their family.

So many people live their whole lives trying to get other people to love them. Many have the desire to be loved the most or be the only one to be loved. It is a "me first" problem. Scripture tells us that they who want to be first will be last. The people who want to be loved the most usually (if not always) feel unloved, as the Bible tells us. The Bible is true and our lives are judged by what is written in it whether we believe it or not or whether we know it or not.

When we believe someone is loved more than we are, we will be envious and angry with him or her and the one we think is being unfair to us by loving someone else more. We will say and do things to hurt and/or embarrass them. Therefore, we will be hurt and embarrassed also. It may not come from them but it will come. We reap what we sow—another scripture by which we are judged. The Bible tells us the greatest spiritual gift is love. Give and it will be given to you, pressed down, shaken together and running over.

Jesus blesses us for our obedience by loving us through others. He gave us the instruction book to teach us how to live our lives so we do not have to suffer. Love forgives, thinks no ill will, nor returns evil for evil. Love fulfills the law, does not lie, cheat or steal. It does not commit adultery, it does not covet or murder. It naturally obeys God's laws.

Love should be our most desired gift. We all have a sinful nature that we need to be freed from. It prevents us from doing God's will. So look within. What is your desire? To love or be loved? To give love or take it away from someone else? Your future happiness depends on your answers. Our actions today determine our lives tomorrow. Jesus said, "If you love me keep my commandments."

I asked the Lord one day, "What is the basic meaning of the Bible?" He gave me the same scripture that He gave when I asked Him what life was all about. Matthew 22:37-39, "Love God with all your heart, soul, mind and strength and your neighbor as yourself."

The devil gives us the opposite of God's will. He wants us to focus on self and trying to get people to love us. If we do, we will never be happy. God's will is the only thing that will make us happy. If we are not happy, we need to examine ourselves and find out what is in us preventing us from being happy.

We are born being self-centered and self-absorbed. Our parents are to show and teach us to love. That should be the first thing we learn in life—to love. Now-a-days parents are usually too busy or self-absorbed themselves to express much love. Some are too damaged from their own growing up that they never learned how to show love. My brothers and I all grew up without being taught how to love. We were all hurt and rejected so that we all had a fear of expressing love. Then we were unable to teach love to our children.

There is a scripture that tell us the sins of the parents are visited on the children. We pass them down and teach them to our children—generation to generation. Someone made the point one time that in the 1800s some people complained as our generation does, that the next generation was worse than their generation had been. I think they do get worse with every generation because each one passes on their sins. Thank God He intervenes and saves, and some people are still able to love and teach love to their children.

The 13th chapter of First Corinthians tells us what love is, what it does and what it does not do. Matthew 6:33 tells us to seek God's love above all else and to seek His righteousness first. God is love, which is His righteousness. Jesus said that love fulfills the law. If we have God's love created in us (and it does have to be put in us by God), we will never break His laws. We will not steal, kill, lie, covet, commit adultery, etc. When we do these things, we are acting out of self-love. We matter and others do not.

The problems many people encounter in receiving and expressing God's love are (1) an inability to know and experience God's love and to love Him in return, and (2) the inability to love and receive love from others. God stands ready to produce His love within us (Galatians 5:33). We will know we love God when we love our brothers and sisters in Christ and our fellow man, which includes our enemies. The Holy Spirit told me one time that someone may be my enemy but I do not have to be their enemy.

Jesus said, "If you keep my commandments, you shall abide in my love just as I have kept my Father's and abide in His love. These things I have told you that My joy might remain in you and that your joy might be full." When we accept Jesus as our Savior, we are born of the Holy Spirit. God changes our old nature and gives us love for others, if we will receive it.

One day I was painting my living room when I noticed a woman walking toward my house. I realized it was one of my ex-sisters-in law whom I hated. I was a brand new babe in Christ so my human spirit had been reborn but my sinful soul still had to be cleaned up and restored. When I saw her, I was instantly angry that she was coming to my house. I said, "Oh no, Lord, I do not want her here. I do not even want her in my yard." He put the scripture in my mind, "Love your enemies." " I do not want to love her," I answered. Another scripture came to me, "Love one another as I have loved you." "I do not want to love her. If you want her to be loved, you will have to do it because I don't want to."

All this happened in a second or two. I got down off the ladder and went out the door and through my front yard to meet her because, as I told the Lord, I did not even want her in my yard. I met her at the edge of my yard. I looked her in the eyes and suddenly this great overwhelming love came into me and rushed out of me to her. I put my arms around her and told her I was glad she was there and I meant every word. God had taken me at my word and He loved her through me. In the process He also filled me with love for her. I still love her to this day even though she died some years ago.

She stayed for three days and was saved during that time. She told me later that she had asked Jesus to save her because of the love that came from me which was God's love that He put in me. I was truthful when I told Him I did not want to love her. So He did it for me and for her.

Another time I had some not-so-desirable neighbors. Sometimes they had drinking parties all night especially on Saturday night. I had to run a fan all night to drown out their noise so I could get some sleep because I got up early Sunday morning for church. They threw their beer cans and chip bags over my fence for me to clean up the next day. I prayed and prayed for years for them to move. They stayed for about twenty years.

One Saturday night I arrived home about 9:30 after visiting one of my brothers and his wife, and I saw these neighbors were having another one of their parties. "Oh, Lord, please give me a break," I pleaded. "They will be out there all night," I complained. As I put the key in my back door lock, I was suddenly filled with love for them. I thought (and was very sincere), "I hope they have a good time!" I went in and went to bed and went to sleep. From then on I loved them. I put their names in at church for prayer for their salvation. I also prayed for them for a few years even though after a couple months they moved. They now attend the same church I attend. The Lord kept them there until I loved them, then He moved them.

So, you see, God is able to create His love in us. We know we can never love our enemies, but God knows He can create love for them in us. With God all things are possible. Jesus said, "Without me you can do nothing." However, In Philippians, Paul tells us, "We can do ALL things through Christ who strengthens us."

We may have our NATURAL feelings of love but a lot of the time it is selfish love. We want to be loved back or we get hurt or angry if that love is not returned, but God's supernatural love is perfect love and, as I wrote earlier, perfect love casts out fear. It also casts out selfishness and self-centeredness, which causes most of our unhappiness. We can choose satan's way and be unhappy or choose God's way (love) and have His joy and peace in our lives. Love creates joy.

So, if you are seeking someone to love you, please change your desire and desire that God's love be created in you. Why? Because the more we love, the more we are loved. It is a natural consequence of we reap what we sow. I asked Jesus one time if He loved me, how did He show it? He said, "I love you through other people. I put love for you in their hearts as I put love for others in your heart, so when you love someone, I am loving them through you."

As I wrote before, perfect love casts out fear. Fear of opening our hearts and minds to others. Most people have their guard up, but God's perfect love takes away the fear of being hurt of shamed. We have no reason to fear because we are living God's will then and we can reap only good because we will be sowing only good seeds. Let's look deeply within ourselves and ask Jesus to dig out by the roots anything that prevents us from being filled with His perfect love. This is what the whole Bible is all about. It is the basic meaning to His instruction book to us.

We suffer because we are missing the mark. Our enemy, the devil, has darkened our understanding. As we read, read and re-read the Bible, our understanding will be enlightened and we will be transformed from the devil's darkness to God's enlightenment. We can become a new person by seeking first the kingdom of God and His righteousness. We usually seek for the flesh, which is health, happiness, money, fame and things we think will make us happy. What do you pray for the most? What do you want more than anything else—what are you seeking first? I hope it is to have the kingdom of God. Him to fill you with Himself. He Himself is love.

I pray that you will seek HIM with all your heart for His word says if we do that we will find Him, our exceeding great reward.

One evening during a Sunday night meeting we were discussing perfection, that is what God meant when He said be perfect as He is perfect. Someone said we cannot be perfect-- that means complete. We wondered what it meant to be complete. I believe if God tells us to do something then it is not impossible for us to do it. So if He says to be perfect then we are calling Him a liar if we say it is impossible.

I went home and looked up "perfect" in my dictionary and it said to be complete. I had not learned anything so I went to the one who knows everything. I asked Jesus what is perfection. I went to sleep and when I awoke He told me perfection was explained in Matthew 5:43-48. The main part is Matthew 5:44, "But I say to you, love your enemies, bless those who curse you, do good to those who hate you, and pray for those who spitefully use you and persecute you." Then verse 48 says, "Therefore you shall be perfect just as your Father in heaven is perfect." THEREFORE, BE YE PERFECT.

The rest of this book explains why we do not love as God wills us to. How we can be free of the reasons we don't. How we can learn and become mature adults and spiritually mature.

Seek FIRST the Kingdom of God and His righteousness (His kind of love) and He will supply all of your needs.

CHAPTER 2

The Breaking of My Spirit

I was the only girl in a family of four children. I had one older and two younger brothers. John was the older one, Jim, and then Mike was the youngest. When John was born, of course he took a lot of my mother's love and attention. My father was one of those people who wanted to be the first or the only one who was shown love and attention. He became abusive to my brother and mother.

When I came along, of course, the marriage was already destroyed; so another child was not wanted. My father, though, did not seem to resent me, but showed me kindness and attention when he was at home. He was an alcoholic and he went from one woman to another. Of course my mother lived with a lot of anger and hurt.

When my father was home, she just could not restrain herself from showing this anger. The times my father was home they argued most of the time. My mother was resentful and abusive to me, I can only guess that it was because I was a female and my father did show kindness and attention toward me at times. Mom couldn't show her jealousy and anger at the women he went out with, so a lot of it was focused toward me.

I remember when I was almost three years old when my brother and I had gotten up on Easter morning and found our Easter baskets in the kitchen cabinet. Dad told us about the Easter bunny leaving them. John grabbed his and ran outside with it, but I wanted to know all about the Easter bunny. I remember standing in front of Dad with my elbows on his knees looking up at him and asking him about this. He was explaining it to me but all the time my mother in the background was swearing and cooking breakfast and banging the pots and pans and things. I can remember willing myself not to pay any attention to her but to keep my mind focused on Dad and what he was saying. I thought she didn't want him talking to me. I tried to close out her angry words.

When I was three years old, my mother's cousin came to visit. Mom fixed a nice lunch. I couldn't talk plain. I asked my mother's cousin, whose name was Lloyd, if he would give me some green beans. As a child I'd thought I had said green beans, but I said "green bean." So he picked out one little bean from the dish and put it on my plate and handed it back. When I looked down and saw that one bean I thought that was so funny that I could just feel the laughter inside of myself so that I laughed very hard. While I was laughing, I happened to glance up at Mom. She was looking at me as though she hated me. Of course that killed all the laughter. I can never remember ever laughing like that again with such feeling until after surrendering myself to Jesus. It was still many years after that before I could.

My brother, John, felt that I had taken love from my father away from him. He was jealous of me too, so he did a lot of cruel things to me. I was told that when I was three weeks old, he climbed onto the bed and began hitting me with his fists. When I got older and could sit up, he poured a bucket of paint over my head and another time, a bucket of syrup.

Mom had to scrub and scrub to get all that off. One time he took me out into the driveway and sat me down and threw rocks at me. The neighbor man had to rescue me that time. One time he took me out into the garden where my grandfather was plowing. Grandpa had a hand plow and made a little garden in the lot beside our house. My brother took me by the hand and sat me down in front of the plow and my grandfather walked around the plow, grabbed me by the arm and threw me. Luckily the ground had been plowed and it was soft so I was not injured. My brother mistreated me so much for so long that I began to fight back. When I was two years old, I blacked both of his eyes and another time he picked at me until I wanted to really hurt him so I went into the kitchen and got a knife. I went back into the living room where he was and told him to put his foot upon the footstool. When he did I hit his toe hard with the butcher knife and cut a big gash in it. My mother became very angry and wanted my father to spank me. He wouldn't do it, because he said John had it coming, that he had been tormenting me all evening. Of course that made my mother even angrier with me. But that's the way our lives went, my mother and father fighting and arguing and my brother and me fighting and arguing.

My mother understandably was very jealous of my father. I can remember one evening my uncle took my father, John and me to the grocery store. Dad was smiling and talking to the cashier who was a young woman. As soon as we walked through the front door, my brother told Mom, "Dad was flirting with some girl at the grocery store." We could see Mom puff up, getting ready to attack. My uncle, behind my father's back, put his hand down about thigh high, indicating that it was just a little girl, which it wasn't, but he knew what would happen if Mom had known the truth. She would start cursing my father and then my father might hit her.

My brother, Jim, was born when I was just a little over two years old. When I was four years old, we moved away from that house into a house where the living room floor wasn't even finished. Dad did put a floor in and did a little bit of work on the house but we had no electricity. We had no curtains on the windows, no rugs on the floors. We also had an outhouse. This was just outside of Indianapolis and we rode the Greyhound bus to get to town and back to our house.

We lived at the end of Lyndhurst Drive. There was a woods about a block and a half from our house. We hadn't lived there very long until Dad had moved out and moved into an apartment in town with some other woman. He would come home on weekends sometimes, not always. He gave Mom enough that we could just scrimp by; we mainly lived on beans and potatoes. Dad came home one time long enough to get Mom pregnant. My brother Mike was born nine months later, just before I turned six years old. When he was born he was blond headed. The rest of us had very dark hair. My mother had dark hair but a lot of people in her family had blond hair. Dad swore up and down that Mike did not belong to him. They had a big argument when Mike was born. I loved Mike dearly and took over watching him as much as I could. I tried to protect him. I wouldn't let anyone say or do anything hostile toward him. If they did, I was ready to fight. I did have a lot of fights because of him. The neighbor kids would try to hurt him. My uncle used to pretend he was whipping Mike and I would try to kick and hit him and yell at him to leave Mike alone. He thought that was cute.

As time went on, Dad began to beat Mom more and more. He would come home and she would be upset because he was living with another woman. All the time he was gone, the hurt, jealousy and anger was churning inside her.

When he would come home, she just could not keep it to herself, which most people couldn't. They would get into an argument and it would escalate into Dad beating her. My brother, John, and I would try to help her. One time John threw a big apple and hit Dad in the head with it and that brought him to his senses and stopped hitting Mom. Another time John swung at him with an iron poker that would have really damaged Dad's skull if it had connected. But Mom saw him over Dad's shoulder and screamed. Dad ducked just in time. That stopped him hitting Mom. Another time, my paternal grandmother was at our house. She lived about a half a block from us. Dad was home so she came to visit. He and Mom were arguing. Mom called Dad a bad name that concerned his Mother too so my grandmother told Dad to hit Mom for saying that and he did. He knocked her out of the kitchen and onto the bed in the bedroom. He got her arms behind her and told her he was going to break her jaw so she couldn't call anyone names for a while. He straddled her on the bed. I was about nine years old. I jumped on his back, locked my legs around him and when he would try to hit her, he raised his arm into the air. When he would bring it down to hit her, I would hit his arm as hard as I could with both of my closed fists and knock it out of his intended path. He would hit the mattress or the head of the bed. When that was over, he had not been able to hit Mom in the face.

While this was going on, she had worked herself loose. She had on high heels. She started kicking him in his abdomen and chest area and had broken a heel off her shoe. The nails from it had started cutting his chest open as she kicked. The pain of that brought him to his senses and he let her go. While she was kicking she was screaming, "I'm going to kill both of you when I get up!" We had a little pistol that Mom kept there because there were prowlers occasionally. As she was getting up, I ran and got the gun and moved it to another shelf in the closet. When she went to get the gun she couldn't find it. While she was looking, Dad took his mother and steered her out the back door and home. Mom kept searching the shelf where she had left the gun. She couldn't find it of course because I had moved it. Otherwise I know she would have shot both my father and my grandmother that day.

Another time they got into an argument, John and I woke up in the middle of the night. They were arguing and Dad had Mom down in the chair setting on top of her. They were arguing about something and wanted us to make the decision about who was right and who was wrong. How could we do that? If we'd said Dad was right, Mom would be angry with us. If we'd said Mom, Dad would be angry with us.

There were times though when we weren't able to help her. One time in the middle of the night we woke up and Dad had beat her. He beat her so bad he had called the doctor to come help her. The doctor had to put clamps in her head in two places to keep her from bleeding to death. In those days, doctors made house calls. Dad had hit Mom so hard he had broken his hand. He asked the doctor to do something for his hand but the doctor told him to get help some place else. He wouldn't help him because of what he had done to Mom.

My brother and I woke up after this. Dad's mother was there. When I awoke, I heard her say, "Lets get this blood cleaned up so the kids won't know what happened."

John and I were afraid to go to sleep after that. We were afraid Dad would kill Mom if we weren't awake to help her. Dad always had a job and made pretty good money, but he spent it on himself and other women. My brothers and I had barely enough to eat. We were four dirty, ragged kids. Most of the neighbors wouldn't let their kids play with us. Mom just seemed not to care. She was trapped with four children she didn't want.

Dad came home drunk one time and he and Mom got into an argument. We had one of those old fashioned dining buffets. It was a very heavy piece of furniture. Dad became angry. He just picked the buffet up and threw it across the room. That terrified me. From that time on I was terrified of anyone who was, or had been drinking.

No one can realize what terrible damage it does to a child's mind and emotions to see their father do those things to their mother.

When Dad would come home, I would just hope that Mom wouldn't say anything to anger him, that she would be nice and pleasant. The visit would be pleasant and Dad would go on his way. It never worked out like that. It's so strange though, that I still loved Dad even though he did all those things. I still loved him, I guess, because he was the only one who showed me any attention or caring. I can never remember him putting his arms around me or holding me or anything like that except when I was about two years old. We watched Snow White and the Seven Dwarfs at a movie one time. I became frightened and Dad held me on his lap during the movie. That is the only time I can ever remember him really touching me except when he hit me. I know Mom held me when I was a baby but I can never remember her ever holding me or kissing me. I think that her relationship with my father before I was ever born had killed her ability to love. I think she just lived in the hurt, shame and embarrassment of what goes with a husband like my Dad was.

She did stay home with us, she fed us, she didn't get out and run around or anything like that until after Mike was about one year old. My mother had gone to her parents and had asked her mother if she could bring my brothers and me and move in with them until she should get a job and get on her feet. My grandmother told her to take her kids and go back home to her husband where she belonged. I think Mom just felt trapped after that, but finally she got enough courage to go into Indianapolis and get a job. She went to work in a factory. After she went to work, she began to meet men and began to go out with them.

The devil used my mother many times and in many ways to try to destroy me. She let it slip after I became an adult that she had purposely done things to break my spirit.

The devil had not only used her, but many others as well. It states in Ephesians 6:12 that we do not fight against flesh and blood but evil spirits of darkness. If we don't realize this we believe it is the person we are being attacked by, but the person or persons are being controlled by evil spirits.

The Holy Spirit told me that satan gives us a dark subconscious from the time we are toddlers and when we become adults he controls us with what he has programmed in us. Like me with the shame He controlled me with that until I was in my forties. The Lord freed me of it finally. The Bible tells us Jesus came to set the captives free. Those who are captive of sin and satan.

I used to like going to my maternal grandparents in Martinsville and stay with them in the summer. Usually, when it came time to go home, I didn't want to go. I just wanted to stay with them. But after that happened, the next time I went to visit, I was older and I got homesick. My grandparents put me on a Greyhound bus in Martinsville. I could get off on the road I lived on and walk about three blocks on a gravel road to my house. As I got close to home, I could see that my cousins were visiting. They and my brothers were out playing in the yard having a good time. I thought to myself how happy I was to see them and they would be happy to see me. As I walked into the yard, I waved and said happily, "Hi, everybody!" No one paid any attention to me. A couple of them did turn around and say "hi," but then went back to their play as though I had never been gone. This hurt my feelings but I thought I'd go in to see Mom. Maybe she would be glad to see me. When I walked into the house, my mom and aunt were in the kitchen. My aunt had brought some chocolate pies and they were on the kitchen table. She and Mom were sitting there talking.

I said "Hi' as I went into the kitchen. They didn't say hi back. Mom just cut a piece of chocolate pie, handed it to me and said, "Here, go out and play." Instead of going out the front door where the other children were, I went out the back door and sat down on the back steps and ate that piece of pie. As I ate it, If felt that no one in the world loved me. The devil had struck another blow. I felt like I was all alone in the world, no one loved me, no one cared about me. My family was a family, they were a group and I was all by myself. I was an outcast.

I was ten years old and had just gotten out of the fourth grade when we moved from the west side of Indianapolis to the east side. A farmer was selling off some of his property and people were buying up acres of land and building houses there. My parents bought an acre and built a house out in the middle of a field. Dad built a one-room tar paper building. We lived in it for a while until he built a cement blockhouse. They put up two beds at the far end and when you went into the door, you walked into the kitchen area. That was all we had, a kitchen area and a sleeping area. No partitions, just one room. Mom slept in one double bed, my brothers slept in another and I slept on a cot at the foot of my brothers' bed. This was until my Dad got the cement blockhouse built.

Dad was so busy with his women friends that he didn't get half of the roof put on the blockhouse so we lived in two rooms of it with a tarp hanging down one side. That was one side of our house. For one winter we had a kitchen and Mom's bedroom. My brothers and I slept on old clothes again.

Dad finally got the roof on the next summer. It was a gray cement building—no paint, no carpet, no curtains, no screen doors. But we had walls and a roof over them. It was very cold that winter.

Dad had a pile of sand out in the yard. When he was building the cement blockhouse, he used the sand to mix with the mortar to lay block. One day he was working on the house and my brother and I were playing. Earlier my father had told us to stay out of the sand. My brother was tormenting me and I had forgotten what my father had said. John had set a trap for me. He enticed me to chase him. He ran to and around the sand. I was running to get him, not paying any attention to where I was going. I ran across the sand pile. My father saw us, came down off the scaffold and came after me. By the look on his face, I knew I was in bad trouble. I ran from him. I ran into the house and ran to the back. He caught me and knocked me down between the beds. He beat me with his fists. He kept beating me until I thought in my mind, and I really believed he was going to kill me, beat me to death. Eventually he stopped beating me. My love for him was almost gone and in its place was fear. We had a heating stove that Mom kept a fire in to keep us warm, while Dad lived in a nice warm apartment in town with another woman. Eventually he did finish the house.

It was just an old gray, cement block square house set down in the middle of a field. Mom had quit working when we moved, but now she went back to work. She was gone most of the time. Sometimes she would work two jobs, sometimes she didn't and she would date a lot. Occasionally we saw her on the weekends. I kept the house going. I took care of the boys and cooked our meals, cleaned the house and did the shopping. Mom talked to the man who owned the grocery store on the corner and asked if I could buy things there on credit through the week and she would pay for what I had bought at the end of the week. I wasn't allowed to buy any sweets or soft drinks or anything like that. It had to be staple foods. So I would buy things to bake with—flour, sugar, and so forth. I had a cookbook. I would make cakes and cookies and things for my brothers and me. At first the only thing I knew how to cook was boiled potatoes with butter and then I learned how to make macaroni and cheese. So one night we would have potatoes for supper, the next night we would have macaroni and cheese.

I had wanted a baton for years, since I was in the second grade, I believe. There was a little girl in our class who could twirl a baton and I wanted one. Finally when I was twelve years old, Dad bought me one for Christmas. The only time he bought us anything for Christmas.

Dad came home one evening and he and Mom got into an argument that escalated into a fight. He started beating on her again, but my brothers and I were bigger now and we attacked him and were fighting him, too.

When he began beating on everybody, I grabbed my baton and was going to hit him in the head with it. He saw me, turned and grabbed the baton and lifted the baton and me off the floor. I let loose of the baton and he turned around and hit me in the abdomen with his fist and knocked me against the back door. It knocked the wind out of me and I just slid down the door to the floor. Then I panicked. I saw that he was too strong for us and we couldn't protect ourselves. I ran out the back door to the neighbors and called the police. When I came back, I told them I had called the police and Dad left. It was cold weather and he had his shirt off. He left without any warm clothing. All he had on was his undershirt and his pants. Pretty soon the police came and had Dad with them. He had gone to the corner to wait for the bus to go into town, and they knew he was the one the call had been made about since he wasn't warmly dressed. They had him get dressed, and then they took him away. It was such a terribly, terribly upsetting time. We had been through it so many times.

My older brother and I told Mom is she didn't divorce him; we were going to run away from home. I know it wasn't us that caused her to get the divorce but she did file for divorce and went through with it. It didn't do much good because she started going with another man by the name of Bob. She had me, for some reason, meet her in town one evening and eat supper with them. She wanted me to meet him to see what I thought about him. So we ate and talked, then Mom and I left to get one of the late buses home. As we walked down the street to the bus stop, she asked me what I thought of him. I asked her not to marry him, because I told her he would drink all the time and be mean to my brothers and me and would be mean to her. Looking back, where all that knowledge came from, I don't know but it was in my head and I told her just exactly the kind of person he was and how he would be if they married.

Of course she ignored me and married him anyway. Years later she told me she wished she had listened, because everything I told her had come to pass.

The first night Bob lived with us I was sick and didn't want to eat anything. He got the belt and said I was going to eat whether I wanted to or not. I sat there and forced down the food. Then I went into the bedroom and lay down across the bed. My youngest brother, Mike, was so upset because of the way Bob had treated me; he didn't want to eat any supper either. So Mike came into the bedroom with me.

Bob came in the bedroom with the belt and whacked Mike on the rear end one time. Nobody hurt Mike without fighting me! I jumped up off the bed and slapped him across the face and told him to never touch Mike again. He never did. He would drink all the time, drink all his money up then want my mother's money to eat on during the week, to buy his lunch and things at work. Mom had to have surgery again. My father sent support money and I was to get the support money and buy groceries with it. While Mom was in the hospital I was responsible for feeding my brothers and myself that week. I was twelve years old, but I'd had a lot of responsibility and I could do that. But Bob had spent all of his money, then came to me and wanted me to give him our support money. I refused to do it. He was very angry. I was to go visit Mom that evening at the hospital. While I was there, he came in to visit also. He started telling her that I wouldn't give him any money and he needed it for his lunch at work, etc. Mom made me give him the money.

I was so angry I would not sit with him on the bus going home that evening. He bought liquor with the money. The grocer let me get extra food even though I couldn't pay last weeks bill.

I found out later that Bob had told her to make me give him the money. That was why she wanted me to visit that evening. She said I had to give it to him, so I did.

After Mom got out of the hospital, Bob got into an argument with my brother. Mom was cutting my brother's hair. Bob walked around and took the scissors out of Mom's hand and cut a big whack out of my brother's hair right in front where it couldn't be repaired. John was fifteen and knew he had to go to school like that. John was so angry; he jumped up out of the chair, grabbed Bob and backed him against the wall. He had both hands around Bob's throat and was choking him to death. My mother and brothers and I grabbed John and wrestled him to the floor in the living room and were holding him down. Mom told Bob to get out because she knew someone would be hurt very badly if he stayed. John was sitting on the floor and I was sitting beside him holding one arm. Mom was on the other side holding the other arm. Bob walked into the living room, looked at John and called him a bad name and said, "You yellow coward, I ought to just kick you right under the chin." When he said that, I saw in my mind him doing that to John. I panicked and I felt inside of myself that I had to protect John. I stood up and as I stood up, I doubled my fist and hit Bob under the chin as hard as I could hit him. I knocked him across the living room and onto a big overstuffed chair. The chair fell over and he fell over with it. He got up and sort of sidled along the wall, away from me and around the other wall to the front door and left.

When I was a little girl, my Dad's family used to come and get John and take him places with them—to the movies, skating, swimming, to the museums and different places. They would never take me and I could never understand why. One day they were taking John somewhere. As they left I asked Mom, "Why do they always take John and never take me any place?" She looked down at me with contempt in her face and said, "Because you're a girl." From that moment on, I didn't want to be a girl. I knew I couldn't be a boy, but I thought I would do things better than boys did and that way people would like me. (More of satan's tactics. I thought no one liked girls so no one would ever like me.) So I competed with my brothers and the boys in the neighborhood. I could run faster, climb trees higher, fight better and I could be tougher and meaner. From that time on, I was the worst tomboy anyone had ever seen. Now it came in handy because I knew how to fight. I used that to protect my brother. Bob told people that he wasn't afraid of John, but he was afraid of me because I was crazy. Eventually Mom and Bob were divorced.

When we moved to this new neighborhood, my brother met a boy who lived a few blocks away and they became best friends. They were inseparable. I'll call him Dan. Dan was at our house most of the time. John didn't go to his house much because Dan's father was a very angry man and didn't want anyone around his house. If anyone went to visit, he made it clear to them that he didn't want them there. For a long time Dan was just John's friend. We were acquaintances. When I was thirteen and Dan was fifteen we began to like each other as girlfriend and boyfriend. I was very shy and he was too. We never even kissed. John got jealous when Dan began liking me.

I had heard him tell Mom one evening that I was taking his friend away from him. The next Saturday Mom didn't go out. She stayed home, dressed in her sexiest outfit and put make up on. When Dan came over she seduced him. They had sex in the front bedroom. There was no door between the bedroom and the living room where I was. Mom intended for me to see them.

That was her way of making sure that John didn't lose his friend. I didn't realize her motive for many, many years. That day I went into the kitchen and sat down at the table. I think I was in shock. I didn't remember what I did then until some time after I turned my life over to Jesus and He was working to heal me of the past.

Jesus brought to my memory what I had done sitting at the kitchen table. I had banged my fist on the table and said, "I will never let anyone do that to me again." I meant hurt me like that had.

That went into my subconscious mind. It was so painful to me that I buried it there and forgot it but it controlled me just the same. I was never able to feel love after that because I associated it with suffering. If you love, you suffer. I feared the suffering.

When I was still thirteen I was kidnapped by three young men. You can guess what they did to me. Later my brother tried to get me to go on dates with his friends. One night two of them came to see me. I hid in the house and told him to tell them I wasn't home. He coerced me to go talk to them. They got me in the car and drove off with me against my will. Again, you can guess the outcome.

The first time I had sex it was rape, and then these two kidnappings took place after that. When I had just turned fourteen, Mom told a young man, who was twenty-one at the time, that he could have sex with me. I avoided that for about four months. But eventually he cornered me.

I got pregnant at fourteen. Mom then told him if he didn't marry me, she would have him sent to jail. We got married and I had my first child at the age of fifteen. He tried to kill my baby and me because his friends made fun of him for "robbing the cradle." Because I was so young, also he never loved me. I was a conquest. I never loved him. We were divorced when I was sixteen. I lied about my age and went to work in a factory.

I started dating a young man. He fell in love with me. He wanted to marry me but I didn't want to be married. He cried and begged me. I married him because I felt sorry for him. I really didn't know beans from apple butter, as the old saying goes. I didn't realize just what I was doing.

I cried all day the day after we were married. I got pregnant nine days after we were married. My past experiences had killed all sexual desire and feelings. He knew I felt nothing for him.

I stayed with him for two years and had two children. He got another young woman pregnant. I divorced him. I was eighteen years old, divorced with three children.

I had moved to Martinsville, Indiana when I married the first time. My father got me a job in Indianapolis. I had a struggle trying to keep a good sitter for the children. Finally a friend moved in with us. She took care of them for her room and board. We all got along well so things were easier. As time went on I grew more and more depressed.

When I was twenty-three a man ten years my senior began pursuing me. He was very much in love with me. He was very good to my children and me. He had been married and divorced. The business I worked for lost a lot of business. They had to let some of the newer employees go. I had only been there about three years so I was one of the ones let go.

To make a long story short, I married my husband for security. Because of the time Mom had sex with Dan I was never able to love a man.

My husband was very disappointed in our marriage. He became very angry and stayed that way for twenty-three years. He was a workaholic so he was gone a lot of the time. I was glad because when he was home his favorite thing to do was to punish me. I was afraid to leave—afraid I couldn't make it on my own. So we both lived in depression and were miserable living with each other. I wanted to die. My spirit was broken. I couldn't fight to survive any longer. In despair I decided to kill myself and get out of the pain. I write about that in the chapter on satan.

CHAPTER 3

The Beginning

I turned my life over to Jesus just a few weeks before my 30th birthday. The next day, and for months, I could feel His presence. I was aware of Him. I lived in the joy of the Lord.

He gave me a hunger to read the Bible. I was ignorant of everything spiritual except for the fact that Jesus had died on the cross so sinners could be saved.

I read the Bible every spare moment I had. I got very little understanding at first. I would ask Jesus what this or that meant and He would (in my spirit) give me the answer.

He would also tell me things He wanted me to do. Sometimes I did and sometimes I didn't do them, but He didn't chastise me as He did later when I had grown some.

When we first accept Him as our Savior or (better yet) surrender our life to Him, we are newborn babes in the spiritual realm. Jesus picks us up and carries us for a while like our parents do in the physical world.

He answers many prayers and will heal things for us. This is to establish that we are saved, that He is with us, and that He loves and will take care of us. After a while he begins to set us on our feet and helps us to begin learning to walk.

Our spiritual growth is progressive just as our physical growth is. After a while He lets us begin Kindergarten.

When this happened with me (you remember I felt His presence all the time), I awoke one morning and no longer felt Him there. I was devastated all day long.

That night I had a dream that Jesus called me on the phone (a phone call in a dream means this is an important message for us) and asked me if it would help me if He held my hand once in a while. He said He had withdrawn the feeling of His presence because He wanted me to learn to walk by faith and not feelings.

He wanted me (as He does everyone that grows out of the baby stage) to learn by faith, not just believe but know that I messed this up.

He was and would always be with me. After that I would believe He was there. Knowing He was there, watching everything I did. Listening to every word I said, every thought that went through my mind. I tried to always please Him.

Now comes the next step in my growth. Hurtful and upsetting things began to happen.

They happened before too but I always had His joy to get through them. Now the upset, hurt, fear, guilt, whatever came into my mind.

He began to let satan cause things to happen that were very upsetting to me. I would pray and still know Jesus was with me so I asked Him why it happened. He would put the answer in my spirit, inside my head.

Usually it was satan attacking me in some sin or weakness. Jesus would show me. I would admit it to Him and He would help me get over it.

I knew I had no power over satan and was afraid of him.

I began having a lot of guilty thoughts. Instead of asking Jesus to forgive and help me get over it, I tried not to think them.

Finally Jesus showed me that it was satan using my brain to make me think what he wanted me to think.

One time he did this. I knew I was helpless against him so I cried out to Jesus. "Jesus, the devil is making me think these thoughts! I have no power to stop him! Please, Jesus, you take over and fight him for me!"

Immediately the thoughts stopped. This happened a few more times but I would say, "Here he is again, Jesus. Please fight him for me." And it stopped.

Many things happened as time went on and I was growing spiritually. Then came a time Jesus didn't respond to my cry for help in fighting satan.

Then I had a dream that Jesus came and told me it was time for me to begin using my spiritual weapons to fight spiritual battles. He taught me that I could use His name to fight these battles to gain the victory over satan. The power is in the name of Jesus. I could use His name anytime I needed.

Well, I had a lot of times. After some years of this, He began to deal with me about using His name to help others be free of satan and his evil soldiers.

I have written all of this as an example of our experiences of growing in Jesus. To become a mature human spirit. We go through growth periods in the spiritual just as we do the physical, mental and emotional stages.

Jesus carries us for a while. When He puts us down and we must begin to struggle is the time many people turn away.

They, like me, believe Jesus has rejected them or just left them for good. Many people have told me they just can't feel Him with them any more. I tell them it is time to begin walking by faith, and they will grow spiritually. I pray this book will help all who read it grow much, learn satan's tricks and how to defeat him.

Hang in there. Jesus will help you even though you don't FEEL Him with you. He is there and always will be, and you will learn the meaning of life.

CHAPTER 4

Body, Soul and Spirit

We are a spiritual being. God created our (I will call it a human spirit) individual spirit being. He then put it in our human body.

Ecclesiastes 6:6 &7 tells us that before we die we are to remember our God, for when we die our body returns to dust, but our spirit goes back to God who gave it to be judged. James 2:26 states that without the spirit, the body dies.

Luke 8 tells of a little girl who died. Jesus went to her and said, "Little girl, arise." Then the scripture tells us that her spirit returned and she immediately arose. In Acts 7:59, the Jews stoned a man named Stephen to death. As he was dying, he said, "Lord Jesus, receive my spirit."

In First Corinthians 6:20, it tells us we are to glorify God in our body and spirit, which are God's. In Second Corinthians, it tells us to cleanse ourselves from all sinfulness of the flesh and spirit.

Hebrews 12: " God, the judge of all, to the spirits of just men made perfect."

Romans 8:16: "The Spirit Himself, (the Holy Spirit) bears witness with our human spirit that we are children of God." First Corinthians 2:11: For what man knows the things of a man except the spirit of the man, which is in him.

From these scriptures, we may understand that we are a spirit created by God and placed in a human body. He also created a soul to live in the body with the spirit.

It is written in Genesis that, this soul (Adam) disobeyed God and fell into sin. Everyone born after that was born with a sinful soul. Our human spirit was sent here to earth to make choices.

God creates a spirit and sends it to earth to learn and grow spiritually. That is the reason we are here. Everything that happens is for our spiritual growth; i.e., for the human spirit to grow into the kind of person who loves God and his neighbor as himself.

I asked Jesus one time why we all have to suffer. He told me it is to show people their helplessness and their need for Him.

God created the human spirit. It will never die. It will live forever either with God or with satan. The choice is ours.

The spirit is sent to earth to learn of good and evil. It is to make a choice to live for sinful pleasure and spend eternity with satan, or to choose Jesus and God's eternal values and live with Him eternally.

To live an earthly life, the spirit has to have a physical body to live in because it will be living in a physical world. Now in the physical body, it will also be living with a sinful soul. It is like two people living in one body and both trying to control the body.

The real us (spirit) is sent here on a mission. It is to see both good and evil and to make a choice. We are to learn God's rules and live by them. In the Old Testament, God instructed the people to teach their children His laws constantly.

It tells us in Psalms 51 that we are conceived in sin—born in sin. We are born with a sinful nature. It is our nature to sin. We are supposed to be taught right from wrong. The parents are to punish for wrong and reward for good. That is to train the child to control the sinful nature, and to learn to treat others as God wills.

In the Old Testament, God instructed the people to sacrifice their best animal to Him if they sinned. That way they had to give something up, and the lamb they killed took their place. Instead of dying for their sin, the lamb died for (paid for) their sins.

The Lord forgave them, but they still were of a sinful nature. They were not changed, just forgiven. So, we, in ourselves, without Jesus, are completely and utterly sinful.

I remember years ago when that was revealed to me. I went into shock and was overcome with shame. I saw and understood that I was completely and utterly sinful. Immediately, though, the Holy Spirit stopped the shame and said, "Why should you be ashamed when everyone in this whole world is JUST LIKE YOU?"

I could not understand why God would create something that was no good. For three days my mind was in complete confusion. Why did God make us? He must have made a terrible mistake. Over and over this went through my mind. Why, why, why?

On the fourth morning as I was doing my morning dishes, I began it again.

Why did God make something that was no good? Suddenly the Holy Spirit answered me. He said because God has to create. He takes this no good, worthless lump of clay and begins to clean out the unrighteousness and then begins to create His righteousness in it.

Any good you see in any human being, God put it there or it would not be there.

No one can take pride in themselves at all because they cannot create anything good in themselves. It all comes from God. We cannot create righteousness. We can only let God create it in us.

I saw that we are all nothing but sin. In Romans 7, Paul tells us there is nothing good in man. The Bible tells us that in the beginning man did what was right in his own eyes. This means he did as he pleased. Mankind, therefore, became so evil and corrupt that God had to wipe the earth clean of them and start over.

He had one righteous man left who was Noah. So, God had a beginning to work with—Noah and his family. Then, after many years, Moses came on the scene. God chose through him to bring forth and establish His laws. The laws were to teach people right from wrong and to establish that God existed, and that there were consequences to breaking His laws. He wanted to teach mankind that they were to treat one another fairly and with kindness and love,

When God created the universe, He created two universal laws. He told us all through the Bible what they were: (1) If we sin, we suffer; and, (2) if we obey, we are rewarded. We reap what we sow, both good and bad. He told us He is no respecter of persons in Act 10:34. This means that we are all treated the same. If we sin, we suffer. If we obey, we are rewarded.

In the law, we could make sacrifices for our sin and be forgiven, but the law could never change our sinful nature. Then, after about two thousand years of the law, He sent Jesus into the world.

In Romans 7, Paul tells us there is nothing good in us. We are under the law of sin and death. Sin has power over us. In Romans 7:24, Paul asked, "Who shall deliver me (and us) from this body of sin and death?" In Romans 8:2, Paul says, "The law of the Holy Spirit of life in Christ has made me FREE from the law of sin and death." Praise God!

When Jesus died, He was our sacrifice, given by God, for our sins. Not only can we be forgiven, but also we can be cleansed of sin and freed from the sinful nature. We can have the nature of Christ created in us (II Peter 1:3 & 4).

So, when we are born, we are born with a sinful nature. It is our nature to sin. We cannot, not sin. The soul is sinful. This sinful nature is put into a body of flesh. The body has needs. It needs food, water, air and shelter. It is our job to fulfill all of these needs; according to God's will not our sinful nature's will or satan's will.

We not only live in a body with a sinful nature, but we also live in a world with an evil being (the devil) who hates us and wants to destroy us. So when we enter this world, we have entered a spiritual battle.

Now, we can understand why we need a savior. WE NEED HELP. Ephesians 6:20 tells us we are in a spiritual battle, and that we cannot fight this battle alone. We try to fight them (anger, fear, selfishness, self-centeredness, pride, immoral thoughts, hate, revenge, lust and so forth) with our mind and will power, but the Holy Spirit revealed to me that we can never win a spiritual battle with physical weapons. Paul called them carnal weapons in Second Corinthians 10:3 & 4.

We have to use God's weapons, which are our spiritual weapons. These weapons are the name of Jesus, the Bible, faith and knowledge of God's instructions, which He gave us in the Bible. We need to read it every day. The more we read the Bible, the more we understand it. The more we understand it, the more we can apply it to our lives. The more we apply it to our lives, the more we will receive the rewards for obeying God. The more we are rewarded, the less we suffer. The less we suffer, the more we enjoy life.

The more we apply the Bible, the more we are submitting to God's will. Gradually our sinful nature is being done away with, and God's nature is being created in us BY THE HOLY SPIRIT. We make the choice. He does the work. Without Him, we can do nothing. (John 15:5)

We have learned that the soul is sinful. It uses the body to do its will. Now, we come to the human spirit. God created it. It is the real us! The body will die, but we leave the body and go back to God who will judge us for our works on earth. (Ecclesiastes 12:6 &7 and 12:13 & 14.

The spirit is sent here to learn about good and evil. Do we choose to live for pleasure then live with the devil forever, or do we choose God's eternal qualities, and live with Him forever?

It tells us in Romans 8 to walk in the Spirit and not in the flesh. As I read that one day, I could not understand what it meant, so I asked Jesus to help me understand it.

The next Sunday in Sunday school another lady and I expressed different opinions on the scripture we were studying. After class, she said to me that she hoped that she had not confused me when she gave her opinion. She was sincere in hoping that she had not confused me and that I understood. I assured her that I had not been confused. I sincerely wanted to put her mind at ease over the situation.

She then said something to the effect that she was sure her superior intellect must have confused my inferior intellect. Then, I retorted, no I think you are the one who is confused. When I got home, I began crying and asking Jesus to forgive me. I had not even known I was going to say that. It just came out. Please do not let me say anything like that to anyone again, I pleaded.

He said to me, "Remember you asking me to help you understand what it means to walk in the Spirit and not in the flesh?" "Yes," I replied. "Well, He said, "You both started out in the Spirit, sincerely thinking of the other's welfare, but you both ended up in the flesh, only thinking of yourselves and your own ego." So, I learned that when we are being loving, kind and thinking of the other person's welfare, we are walking in the Holy Spirit. When we are being selfish, self-centered, proud, or when we are saying harsh words that hurt or embarrass someone, we are in the flesh and we are sinning. The Holy Spirit taught me that all harsh words come from the devil.

We believe the devil's lie that it is all right to talk to others like that. They offended me or rejected me, refused to do what I wanted, and so forth, so I am justified in hurting and humiliating them. I know that satan had programmed my mind to have all these sinful thoughts and attitudes.

God's instructions about this are to be kind and tenderhearted toward everyone. This takes time and growth. With the help and guidance of the Holy Spirit and the reading and study of the Bible, we can become what the Lord wants us to become.

His will is for us to be transformed by the renewing of our mind. My mind needed to learn to let the Holy Spirit teach me what God's thoughts are. I had been thinking the devil's thoughts (worthlessness, self-hate, inferiority, anger, selfishness, pride, guilt, shame, fear, etc.) most of my life. So, our human spirit needs to yield to Jesus and the Holy Spirit so we may be transformed from sin to righteousness.

We are a spirit who lives in a body with a sinful soul. They both want to be in control of the body. They both want to use the body to manifest themselves, to let themselves be seen and heard.

I began to watch my thoughts to see if they were thoughts Jesus would want me to have. I learned when the sinful soul, and/or the devil were trying to control me, when they were trying to control my thoughts, words or actions. I learned to discern what was going on inside my spirit, my soul and my body that was trying to control (me) the spiritual being inside my body.

How do we become transformed? We become transformed by the renewing of our mind. How is the mind renewed? We have been programmed or trained (as the Bible says) to think and feel as we did before we asked Jesus to save us from sin and Hell.

After we are saved, we are to read the Bible (the instruction book), and learn God's rules for our lives so we do not have to suffer the consequences of sin if we obey the instructions. As we read the Bible, we begin to see how wrong we are and have been.

The Bible tells us that God's ways are above our ways, and His thoughts are above our thoughts. As we read His instructions, He teaches us what is right and what is wrong. He gives us a desire to get rid of our old ways and begin doing things His way. As we learn and ask Him to change us, He begins to clean out the old thought patterns and create His in their place.

Before I turned my life over to Jesus, I was an angry person. I was taught as I grew up that you did not take anything from anyone. I was a fighter because my older brother bullied me all of our growing up years. One of my uncles hired me to beat up a bully who was hurting his children. The boy was bigger than me, but I won the fight. I came close to killing someone twice in my life. If someone had not intervened, I would have.

I stabbed my husband once, but just as the knife entered his body (even though I had not turned my life over to Jesus as yet); something stopped me from sinking the knife into his abdomen. I just broke the skin. After I turned my life over to Jesus and read the instruction book, I learned it was sinful to be angry or hurt or embarrass others. I learned we are to forgive, to love and to help others. The Holy Spirit revealed to me how sinful I was.

I prayed for Jesus to clean me up and make me the person He wanted me to be. I continued to read the Bible and do my best to do and be what it instructed me to. We cannot just stop doing the wrong. We have to put something right in its place. Gradually, I became a different and better person.

I have had my mind renewed by putting in God's thought and attitudes instead of the devil's and mine. As an example of my thoughts versus His, all my growing up years, I knew my mother did not like or want me. She cared about my brothers. She especially favored my older brother. I competed with him. I wanted to be the one to be loved. All my growing up years I wanted to be number one. Jesus taught me that was a sin. "They who want to be first shall be last" (Matthew 20:12-16). I was always last in favor or not favored at all.

One morning just before I awoke, I dreamed that Mom, my brothers and I were all sitting on a bench in a locker room (it represents change).

My brothers were all sitting on Mom's left. I was on her right. She turned her back to me and put her arms around my brothers. In the dream, I said (and I sincerely meant it), I love my brothers and I want them to be loved whether I get to be loved or not.

When I awoke, I knew that was the attitude Jesus wanted me to have. It was also the one I wanted to have. It made me happy to have that attitude. When I wanted to be number one and I knew I was not, that made me unhappy.

God's ways are higher than our ways. His ways make us happy. He had renewed my mind in this area with His thoughts that would give me peace and happiness. He was working to transform me by renewing my way of thinking. By doing this, He was breaking the hold that the devil and my sinful soul had over me, the real me, the human spirit me. Most of my thoughts and attitudes were wrong, sinful and self-centered. Jesus had much work to do in me. After I gave my life to Him, He immediately began and continues the work. Thank you, Jesus!!

So we have learned our body is just a vehicle in which the soul and spirit live, and they both want to be the driver, so to speak. They both want to be in control. They both want to manifest themselves to the outside world through the body.

The spirit is the part that wants to serve, obey and love God and others, and to be what God wants us to be after we accept Jesus as our Savior. The soul wants to feel good, look good, have its own way, be number one, be looked up to and worshipped. It is full of pride, jealousy and envy. It feels superior. It is selfish and self-centered. It takes pleasure in hurting and embarrassing others, and it wants control of everyone and everything.

The spirit is the one who feels shame, guilt, fear, regret, and remorse at the things the sinful soul does. It is God's will that the body, soul, and spirit are to all work together in harmony for the good of all—not against each other. He wants us to be a clean vessel in which He can use us when, where, how and/or why He chooses without resistance from us. As David said in Psalm 51, "Create in me a clean heart and a right spirit then I will teach transgressors your ways and sinners will be converted."

First, the hold the sinful soul and the devil have on us, have to be broken so our human spirit can be cleansed and healed of the destructive things of the past, i.e., self-hate, shame, guilt, fear, hurt, hopelessness, depression, and the lies about ourselves that satan made us believe. In other words, the soul has to be broken so the spirit can be set free. The spirit can be set free to do God's will. This is so satan and sin have no more power over us. The devil wants to destroy the spirit first so we will turn against God, or kill ourselves before we accept Jesus. Even if we do accept Him, satan tries to keep us from doing what God sent us into the world to do and be. To help more souls be saved through accepting Jesus as their Savior. As David wrote in Psalms 23, "He restoreth my soul." The hold the soul has over our human spirit has to be broken. As the cleansing and breaking of the soul takes place, the human spirit gains more control. As the spirit is cleansed and healed, the Holy Spirit gains more control. This is so the soul and spirit yield to Him more and more. We walk more and more in the Spirit, and less and less in the flesh.

If we continue to read the Bible every day, we gain more understanding, faith and trust in what God tells us, through it. The more scripture we put into our memory bank and subconscious mind the more we have to help us when we need it. Ephesians 6:16 states that faith quenches all the fiery darts of the devil. When we need a scripture, the Holy Spirit will put one into our mind to teach, encourage, comfort, enlighten or whatever we need at the time or to help or teach others.

Our sinful soul is cleansed of sin and restored to God's will and ways. We no longer have to fight the battles with self because we are now both working for one goal, which is to please and serve God. In Psalm 51, David asks God to give him a clean heart and right spirit. Then he could teach transgressors God's will and sinners would be converted. He wanted a clean soul and a spirit right with God. It is all about being cleansed, changed, restored to God's will and ways so He can use us to win sinners to Him and His kingdom.

In First John 1:9, it is written, "If we confess our sins, He is faithful and just to forgive us our sins and to cleanse us of all unrighteousness. If we say we have not sinned, we make Him a liar." We are forgiven and cleansed of the sin we confess. If we refuse to look within ourselves to search out the sin, we stay in that sin and reap the consequences of it. If we sin, we suffer. If we obey, we are rewarded.

I have heard preachers say that our human spirit is perfect because God created it, but they did not understand that God sent it into this world, into a physical body to learn and grow. He wants it to be perfected. Second Corinthians 7:1 tells us to cleanse ourselves from all filthiness of the flesh and spirit, perfecting holiness in the fear of God.

Everything that happens in our life is for our spirit to grow. Romans 8:28 states that all things work together for our good. I believe that is telling us all things work together for our spiritual growth—our spirit to grow. When one or the other of my four daughters would suffer something, I would suffer, too. I would try to pray away their suffering. One night I was in mental torment because of one of them when the Holy Spirit told me that everything that happens to them is for their spiritual growth (for their spirit to grow). He said if it were not, He would not let it happen.

He also said that is the reason anyone is put into this world. It is all for the spirit God sent here to grow, so when we return to God, we will have nothing to be judged for. We are not sent here because we are perfect. We are sent here to become perfect. Here are some scriptures telling us that is God's will. Colossians 3:14, "Love is the bond of perfectness," Colossians 3:11, "Be thou perfect," Colossians 1:28, "That we may present every man perfect in Christ Jesus," 1 Corinthians 13:11, "Be perfect," Genesis 17:1, "God told Abraham 'walk before me and be thou perfect," Hebrews 6:1, "Let us go on to perfection," James 1:4, "Let patience have her perfect work that we may be perfect and complete (perfect and mature),"Colossians 4:12, "That you may stand perfect and complete."

That is why God sent our spirit (us) into this world. He created a spirit and sent it to the earth to be perfected.

LOVE. GOD'S LOVE. It is God's will for us to be like Him. It is the devil's will for us to be like him. God is love. The devil is hate.

When the Holy Spirit told me that everything that happens is for our spirit to grow, He also told me that many things happen to break our self will. It is better that we suffer whatever it takes to break our spirit and soul than to be cast into Hell because of our rebellion and self will.

Jesus said it is better to go to Heaven without a hand, foot or eye than to go to Hell with them. It is better to suffer whatever it takes to break us. The breaking is for our spiritual growth. Things may seem terrible in the flesh, but they are for our spirit's good.

God sent us here on a mission. He wants us to go home better than when we left there. I have heard people say they believe God sent them here for a purpose but they do not know what that is. It is the basic meaning of the Bible. We are to choose Jesus as our Savior and then yield our will to Him so He can get us to the place that we love God with all our heart (spirit), soul and mind, and our neighbor as ourselves.

The trouble is that the devil and his evil spirits are working all the time to prevent this. Jesus, by the Holy Spirit, has to clean us up, and train us to be what God wants us to be when we leave this world and return to Him.

We need to (as the Bible tells us) examine ourselves, and humble ourselves, and look at the sin in ourselves – not others—ourselves. Ask God to reveal them to us as we can stand to see them. I believe this is the greatest hold up to our growth. We do not want to see the sin in ourselves, so I believe many people who have asked Jesus to save them just stop there. They will not go on through the cleansing. They go to church for years, but still say hurtful things to and /or about others.

The Holy Spirit told me one time that "first comes the salvation and then comes the cleansing." The cleansing time is the suffering time. If we resist it, then it will last longer. If we turn our life over to Jesus, He can get it over with quicker.

I asked Him one time why was it taking so long to get me cleaned up. He said, "That is your choice, not Mine. You are afraid to turn it all over to Me so I have to take you a step at a time. One step at a time."

I asked Him another time why did I have to suffer so much to learn. I suffer, suffer, suffer and then learn. He said, "Because you won't do it the easy way and let me take over and get the work done quicker." So, do not think I learned the things I have put in this book quickly and/or easily. It took me years. Which is a sad thing, but I am very grateful that Jesus has not given up on me. My hope in your reading this book is that you will learn much faster than I did.

When we give our lives to Jesus, He gives us the gift of the Holy Spirit. The Holy Spirit is to be our helper. He helps us see the sin in us. He helps us repent of it and He does the cleansing, changing, setting free and transforming us.

The Father, Son, and the Holy Spirit are all in one accord, one in purpose, intent and deed. They never disagree. They all work as one unit, so do we after the Holy Spirit transforms us. As body, soul and spirit, we will work together as one. We will all work for the good of all. We will be one in purpose, intent and deed. We will no longer live in conflict with ourselves, but we will live in perfect peace and be at one with God. That is His will for us, but most people never make it that far because of fear, self will and pride.

"Eye has not seen and ear has not heard, nor has it entered the heart of man the things which God has prepared for those who love Him," First Corinthians 2:9. How many wonderful things we miss out on in this life.

I pray that you who read this book have already or will seek God's will and His righteousness above everything else. His will and righteousness are the only things that will make us happy. Matthew 6:33 states if we seek God and His righteousness FIRST, He will take care of all our needs. His Word also states that God is a rewarder of those who diligently seek Him. So, He will supply all of our needs and our wants if they are within His will.

Throughout this book, when I write of me, I or we, I am referring to the human spirit. The real spiritual person who lives in the body.

Now a question often asked. Will there be marriages in Heaven? Jesus said that in Heaven, we would be like the angels. There will be no marriages in Heaven, Matthew 22:30. He said we would be like the angels. The angels do not have sex organs and neither shall we. That is only for physical beings for the purpose of bringing more spiritual beings into this world.

When we leave this body, we will be nothing but a spirit. We will leave all of the physical here on earth. In the Bible, (Jeremiah 1:5), God tells us He knew us before we came here. How long we lived with Him there, we do not know. Heaven was our home. We are here on assignment. Let us pray that we accomplish what we were sent here to do.

The Holy Spirit gave me the following illustration years ago to help me understand what His goal is for those who ask Jesus to save them. I saw a transparent glass filled with pebbles (small rocks). Then I saw a transparent pitcher filled with water.

I saw a hand pick up the pitcher and pour the water into the glass of pebbles until the water was near the rim of the glass. Then the hand removed a pebble or two from the glass. The water level then dropped. The hand poured more water into the glass and the water rose.

Then more pebbles were removed, the water level dropped. More water was added until the glass was almost full again. This went on until all the pebbles were gone, and the glass was completely full of water.

The understanding I was given was that the glass represented our body, the pebbles our sins, and the water was the Holy Spirit. The hand of God poured His Spirit into us. Just the little there was room for. He took out some sins and there was room for more Holy Spirit. He took out more sins and that left more room for more of the Holy Spirit. Eventually, all sins were removed and the body was filled with the Holy Spirit.

This next statement is very important for you to understand. The complete filling (complete removal of all sin) by our Heavenly Father and replaced with His Holy Spirit is the Kingdom of God within us. It is the pearl of great price.

This is why it tells in First Corinthians 6:10 that thieves, liars, immoral people, etc., cannot enter the Kingdom of God. We have to let ourselves be cleansed of all sin. A person in my family tells me we can never get rid of all sin. My question is, which sin is God not able to cleanse us of?

After learning what the Kingdom of God is, we can understand why in Matthew 6:33 Jesus tells us this is what we are to seek above everything else. He said seek the Kingdom FIRST.

I believe the truth and reality of the Kingdom of God and the pearl of great price is the best-kept secret of all times. The devil does not want humanity to know this. Being FILLED with the Holy Spirit is what God wants for us when He welcomes us home with, "Well done, my good and faithful servant."

Can you imagine what a person could do for the Kingdom of God if it was created in them? People need to know that our spirit can become one with God. We can be conscious of Him all the time.

When the LORD first showed me this, I dreamed I was in darkness. I could only see an outline of a person's body, but then light began to fill this body until it was full. It glowed from inside out. As I saw this, someone spoke to me in an urgent voice and said, "If you want to pray about anything, do it now!" The light was beginning to leave when I heard this order.

I searched quickly to determine the best thing to pray for, and I prayed to be freed of all fear. Then I awoke. My whole body was tingling with ecstasy. The Holy Spirit then told me, "That was the Kingdom of God. The pearl of great price."

I then was given the understanding of the scripture Romans 8:11: "If the Spirit of Him that raised up Jesus from the dead dwells within you, He that raised up Christ from the dead shall also quicken your mortal bodies by the Spirit that dwells in you." Believe me, when I awoke, my body was quickened. It was alive with the Holy Spirit.

It is so sad that God has that for those who will let Him cleanse them of their sin, but we fight so hard to refuse to even look at our sin, let alone let God get rid of them. As Paul said in Philippians 3:14, "I too press toward the mark of the high calling of God in Christ Jesus." I pray that you do too. When our spirits go back to God, who gave them, we will have nothing to be judged for.

We will place our crowns at Jesus' feet and praise Him that He earned them for us. Thank you, sweet Jesus.

CHAPTER 5

Holy Spirit

When I began reading the Bible about the Holy Spirit, I could not understand what kind of being He is. I had a dream that I was going to receive the baptism of the Holy Spirit. It frightened me because I did not know what it was.

My oldest daughter, Freda, and I went to a church that taught that speaking in tongues was the baptism of the Holy Spirit and salvation. We took Freda's friend with us. The preacher was someone Freda knew and cared about when she was a child and we wanted to hear him preach. He had moved to Georgia years before and was here visiting family. He would be preaching here a few nights. He believed as this church believed and preached on it.

After the preaching, Freda's friend wanted to receive Jesus as Savior. She was prayed for and spoke in tongues. That night I was very upset. I could not understand why she went one night and got the baptism (I still did not understand anything about it), and I had been going to church four years and had not yet received the baptism. I knew it was a good thing.

To this day I do not know how I knew to say this, but I said, "I want Jesus, Himself, to tell me why. I do not want the Holy Spirit to tell me. I want Jesus to come, Himself, and tell me why she got it and I did not." The Holy Spirit said to me, "Be at peace now. He will speak to you in the morning." Instantly, I was at peace and went to sleep. When I awoke the next morning, Jesus was standing by my bed. He said, "They are given the experience but not the power. They have to have the experience (speaking in tongues) to believe they are saved." Then He was gone.

I knew I was to wait. I would receive the baptism in His time. There are very many scriptures in the Bible that tell us what the Holy Spirit does. He is God's gift to us. After we ask Jesus to save us, we receive the gift of the Holy Spirit. He is to be our helper, comforter, teacher, guide, counselor, and healer. He is to convict us of our sins or else we would not see them as sin. By ourselves we can never free ourselves of sin. We could not learn of the spiritual understanding of the Bible, God or Jesus. He is given to us to lead us out of the nature of sin into the nature of Jesus.

Before we ask Jesus to save us, we can never be free of our sinful nature, but the wonderful truth is Jesus came to set the captives free. Free of the power of satan and sin. He made it possible for us to be cleansed of sin. Jesus gives us the Holy Spirit to lead, guide and help us through all of our trials and tribulation.

In the past I lived my whole life in fear. One day I was being tormented with the fear of something destructive happening to my youngest daughter. My husband and I were at the grocery store. All the time we were there I was worrying (worry is fear) about my daughter. When we got to the check out, my husband began putting the groceries on the counter. Suddenly I was unaware of my physical surroundings. I know now that somehow my spiritual eyes were opened, and I was seeing wave after wave of light. I was in the light. It was everywhere, above, below, all around. I was immersed in it. I could not have gotten out of it if I had tried.

I saw these waves of light come toward me, and then pass through me and then more came and passed through. I knew it was a constant thing. When this was happening, a voice spoke to me and said, "You see, you have no reason to fear." I was given the scripture, "In Him we live and move and have our being." Acts 17:28; also, Ephesians 4:6, "God is above, all through all and in all."

The Holy Spirit revealed Himself to me. He is everywhere all the time. My science teacher taught that the only thing that exists is energy and all matter is created from that energy. I could not understand that either but wondered about it often through the years. One evening I was sitting in church wondering about this again. Suddenly the Lord said to me, "Energy is the Holy Spirit. The Holy Spirit is energy." The only thing that exists is God and the matter He has created and is creating. While I was watching TV once, a scientist said, "We have found that there is some kind of energy everywhere, but we do not know what it is." He should read the Bible.

This experience that I had at the grocery helped me understand more about the Holy Spirit. God's Holy Spirit. He is everywhere and knows everything. He knows our thoughts and feelings. He never leaves us, and we cannot leave Him. We may shut our minds and hearts to Him. We may resist Him. We may not feel His presence, but He is always with us.

He knows everything we have ever done. He knows everything that is stored in our memory bank. He knows all the things we have buried in our subconscious mind that are too painful for us to deal with. If we let Him, He will bring it out and help us deal with it and get over it. No matter what we have ever done wrong in the past, He will forgive us.

The fruit of the Spirit is what the Holy Spirit will produce or create in us. The fruit is love, joy, peace, patience, kindness, goodness, faithfulness, gentleness, self-control and long-suffering. These are all God's qualities.

An apple tree produces apples, a peach tree produces peaches. The Holy Spirit produces God-like qualities, but the seed of the tree has to be planted, then grow and mature; then the bud, then the fruit. This is a growth process. The Holy Spirit is always there working to produce His fruit in us.

As I wrote elsewhere, we cannot just stop the wrong; we have to replace it with something. The something we need to replace it with is something God-like. Replace anger with mercy, unforgiveness with forgiveness, hate with love and so forth. That way our mind is renewed with God's thoughts and attitudes. Our old ones are done away with.

All this is done by the Holy Spirit. We make the choice to let Him do it and yield to Him when He is doing His work. We think all day long. Are we thinking God-like thoughts? If we look at our thoughts, we can begin to bring them into captivity as it is stated in the Bible in Second Corinthians 10:5. We can learn to reject all thoughts that we know are not God-like. In Philippians 4, it tells us the kind of thoughts we are to have. We have the power to change our thought habits.

We have to admit it when we are thinking thoughts other than God-like thoughts. We can ask the Holy Spirit to reveal this to us. He knows our every thought, remember? He knows all of our past. He will bring things to our remembrance, and also tell us things to come.

It is always safe to trust the Holy Spirit, Jesus and God. The minute we ask Jesus to save us from the power of satan and sin, the Holy Spirit begins acting in our lives for our benefit, for our spiritual growth and spiritual freedom. He never leaves us. He is always there, always trying to teach and help us. He will heal us of past hurts. He will help us forgive ourselves as we forgive others. He will teach and equip us for the job we have to do to further the Kingdom of God. He told me that everyone in the Kingdom of God has a job to do. We all have something we can do to help others. He will help us find and use that if we yield to Him as He works with us.

Jesus said that everything He did was by the power of the Holy Spirit. After He was tempted by the devil, scripture states that Jesus returned in the power of the Holy Spirit (God's Spirit), Luke 4:14. After we accept Jesus as our Savior, the Holy Spirit begins to help, teach, comfort and help us grow spiritually. The Holy Spirit helps our spirit (the real us) to grow into what God wants us to be.

Acts 10:38 says, "God anointed Jesus with the Holy Spirit and with power who went about doing good and healing all who were oppressed by the devil." The Holy Spirit is God with us, Acts 17:28, again. There are many scriptures about the Holy Spirit. There are too many for me to write. If you want to read and learn more about Him, get a concordance and look them up. We should learn all we can about Him.

God knows how helpless and ignorant (meaning we have no knowledge of) we are about Him and His ways. The Bible states that He pities His children. He remembers they are dust (Psalms 10:3). He knew we would need constant help in our spiritual walk, so He gives us the Holy Spirit to be our constant helper.

We must yield and not resist Him. He is God's Spirit, which is love. So, everything He brings about in our lives is for our good. It will be either to protect us and/or others from hurt or suffering or help us to grow. Everything that happens is for our spiritual growth. If we really realize that fact, we will yield more to the guidance of the Holy Spirit and grow.

The Bible tells us God speaks to us in a still small voice (First Kings 19:12). At times we will be puzzling over (meditating on) something and suddenly "the light bulb goes on." We get the answer. That is the Holy Spirit revealing the truth to us. We will be asking if we should or should not do this or that, and a scripture will pop into our mind that will give us the answer. That is the Holy Spirit giving us the answer. Through these many years the Holy Spirit has taught me when He gives us something, He expects us to use it to help others. When I would pass on to others the things He would tell me, I would say He told me this or that. One time a young woman ridiculed me for saying He spoke to me. Later, I prayed and asked how I could help her understand. He told me to tell her that He is Spirit. He has no physical mouth to speak to our physical ears, so He speaks to our spirit that lives inside of our head.

God knows that we, ourselves, have no spiritual understanding. We only have our natural understanding. The Bible tells us that spiritual things are foolish to the natural man. When we accept Jesus as our savior, the Holy Spirit begins to teach us and give us spiritual understanding. We have been born into the spiritual world.

We are first born into this physical world, see and learn about physical things; then when we ask Jesus to save us, we are born (brought forth, carried) into the spiritual world. We have become a new person, spiritually. We are a new spiritual person, but we still have the old sinful nature living in the same body as our new spiritual nature. The sin has to be cleaned out of us, so the Holy Spirit begins to do this job.

The Holy Spirit begins to teach us and give us understanding. After I turned my life over to Jesus, I prayed everyday for wisdom, knowledge and understanding. I also prayed for faith and love. I began praying for spiritual things and not just things for the flesh to feel good.

By the way, there is a difference in asking for salvation, and surrendering our life to Jesus. Jesus wants us to surrender everything to Him so He can cleanse, heal and set us free quickly. If we ask for salvation but will not surrender to Him, we will suffer more because we are holding on to our sinful attitude of wanting to be in control. When we first come to Jesus (as I have written before), we are sinful beings. The Holy Spirit calls and draws us to Jesus. He empowers us for service. When He has come, He guides us into all truth, John 16:13.

Job 33:4, "The spirit of God has made me, and the breath of the Almighty has given me life."

Psalms 137:7, "Where shall I go from your spirit? Or where shall I flee from your presence? Verse 8: "If I rise up into Heaven, you are there: if I make my bed in hell you are there."

Acts 1:8, "But you shall receive power after the Holy Ghost is come upon you: and you shall be witnesses unto me."

Ephesians 4:30, "Grieve not the Holy Spirit of God, whereby you are sealed unto the day of redemption."

Titus 3:5, "Not by works of righteousness which we have done, but according to His mercy He saved us by the washing of regeneration, and renewing of the Holy Ghost.'

Second Peter 1:21, "For the prophecy came not in old time by the will of man, but holy men of God spoke as they were moved by the Holy Ghost."

Romans 8:11, "Looks ahead to the time of our future resurrection, reminding us that just as the Holy Spirit was the active Agent in resurrecting Christ, He will also bring about the resurrection of the righteous who have died."

Thessalonians 4:14-17, "His presence in the lives of believers is evidenced by the fact our lives are controlled by the Spirit rather than by our old sinful nature."

In First Corinthians, we learn that the Holy Spirit knows all things and shares God's wisdom and knowledge with us. Scripture tells us (Proverbs 3:13-18) how precious is knowledge, understanding and Wisdom. All of these are given by the Holy Spirit. The 13th chapter of First Corinthians tells us the importance of love. The greatest commandments are to love. The Holy Spirit gives us this. Faith quenches all the fiery darts of the wicked one (Ephesians 6:16), and faith is a gift given by the Holy Spirit.

As a member of the Godhead, the Holy Spirit reveals and conveys the mind of God perfectly. He continues the ministry of Jesus in the life of the believer. He is the One who convicts a person by the message of the gospel. He encourages, instructs and intercedes through believers. He is never away from us. We can have conversation with Him. He is always there to help us learn and grow spiritually into the likeness of Jesus.

Jesus knew how helpless we were. He knew that we needed someone to care for us. He gave us a spiritual caregiver to meet all of our needs. He is to cleanse us of sin, heal us of the past, equip and train us for our ministry; what we were sent here to fulfill. Besides learning to love, we all have work to do here. Different people have different jobs. The problem is that many people resist the Holy Spirit and never reach that goal. They live their lives for themselves. Their time on earth is not only wasted but spent doing things that they will be judged for when they leave here.

Jeremiah 17:9 and 10, "The heart is deceitful above all things, and desperately wicked. Who can know it? I the Lord search the heart. I test the mind, even to give every man according to his ways (deeds) according to the fruit (results) of his doings."

The Holy Spirit can only do what we choose to let Him do. He does not force us to yield to Him. God's Word tells us that we grieve the Holy Spirit when we resist Him. It is like telling our children how to live so they can be happy, healthy, productive adults, but they do the opposite and destroy all of this in their lives. How we grieve over them, so the Holy Spirit grieves over us also, when we choose the destructive ways of life.

When we choose to yield to the Holy Spirit, then He works to accomplish that choice we make. When we choose to resist so we can do our own sinful thing, then an evil spirit takes over and accomplishes what we choose. All we do is make the choice. A choice we will suffer for. Meanwhile, satan is laughing with glee that he got to be in control of us and made us sin against God, ourselves and/or others.

Jesus did not leave us in satan's power without an escape. The Holy Spirit was given for the purpose of leading us out of the power of satan and sin into the wonderful protective power of the Father, Son and Holy Spirit. All we have to do is choose to yield and obey, and let the Holy Spirit accomplish what God's Will is for us. It is all good.

We can converse with the Holy Spirit. He is here to help us. I talk to Him about everything. He listens and understands. He will help us with our daily life and problems. One time I wanted to have some new mauve colored carpet put in my TV room. In the past, I was always afraid to make a decision. I asked the Holy Spirit if I would be happy with a mauve colored carpet. Instantly, I saw myself cleaning one. I was angry with myself for buying it. I was saying, "All I ever do is clean this darned carpet." I knew the Holy Spirit had answered my question. If I need something but cannot remember where I put it, I ask Him. Instantly, I know where it is.

Sometimes I play games on my computer. A few times I have gotten stuck on a level that I could not pass. I would say, "Holy Spirit, please help me understand this." The next time I looked at it, I knew how to do it. We just have to believe He is there, and that He cares about everything concerning us. He is willing to help us. People ask me if I get lonely. I tell them no because I am never alone.

I can talk to Him about everything. He always understands and helps me with it, or through it. He would do and be the same with everyone if only they understood more about Him. But, the devil works to keep people from this knowledge. I was about to close this chapter about Him. I stopped and asked Him if there was something special He wanted me to write. He said to write that He dances with joy when He can have a close, personal relationship with one of his own.

He has different ways of getting His messages or answers to our questions. Usually, we just suddenly understand or hear the still, small voice inside our head where our spirit lives, or as with my question about the carpet, He plays it out for our spirit to see and understand in our mind.

It is wonderful, wonderful, wonderful having Him as a friend and companion and helper. He will speak through us to help others. He heals the sick, raises the dead, and delivers us from satan's power. The devil does not want us to know anything about the Holy Spirit. He will confuse our thinking or simply rob us of any understanding or belief in Him.

I heard the following little story years ago. It gives us some understanding on this.

Once there lived a little fish with his mother and father in a little pond. One day a frog came hopping by and saw the little fish. The frog said to the little fish, "Hi, little fish. Do you know you are in water?" "What is water?" asked the little fish. The frog said, "Go ask your mommy." The little fish swam to his mother. "What is water, Mommy?" he asked her. "I do not know," she replied. "Go ask your father." The little fish obeyed and swam over to his father. "Daddy," he said, "The frog said we are in water. What is water, Daddy?" The father told the little fish, "Do not pay any attention to the frog. There is no such thing as water."

This story gives us a mental picture of people's various thoughts and attitudes about the Holy Spirit. What we do not understand, we tend to dismiss it, deny it, disbelieve it, fear it, or hate it. What are your thoughts and attitudes about Him? You might ask Him to help you understand the truth about Himself. Get a good concordance if you do not have one, and look up the scriptures about Him.

In Him we live and move and have our being. Jesus did what He did by the power of the Holy Spirit. Luke 4:14 tells us that after Jesus was tempted by the devil, He returned in the power of the Holy Spirit. Jesus, Himself, said that He did what His Father told Him to do, and He did it by the power of the Holy Spirit.

We cannot see the Holy Spirit with our natural eyes. Jesus told that the Holy Spirit is like the wind. We cannot see the wind, but we can see where it is and what it does. We can feel it, but we cannot touch it with our physical fingers. It touches us. We cannot touch the Holy Spirit, but He touches us. We can see Him heal, protect, and change a person. We can see what He does, but we do not see Him.

Sometimes we can be aware of Him. We can experience Him at times. We can hear Him speak to us with that still, small voice. We cannot hear Him with our physical ears, but with our spirit who dwells inside of our body. Just as Jesus moved through a closed door, the Spirit can move through, and indeed dwells in, our physical being.

Our physical eyes are blind to the spiritual worlds around us. We really live in two worlds at the same time. One we see and one we do not. It tells us in the book of Hebrews that we have angels around us to minister to us.

We also have a cloud of witnesses around us. We are not alone here. We have more help and protection than we can ever really understand, because we are part of this spiritual world (we are a spirit) enclosed in a physical body.

At times, the Holy Spirit lets us experience a spiritual awareness of Him. We can at times experience a feeling of His love or presence, but usually we do this on the inside. Sometimes it permeates our physical body, but that is still the work of the Holy Spirit's energy. Some people express that feeling as electricity, a tingling or heat.

He tells us of Jesus and the Father. The Father, Son, Holy Spirit. They all work together as one. They are all one in purpose, intent and deed, though they are three separate entities. (Matthew 3:16) The Holy Spirit was given by Jesus to help us poor, puny, pitiful creatures here on earth.

The natural man CANNOT discern these things, because they can only be discerned spiritually; and they can only be discerned spiritually, if we have accepted the Son of God, Jesus, as our personal savior. That is when the Holy Spirit begins to cleanse, heal, and create His fruit and gifts in us. It is He who begins to lead us out of the power of satan and sin into God's righteousness. It is He who replaces our sinful nature and the strongholds of satan with the DIVINE nature. IF WE HUMBLE OURSELVES AND LET HIM.

Most people believe this is impossible, but scripture tells us with God all things ARE possible. He speaks to our human spirit (the real us) to answer our questions. We may ask Him any question. He is always willing to help us understand and grow. A lot of the time we do not realize that we have just been spoken to by the Holy Spirit. The less we focus on ourselves, and the more we focus on God and doing His will, the more we can discern when the Holy Spirit is speaking or directing us.

The natural man will be drawn by the Holy Spirit to accept Jesus as their Savior. It is His job to do that. Sometime ago I prayed for a person to be drawn to Jesus. This person never knew that, but later told me when they had gone through a time when they kept thinking about Jesus, and they had feelings about Him that brought them to tears. Alas, they did not yield to him at that time. Later, things happened in their life that brought them to their knees.

John 14:15-17, (15) "If you love Me, keep my commandments." (16) And I will pray the Father and He will give you another helper, that He may abide with you forever."

"The Spirit of truth, whom the world cannot receive, because it neither sees Him nor knows Him; but you know Him, for He dwells with you and will be in you."

John 14:26, "The Helper, the Holy Spirit, whom the Father will send in My name, He will teach you all things and bring to you remembrance all things I have said to you."

The Holy Spirit brings to our remembrance the things Jesus taught when He walked the earth in a human body. When we need some guidance, comfort or help in some way, the Holy Spirit will bring to our mind a scripture that will help us in whatever need we have.

That is Him speaking to us. He does that as we walk our spiritual walk, but we usually do not perceive that it is Him speaking to us. We think it is ourselves remembering the scripture.

I hope you have gotten some understanding of the Holy Spirit. I hope you will pray to God the Father, in the name of Jesus the Savior, to help you get to really know and understand our helper, the Holy Spirit.

One last thing. He can and will let us see Him as He did for me when I was so fearful about my daughter. As I wrote elsewhere, my whole life was lived in fear, but I was given this experience to help me be freed of that. He will give us what we need to grow or to help others grow. God with us, (the Holy Spirit) the hope of Glory.

Father, Son and Holy Spirit, these three are one. So many people can't understand how this can be.

Their problem is the fact that they are thinking of the *number* one. This is not pertaining to a number, but a state of being, a state of mind.

They are all in one accord at all times in purpose, intent and deed. The Lord gave me this understanding many years ago when my youngest daughter was about six years old.

We have a fall celebration in our town each year. This year, my daughter wanted to go with her friend and her friend's family.

I was not at peace with it but knew her three older sisters would be there too, so we let her go.

My husband and I went to visit his mother while the girls were gone. While we were there, the friend's mother called us and said they had lost our daughter, Missy.

We both panicked. We began calling people whom we thought would be there and might find Missy. We finally found that one of her older sisters had her.

Some time later, I was pondering the question how could the Father, Son and Holy Spirit be one person. The Lord said to me, remember when Missy was lost at the fall celebration?

Yes, I answered. What did you and Harold do? He asked. I knew instantly what He meant. We were both afraid. Everything went out of our minds except what we could do to find her.

We were both thinking everything *we* could think of and then we acted on that.

I understood. *We* were two people but *we* were in complete agreement on our purpose, intent and deed. *We* were two people but we were one in our desire to find our lost daughter. *We* acted as one unit.

That is how the Father, Son and Holy Spirit operate. They are all centered on *one* thing. They are in *one* accord in their desire to find and save lost souls.

CHAPTER 6

God Speaks

God speaks to us very often but many times we do not realize that He is speaking.

In Genesis 1:29 He speaks to Adam and Eve.

Exodus 14: 15 & 16 He spoke to Moses.

Genesis 2:16 He spoke to Adam again.

Psalms 91:15 He answers us.

First Kings 19:9 He speaks to Elijah.

Acts 9:4 Jesus spoke to Saul and later Paul.

Acts 8:26 An angel spoke to Phillip.

Acts 9:10 The Lord spoke to Ananias.

John 16:13 Jesus said the Holy Spirit will speak to us.

John 14:21 Jesus said He will manifest Himself to those who keep his commandments.

John 14:26 Holy Spirit will bring things to our remembrance (our mind).

John 10:3 Jesus' sheep hears His voice.

John 10:16 Jesus has other sheep who hear His voice.

John 18:37 All who are of the truth hear My voice.

John 10:27 My sheep hear my voice.

Mark 13:11 The Holy Spirit speaks through us.

Isaiah 30:21 And thine ears shall hear a word behind thee saying, this is the way walk ye in it, when you turn to the right or left. When I hear the Holy Spirit it seems I hear Him at the right sides of the back of my head.

Isaiah 30:21 says when you hear a word behind thee, I believe He is saying, so to speak, we will hear Him speak in the back of our minds or brain.

I believe that is where our spirit resides. So His Spirit is speaking to our spirit.

In Isaiah 30:21 He is telling us when we wonder off the straight and narrow path He will guide us back to it.

Many times we think they are our thoughts but they have been put there by the Holy Spirit.

We will get a "thought" that tells us we are in the wrong or a scripture that tells us the right way, that is also the Holy Spirit speaking to us.

So we can hear that still small voice of God that Elijah heard in First Kings 19:12, that still small voice in the back of our mind.

CHAPTER 7

The Subconscious Mind

Seek FIRST the Kingdom of God after John 3:16. We are to begin our journey to seek God's will for us, seek to have His righteousness created in us. This chapter is to explain how we get off the track and how we can get back on it.

There is a place in our brain where everything we see, smell, touch, taste, hear, think and do, is recorded. The following is what the Holy Spirit helped me understand what the subconscious mind is and what it does.

He used the tape recorder as an example. When we tape something on a recorder, every time we play that recording, it plays the same thing, over and over always the same. The subconscious mind does the same thing. What we put in, it records. It does not matter whether it is good or bad, right or wrong, it records.

It begins taping when we are born—maybe sooner—and tapes until we die. Studies have shown that by the time we reach our fifth year, our personality is formed.

The Bible states that when we die, the books will be opened and we will be judged for what we did while on earth. I believe that all these memories are also stored in our subconscious mind, and also our spiritual mind. Our spirit that goes back to God. The Bible tells us that when we die, our body goes back to dust and our spirit goes back to God who gave it. Then, we are judged for what we did here on earth.

I believe also that the books that are opened are our subconscious minds, which recorded everything we did on earth. People who have come close to death have said that in an instant their whole life flashed before their eyes.

As we go through life, things happen to us. When they do we will think and feel something about it. What we think and feel is recorded. When something unpleasant happens, satan will put a negative thought in our subconscious mind.

There are two levels of our mind—the rational and the irrational level. The irrational is the subconscious. The rational has the faculty of reasoning. We think with our rational mind. We can reason things out.

Our subconscious is the seat of our emotions, and is the creative mind. It creates according to the thoughts our conscious mind gives it to work with. If we think good it creates good. If we think bad, then bad will follow.

The important thing to remember is once the subconscious accepts a thought or idea, it begins to use that. When a situation happens and we become angry, and it happens again, we become angry. Then when a situation occurs like the first two, our subconscious deals with it the same. Anger. Maybe the rest of our lives.

It has set its course to deal with situations similar to the first ones the same way. We may live the rest of our lives being controlled by this rule the subconscious accepted. Once it accepts something, it makes the same response every time. That is why we react to people and situations instead of thinking first.

The devil knows all of this. He knows how our brain and mind works. The brain and mind are not the same thing. The brain is a fleshy machine. The mind is us, using the brain to manifest our thoughts, attitudes and desires.

When any given situation or experience occurs, satan is there to put his thought, attitude and desire into the subconscious mind. If we accept those, they are recorded and programmed. He or one of his evil spirits is always there to take advantage of the situation to record or reinforce something that has already recorded. This is how satan creates strongholds in our mind. When the subconscious accepts these thoughts, attitudes and desires, satan then has the control of that part of our life.

The Holy Spirit told me, as I have written elsewhere in this book, that satan programs our subconscious mind even as we begin to learn to walk. Then when we become adults he controls us with the destructive thoughts he has put in there that we accepted.

This is why scripture tells us to take every thought into captivity, which means to watch the thoughts that come into our mind, and reject every thought that is not of faith. It tells us everything that is not of faith is sin, Romans 14:33.

I have heard so many people say, and I myself said many times, I have bad thoughts I cannot stop thinking. Or I keep doing the same wrong thing over and over that I cannot control. This is because our subconscious mind has been programmed to do or think those things.

The subconscious does not have an opinion of whether something is right or wrong. It is like a computer because it records and programs what ever is put in it. Once it accepts something, only God can change it. I have read and heard that we can change a habit if we replace it with something else for 21 days. Even then it is the Holy Spirit that gives us the ability to do that. All GOOD things come from God.

Philippians 4:8 tells us what kind of thoughts we are to think. If we think these thoughts over and over, we will be programming our subconscious mind with them. When it accepts these thoughts, it brings those things to our conscious mind. We do not have to consciously control ourselves to think them any more. Our subconscious will automatically put them in our mind.

Peace of mind and good health are inevitable when we think and feel the right way. When we think and feel the right way, our actions will be in accord with them. When we give the command to the subconscious, it will faithfully reproduce the idea we have implanted in it. It may take different time lengths for different orders. It may depend on how strongly we give the idea to it.

We have to remember, if it is a stronghold of satan and not just our thoughts, we will need to get rid of the spirit first. Jesus said to get rid of the strong man first and then we can clean out the house, Matthew 12:29.

If it is a spirit, we cannot get the victory until it is gone. We cannot reason with nor can we compel it to leave, nor replace old thoughts with new as long as it is there. WE HAVE TO BIND ITS POWER IN THE NAME OF JESUS AND COMMAND IT TO LEAVE.

Once is it gone, then we can get the victory. Sometime the sin, hurt, fears, addiction, whatever it is, leaves immediately. Other times we may have to fight a battle with our sinful self. That is all up to Jesus. There is always a reason for what He allows, and that is for our spiritual growth.

An example of being programmed, when I was very small, Mom took my brothers and me to her parent's farm to visit. While there, she had a flat tire. Grandpa was going to take her to town to have the tire repaired.

My older brother, John, wanted to go too but they did not want to take him, so they drove away leaving him in the yard with Grandma and me. Their yard went so far and then made a big dip to the road. John ran after them. He ran down the dip in the yard and disappeared from my sight.

In a moment, he came running back as fast as he could with a look of terror on his face. Then I saw Grandpa running after him with a long thin branch from a tree. He was holding it over his head and yelling at John that he was going to beat him to death.

It terrified me. I remember grabbing hold of Grandma's leg, looking up at her and saying, "I'll do anything you want me to." From then on I felt that if I did not do everything everyone wanted, I would be in some kind of danger. I did many things I did not want to do but could not stop myself.

Mom told me when I was about seven years old that no one liked girls. She had a look of contempt for me when she said it. From that time, I became what they called a tomboy. I knew I could not be a boy, but if I could do things better than they could, maybe people would like me anyway. I competed with John and men from then until after I turned my life over to Jesus, and He showed me all of this.

I never thought that I am going to do this or that better than they can do it. I just FELT compelled to try. It had been programmed into my subconscious mind. My subconscious mind compelled me to do it. I did not realize what I was doing or why I was doing it until the Holy Spirit revealed it to my conscious mind that I was trying to get people to like me even though I was a girl. I lost my identity for a long time.

I believed it when Mom told me no one liked girls. The devil put that in her mind to tell me. He was using her again, trying to destroy me. He was working to program my subconscious mind so he could control me with that belief and fear that no one would ever like me.

It worked for many years. I was in the second grade when this happened. I was controlled by it until I was in my thirties, and Jesus began to set me free of it. It took him a while to erase that from my subconscious mind and program His thoughts and attitudes in its place, but He was beginning to renew my mind, cleaning out the old thoughts, attitudes, and beliefs and replacing them with new—His.

Things happened to me in my childhood, my growing up years into my adult life that satan used to program me to believe I was a very sinful, shameful, inferior and worthless person. He does this to many, many people. In fact, I believe he does this to the majority of humanity. He has his army of evil spirits working for him.

It took the Holy Spirit quite a while to get me to feel comfortable in feminine clothing. I was used to jeans, and carried a billfold in my back pocket. You might ask me how I know all this. The truth is that satan took over the control of my life when I was just a child. He did and caused all of these things in my life and me.

He wanted to make my life so miserable that I would kill myself. I fought it for years, but finally I came to live in despair. I saw no hope in the future of ever escaping the mental and emotional pain of depression I had lived in for years so I was going to kill myself.

Jesus stopped that when He appeared to me and gave me the choice of doing that or turning my life over to Him. He revealed all of this that I have written about. He taught me that when we let pride rule in our lives then comes the shame. Shame is one of the most painful things to live with.

We do not want to have to suffer with it. The devil gives us his way of dealing with it. Shame makes us feel very bad about ourselves. Pride makes us feel very good about ourselves so satan's evil spirits of pride begins working on us to cover the shame with pride. We begin to feel more and more pride. We have fallen into his evil trap.

When I encounter someone displaying a strong sense of pride I think the poor thing is caught in the shame and pride trap.

I was talking to someone about his or her pride (I had not yet been freed of mine), and, as I was talking to him or her, the Holy Spirit said to me, "You will never get rid of the worthlessness until you give up the pride." In my inward self, I said (not out loud), "Okay, I give it to you right now." The devil had programmed the worthlessness in my subconscious mind since I was a child. He had controlled me with it for over thirty years. He had put a lot of it in there.

I tell you that to help you understand what I will write now, and that is for the next three days I could think of nothing but how worthless I was. I had suppressed worthless thoughts, but I always had the feelings of it in the back of my mind. But it was in my subconscious mind all the time. It is hard to explain. It is an attitude you have about yourself. You may not think the thoughts of, "I am a worthless person," but you feel that way. At times, I would say to myself, "you are no good to yourself or anyone else," but then bring myself out of that.

After I gave the pride up, which covered the worthlessness of my subconscious mind, I began to tell myself how no good I was. I thought over and over that I was no good as a mother, no good as a sister, no good as a wife, no good as a daughter, just a no-good person. This went on for three days.

I really believed it. I felt so sad and sorrowful all the time. I cried and cried about it. As I awoke on the fourth morning, the first thought I had was that I was no good, but this time the Holy Spirit said to me very compassionately, "Now you know that isn't true," and the worthlessness was gone. Praise the Lord!

He revealed to me that all of that had been buried in my subconscious mind for so long that it took those three days for Him to clean it out.

The pride was gone so there was nothing there to prevent the worthlessness from coming out. I faced it and did not try to hide it anymore, so He was able to clean it out. As long as we hide it from ourselves, it affects our lives in a negative way.

I believe satan has a bag of tricks that he plays on the majority of people in this world. I did not know myself at all until I turned my life over to Jesus, and He began to reveal the truth to me. John 8:32, "You shall know the truth and the truth shall set you free."

I hated myself but He began to show me that there were reasons why I did things I was ashamed of. The devil was controlling me. Slowly, I quit hating myself once I began to see and understand that I did many things that my spirit was ashamed of because so many times I was not in control. Also, I was sinned against many times in my life, especially in my childhood and teen years, and that was satan using people around me to try to destroy me. It worked, but he did not get to kill me.

Jesus took the damaged vessel and repaired it. He replaced old parts with new, sanded it down, which did not feel good at the time, and He replaced the old broken parts with new ones. He got it back into good shape so He could use it for His purposes. Now, I know I cannot take any pride in the change and newness. All I can do is be grateful to the Master builder for repairing me and using me to tell others about it.

He will repair anyone who will humble themselves and let Him. I pray everyone who reads this will do that.

The Bible tells us that satan goes up and down through the earth seeking whom he can devour, meaning destroy. He destroys our mental and emotional health. The Bible tells us he deceives us and makes us believe lies, and that he deceives the whole world.

He had me believing that I was the worst person in the whole world. He programmed my subconscious to believe this. I felt that about myself for years and years. I did not think the thoughts, but the feeling was always in the back of my mind (the subconscious).

I always felt uncomfortable around people, especially people like doctors, teachers, people who had more or did more and/or better than I was or did. The devil had done a good job of programming my subconscious the way he wanted it, and I was controlled by it. I felt that I could never do as well or be as good as other people.

As a child, I learned anger and violence by my family and some of the people around me. I was punished if I did not fight to protect my brothers, even my older brother. I was programmed to feel ashamed and think of myself as a coward (which back then was one of the worst things your could be), if I did not fight for them.

I grew up fighting their battles until I was fifteen when one of my brothers came and wanted me to beat up a boy about his age who had hit him. I told him I was too old to fight his battles anymore, that he would have to fight his own. I never started a fight except one time when one of my uncles hired me to beat up a bully who kept hurting his children.

I have written all this so you will have some understanding of how much control satan through our subconscious can have over us. Now I look around at so many people and see some or all the same things controlling them, but like myself, they do not realize they are being controlled.

I was molested when I was in the second grade. At the time this happened, satan put in my mind the thoughts and feelings of shame. From that moment until I was in my late thirties, I felt ashamed of myself. I did not think, "I am ashamed." I felt it. He put that in my subconscious mind at a traumatic time. My subconscious accepted it was true that I was the one who did something shameful. I believed I was a terrible person and everyone would hate me.

I did not deserve to be liked. All of my relationships were with abusive men. That was because I felt I did not deserve any happiness. I deserved to be punished for my sins. That is why so many women choose abusive men; satan has programmed them to feel isolated because of their shame of the past, so they seek someone they can feel close to. Not all alone in the world.

Because of the shame, they are attracted to abusive men who will punish them, which only makes them more ashamed. Some women, though, are compelled to love a controlling, abusive man by satan's evil spirits. In both cases, it is satan working to destroy them.

I read of a case where a man was allergic to flowers. Through therapy he remembered that when he had been left at the altar by his fiancé, there were many flowers there. After that, when he encountered flowers, his nose would run and his eyes watered. He had wanted to cry when he was jilted, but he would not let himself. When he encountered flowers, his subconscious gave the outward appearance of his inward desire to cry. The flowers triggered the desire and the subconscious created the tears and runny nose.

One time my husband took my daughter and me out to eat at a fast food place. I had been working on eating right. I really wanted a big old cheeseburger, but I ordered a fish sandwich instead because it was better for me.

When our order arrived, there was no fish sandwich. The lady had brought me a large cheeseburger. I told her that I had ordered fish. She, my husband, and my daughter all said that I did not order fish, I had ordered a cheeseburger.

It was on the tip of my tongue to deny that, when the Holy Spirit helped me see they were right. He told me I wanted the cheeseburger so much that my subconscious took over. I heard myself say fish, but I really said cheeseburger.

The Holy Spirit was teaching me about the subconscious, and this was my first personal lesson on how it makes things happen that we give it the information to use. What the devil does through us, or what we give our subconscious, will come to pass — good or bad. I really wanted a cheeseburger, so my subconscious made that happen.

Our habitual thoughts in our conscious mind make grooves in our subconscious, which is very good for us if we think good, peaceful, kind and constructive thoughts.

I read of a woman who kept thinking to herself that she was losing her memory. She began repeating everyday, "My memory is getting better all the time. I will always be able to remember all I need to. It is improving everyday in every way." After three weeks, her memory was restored to normal.

Many times in this world, satan tells children that their parents do not love them when the child is being corrected for a wrongdoing. The child will believe what satan puts in their mind. They may live their whole life believing their parents did not love them.

This was put into the subconscious. The child believed and had a strong feeling about it, which opened the subconscious. Once the subconscious believed that, it would never let the person believe they were loved by the parents again, unless the Lord freed them of this belief.

My husband and I both loved our adopted grandson more than our own lives. When he was 3-1/2 years old, he wanted to play on the roof my husband was repairing. He cried and begged me to let him up there. Of course I could not. He cried himself to sleep. He had a nightmare about it that we did not love him any more.

One of the devil's evil spirits put that in his subconscious. He told me when he was in his early 30s that he could never believe we loved him. The subconscious believed the lie so it never let him believe he was loved. This caused mega problems in his life and mine. That is just why the huge lie was programmed into his subconscious.

This is the beginning of low self-esteem, the beginning of satan's plans to destroy a person. I have known other children who believed their parents did not love them, but I knew the parents and knew they did love their child very much.

The devil makes us believe lies. How many of his lies do you think you may have believed? Do you have negative thoughts about yourself? Do you think you are not as good as others? Do you think you cannot handle new experiences coming into your life?

These thoughts do not come from God. You are not thinking His thoughts. These are the kind of thoughts satan wants you to think. When you begin thinking these thoughts, hit the delete button and print something good in its place. Begin the transformation of your mind, because these negative thoughts are all lies that you have been programmed to believe.

The brain is a very amazing thing. The devil knows all about the brain and how it works. He knows that through it he can control our thoughts and emotions, if we allow it.

At first when we are little children, we do not realize this. We accept as true whatever he puts into our brain. That is why there is such a battle over who is using it. The devil can use our brain to make us have the thoughts and emotions he wants us to have to destroy us.

The Holy Spirit can us it to give us the thoughts and emotions Jesus wants us to have to create God's righteousness in us. We, (our spirit) or our soul can use the brain for its own agenda.

The point is that the emotions are created by the chemicals the brain tells the glands to produce, as whoever is using the brain at the time wills.

It is so terrible in this world that so many destructive chemicals are being put in the things we eat, drink, and breathe. They cause illness, and then we are given manufactured chemicals for the illness that may cause worse things, even death for the person taking them.

We only get one brain to get us through this world. We should take the best care of it that we possibly can.

Those of us who drive can remember when we first began driving. We had to focus on what we were experiencing all the time. We had to watch out for the other guy, keep it in the speed limit, watch for stop signs, stay on the right side of the road, etc.

We were a little fearful of making a mistake and wrecking the car. We were recording all of these things into our subconscious mind every time we drove. As we would drive at various times, this all became easier and less fearful.

Now we get in the car and take off without any of that. We now drive our car automatically. We do not have to focus on telling ourselves to do all of these things right. We can do them automatically while talking to someone in the car with us. Our subconscious has been programmed to do the things we need to do while driving. We are being controlled by our subconscious to do the things it was programmed to do.

This is how our mind is transformed by reading the Bible. We read to learn. We read and try to obey. Every day we will be practicing. Gradually we begin doing and thinking the things we have read. After a while, we do them automatically without thinking about it. Our subconscious has been programmed to God's way of thinking and acting.

We have been changed by recording new things over the old. The subconscious is now controlling us to do God's will. The old recording has been replaced by the new. We do not have to tell ourselves anymore to be that, we have become that. Transformed. Praise God for His wonderful works.

CHAPTER 8

Satan

I want to assure you that Jesus has given us authority and power over all the enemy. Jesus won the battle over our enemy when He died for our sins and was raised from the dead. We have no reason to fear satan if we have accepted Jesus as our Savior.

As God is love, satan is hate, pure hate. There is no mercy or sympathy in him at all. His desire is to destroy as many humans as he can. In any battle, it is best to know your enemy and how they operate. The Bible tells us to stand against the tricks of the devil (Ephesians 6:11). He is a liar. He begins telling us lies when we are children. He tells us our parents do not love us, and that there is something wrong with us, so that is why our parents don't love us. He is controlling the parents' minds to say and do destructive things to children. They do not realize they are being controlled by him.

He tells our parents or guardians to criticize and/or shame us and that will motivate us to do what they want. Criticizing and shaming makes a child feel worthless and unlovable. They develop a low opinion of themselves and believe everyone else has a low opinion of them, also. This is one of the tricks satan uses to begin our destruction. You are lazy, dumb, fat, no good, and will never amount to anything, and words such as these.

The word satan means adversary. He is our enemy. In the book of the Revelation, he is called appolyon (the destroyer). He is the accuser of the brethren, deceiver of the whole world, a murderer, (causes people to kill themselves) and/or others. He is called the evil one. Moral evil is his basic attribute. Jesus told us that satan was a murderer from the beginning and lived not in the truth, because there is no truth in him. When he speaks a lie, he speaks of his own, for he is a liar and the father of lies (John 8:44).

He was banished from Heaven because he had a passion to be above God and to be worshiped. He is still working all this time to be the ruler of God's creatures—us. He rules most people's lives in one way or another; fear, shame, guilt, anger, pride, selfishness, unforgiveness, bitterness, revenge, hate, sexual sin, drugs, or alcohol. The list goes on.

Anything we have in our lives that we cannot get the victory over means we are being controlled by him and/or his evil spirits. The Holy Spirit told me one time that as long as we have a spirit controlling us, we cannot get the victory; however, when we get rid of the spirit, then we can get the victory. We must really want to get the victory. I remember one time I saw how destructive anger was to my family, and I tried to get rid of it, but I could not. I had a dream of a red snake hiding in my house. I knew where it was, but I did not want it to leave because it looked so pretty to me.

The understanding the Holy Spirit gave me was that I really did not want to give up the anger because I used it to try to control people and circumstances. It was my way of trying to make people do my will. I also used it to defend myself against the things and/or people who offended me. The Holy Spirit finally got me to trust Him to defend and protect me, and to know that I could rest and let Him take care of me. He has done a wonderful job of that. I got rid of the spirits that caused the anger, and then I got over the need (my idea) for anger.

The night I turned my life over to Jesus, satan had almost taken me the last step into killing myself. He would have been very gleeful over his ability to murder me. Jesus came and told me there was another way out—to turn my life over to Him, and I took it. I bet satan was very angry when that happened.

Jesus has taught me through the years that we have the power to bind the power of the evil spirits (meaning preventing them from acting against us or others). The power is in the name of Jesus. At the name of Jesus, they have to obey us. Jesus won the victory. He rules! We must always remember to bind their power in the name of Jesus. ALWAYS! When we do that, they cannot manifest themselves against us or others.

My grandson had a spirit of fear. He could not be away from me. If we were out after dark, when we drove into the drive and I turned off the car lights, he grabbed me around the neck and would not let go. I took him to our assistant pastor who could cast out spirits. This was before I started doing that. The Holy Spirit had told me about being able to get the victory over problems and sins after getting rid of the spirit of them.

That night, the assistant pastor silently bound and commanded the spirit of fear to leave my 6-year-old grandson. It was dark when we got home. I turned off the car lights. Instead of grabbing me around the neck as he always had, he opened his car door, got out, walked around the back of the car, and walked to our door in the dark. He was very happy with himself, and so was I. Since then, the Holy Spirit has taught me a lot about satan and his evil army.

The Bible tells us to take every thought into captivity. We need to keep watch on the thoughts that enter our mind. In the past, I would be critical of everyone. I became aware of what I was doing. The devil blinds us to the sin in our lives as long as he can. He had blinded me to the constant critical thoughts. After I turned my life over to Jesus, He began opening my spirit to what was going on in my mind. I did not like what I saw, but I was unable to stop it.

One evening I was sitting in church listening to a visiting speaker. I caught myself being critical of him. I felt guilty and I asked Jesus to forgive me. Jesus asked me if I liked those thoughts. "No, I do not," I answered. He said, "Do you want to have these thoughts?" Again, I answered, "No." He said, "Then it is not really YOU, is it?" He told me that any thought I had that I did not like or want was not me thinking it. It was my enemy, satan, or an evil spirit putting them in my mind, and I was taking the blame. I was feeling guilty for what satan was doing, which was what he wanted.

The Holy Spirit told me that one of satan's tricks and pleasures is to keep us all emotionally upset ALL THE TIME. He will put a thought in our mind that he knows will cause fear, shame, self-pity, worry, regret, hurt, unforgiveness, revenge, and anything he knows will be upsetting to us. If we accept and dwell on that thought, he knows our brain will manufacture the emotion that goes with the thought, and there we are being controlled again. We have taken the bait.

In the past, he had almost complete control of my thoughts and emotions. I would awake in the morning full of self-pity, angry at the world, or guilty about the past. You name it, but it was never a positive emotion. I thought I could learn to deal with it, and get over this by using my mind and or will power. The Lord had led me to study psychiatry to learn about the mind and body, so I thought I would use this to get control of my emotions.

One morning just before I awoke, I dreamed that Jesus came into my bedroom. He stood beside and touched my chest of drawers. The chest of drawers in the dream represents where things are put away or stored out of our sight. Jesus pointed at a full-length mirror on the other side of the room. When I looked where He was pointing, I saw satan standing beside and partly hidden behind the mirror. He was distorting the mirror. It was like the mirrors in a carnival fun house. A mirror represents how we see ourselves or others. Jesus told me that satan was distorting how I saw myself. I saw myself as a terrible, no good, inferior outcast. He was distorting my outlook on the world and other people. I could see no goodness or beauty in them. I lived in depression because satan had control of my thoughts and emotions. I constantly wanted to die so I could get out of the mental and emotional pain.

In the dream, Jesus told me I could not get over this with psychology. He told me to order satan, "In the name of Jesus, to go away!" I was so afraid of satan that I scrunched up with fear. I fearfully pointed at him and told him to leave "in the name of Jesus."

That day I thought of the dream. I understood it. I did what Jesus had shown me in the dream. Relief! He left! The thoughts of and desire to commit suicide left.

I still had some depression that Jesus would take care of later, but the strong desire to die or kill myself was gone. Jesus left some of the depression so I would continue to seek out, repent of, and be freed of the destructive things of the past and the sinful attitudes that I had accepted from satan through all the years of his persecution of me. I learned to keep close watch on the thoughts and attitudes that came to my mind. If I knew it was not what Jesus would want me to think or feel, I immediately bound the spirit "in the name of Jesus," and commanded it to leave. It always did. I still do and will continue to do that.

We can keep our mind free of satan's influence if we do this. The devil only has the power over us that we give him. What we give him becomes a stronghold. We then lose the power to control ourselves or our thoughts in that area, in our own power. We then need to use our spiritual weapons, the name of Jesus, scripture, faith and our authority in Jesus. Unfortunately, he begins to program our way of thinking in our very early childhood as I have written elsewhere about the time my grandfather chased my brother and told him he would beat him to death. God only knows what satan put in his mind at the time, but satan told me that I had to do everything people wanted me to or something terrible would happen to me. I was only three years old at the time. The Holy Spirit showed me that satan begins programming our subconscious minds when we are toddlers. He works on us before we are able to reason things out or even understand or know about him.

My grandson was only three and a half years old when satan gave him the dream that he was helpless and no one loved him. That dream caused him to grow up trying to not be helpless by controlling others with anger. The fear was put away out of sight. Remember the chest of drawers in my dream of Jesus showing me how to get rid of satan? We all have or had things stored in our minds out of our conscious sight. These things satan has put there to control us as adults. Alas, most people never realize they are there, so they control them to their dying day.

My mother-in-law was a very cruel and verbally abusive woman until she was eighty years old. She took a good look at herself, saw the truth, and became a different person. The devil blinds us to the destructive things he programs us to do and be. He uses us to hurt and try to destroy others. He had used my mother-in-law for many years to hurt many people, especially her family. Our families receive most of our abusive words and actions. We are with them more. Jesus said our foes are the members of our own household in Matthew 10:36.

We tend to let ourselves be controlled by evil spirits when we are at home with our family more often than when we are in public. The devil uses us to try to destroy each other. He has destroyed many, many people that way. Colossians 3:21 says, "Fathers provoke not your children to wrath lest they become discouraged." They not only become discouraged and lose their faith, but they become angry, vengeful, rebellious, but also ashamed.

My aunt divorced her husband and brought her three children and moved in with us. One day my cousin and I were playing in the front yard when her paternal grandfather drove up. In those days, the automobiles had what was called a running board on the sides to step on to enter the auto. When my cousin's grandfather stopped in front of our house, she and I went to see what he wanted. We were about seven or eight at the time. He talked to her a few moments and then asked her if she would kiss him goodbye. She stepped up on the running board and kissed him on the cheek and then took off running to the house. Her grandfather asked me if I wanted to kiss him goodbye, too. I did not but I did not want to hurt his feelings, so I stepped up on the running board, kissed him quickly on the cheek, and ran to the house, also.

When I stepped in the door, I saw that my mother, aunt, brothers and cousins had all been watching me from inside the house. They were all looking at me when I entered. Mom began yelling at me with a look of contempt on her face. "How could you kiss that nasty old man?" she yelled. She went on and on about how bad and shameful I was in front of everyone.

I had thought I was doing the right thing by kissing him to prevent him having his feelings hurt. But now Mom was telling me I had done a nasty, shameful thing. I thought I was such a terrible person because I had thought doing something nasty was good. At that instant I lost all confidence in myself to make a right decision. I felt so much shame that I could not stand it. I wanted to run away from everyone's sight, but I was afraid of my mother, so I made my body stand there, but I, me, the spirit being, hid someplace in the back of my head. It seems so strange to write that, but I left somehow. The psychologists call that disassociation. The spirit abdicated the rule of the body to the soul. For many, many years, my soul made many choices that I did not want it to. I felt as though I had no control, which I, my real self, the human spirit, did not have.

When I was in my early forties, a very close friend and I began having a weekly prayer time together. We had heard about praying for Jesus to heal our destructive memories. One evening we decided to pray about this traumatic experience. I sat in a chair and she stood behind me and put her hands on my head and began praying. I closed my eyes and pictured in my mind that I was standing in our living room. I pictured everything as it had been. My mother was saying hateful things to me. I then pictured Jesus come in the door. From there, He took over. He leaned over and picked me up. Remember, I was a child at the time. It was so real I could feel myself sitting on His right arm. He turned and pointed at my mother. When he did, I looked where He was pointing, and I saw satan standing at her right shoulder talking into her ear. When Jesus pointed at her, he said to her, "Quit talking to her like that. The devil is using you to try to destroy her." Then I was back listening to my friend pray. I stopped her and told her Jesus had done what she had prayed for.

Before this happened, I tried not to think about that, because I always relived the terrible shame I felt at the time. After this experience with Jesus, and I know that is what it was, when I thought about it, I always felt happy and safe as I did sitting on Jesus' arm. The memory had been healed. Thank you, Jesus!

As I left for church one evening, a lady approached me. She told me the Lord had given her two words for me. For a few days I had been in torment in my mind and emotions. I had been praying and trying to get rid of it. I thought it was a spirit but did not know what it was called. I had been trying to get over it all through church. When she told me God had given her two words for me, I, of course, asked what they were. She replied, "Mental anguish." I knew the Lord had given me the answer to the question I had been asking for. The terrible feeling was mental anguish. On the way home, I bound the power of this spirit in the name of Jesus and commanded it to leave.

Instantly I felt some kind of invisible creature on top of my head. It had been manipulating my brain. I felt it release my brain and leave. I had been having these bouts with mental anguish since I was twelve years old. Every time I did something wrong or made a mistake. This night that the spirit left me was about twenty years ago. I have never had an experience of the mental anguish since then. Praise God!

Through the years, I have heard so many people complain of having wrong thoughts they hated, but they could not prevent them. I know now that they have no power over these thoughts because they are being put into their minds by spirits. They, of themselves, have no power to protect themselves. They are in a spiritual battle. They (I did the same) are trying to fight a spiritual battle with physical weapons, their brain, their will power or their determination. None of these work because they are not spiritual weapons.

In Second Corinthians 10:3-5, Paul tells us the weapons of our warfare are not carnal (of our flesh), but mighty in God for pulling down strongholds. Things satan has control of in our minds. In Ephesians 6, he explains we have to use spiritual weapons to fight spiritual battles. The Holy Spirit explained to me that I was fighting spiritual battles with physical weapons, and I could not win with them. We know satan is a spirit and our flesh has no power over him.

We have to use spiritual weapons. The Holy Spirit told me that the spiritual power is in the name of Jesus and scripture. All we have to do is command them in the name of Jesus. The Holy Spirit said we speak the words and Jesus does the work.

The most important words we must use are "I BIND YOUR POWER IN THE NAME OF JESUS." Then they have no more power to control us. We do not always have to give them a name. I have learned I can say, "You, spirit that is making me have proud, selfish, guilty, or even making me feel these feelings I do not want, or thoughts I do not want to think, I bind your power in the name of Jesus. I command you to leave and never come back."

The more we humble ourselves and confess what is going on in our minds that should not be there, the more we can be free of them. We will become ashamed or feel guilty for thoughts and feelings we know are wrong, so we will deny to ourselves they are there. We believe we are a very shameful person, take the blame and punish ourselves for the thoughts and feelings that are being put in our brain by the enemies who are the evil spirits.

As long as we refuse to acknowledge them, they will continue to control us. If we do not like them, they are not our thoughts. If we do not want them, they are not ours. If we liked and wanted them, then they would be ours. When we take the blame and feel guilty, we are punishing ourselves. Guilt is self-punishment. That is what satan wants us to do. He gets much pleasure in making us suffer.

I raised one of my grandsons. When he was in the fifth grade, I began having a very difficult time getting him up for school. It was terrible every morning. One morning I had to call the principal to come get him. He went to a small Christian school. One morning I had to manually drag him out of bed. I finally got him to school. When I got home, I laid down for a few moments and fell asleep. I had a dream that I was in bed looking at my ceiling. I saw swarms of tiny creatures flying near my ceiling. They were putting out little clouds of dark, gray smoke. They eventually put out so much smoke I could not see them any more. I just saw the smoke. When I awoke, the Holy Spirit gave me the understanding that they were evil spirits causing the problem of my grandson fighting going to school. He showed me that I was seeing the problem, but I was not seeing what was behind it—evil spirits. He reminded me that one of satan's names is Beelzebub. That means lord of the flies. That is what they looked like, swarms of flies. From then on when I awoke, I bound their power in the name of Jesus and commended them to leave. My grandson still grumbled in the morning but he did not put up such a fight after that.

Years before this I would awaken in the middle of the night, and I would begin feeling guilty about the past, and I would also worry about my children. I would become upset, and I could not go back to sleep. When my husband and I went on vacation to Tennessee, I always felt very peaceful there. One night when I had one of the guilty and fear (worry is fear) nights, I did drop off to sleep. I dreamed I went to Tennessee. I was talking to a woman who lived there. I said, "I wish I could live here all the time like you do instead of just once in a while." Remember, Tennessee represented peace to me, so I was really saying I wish I could live in peace all the time instead of just once in a while. She said to me, "You could if you quit letting satan put those thoughts of guilt and fear in your mind."

From then on when I awoke and he tried to put the thoughts of guilt and fear in my mind. I said, Jesus please come and fight him for me. He tried for a couple more nights, but he could not, so satan quit that tactic. Second Corinthians 10:5 tells us to bring every thought into captivity to the obedience of Christ. We must watch our thoughts. Are they of God, self or of the devil? If we live according to Jesus' thoughts and attitudes, we will live in peace.

When my grandson was small, every time I thought of him I felt sorrow. I felt sorrow for him that his parents did not want him and other situations in his life. One day when I was feeling sorrow for him, the Holy Spirit revealed to me that it was an evil spirit controlling my emotions. From then on I nipped it in the bud before it could get control. We have the power to protect ourselves. We just need to learn the enemy's tactics. God had allowed these things in my grandson's life for a reason—his spiritual growth.

Unforgiveness, anger, fear, sorrow, guilt, self-centeredness, contempt, and so forth, are all from sin and satan. He will make us believe we have the right to all of these and more because they are upsetting to us and others. He gets much pleasure from controlling our thoughts and emotions, and making us and others suffer from that. He loves the power and the pleasure he gets from torturing us. He wants to take to Hell with him as many as he can.

He also wants us to live in misery while we are here on earth. He can cause sickness. Sickness is an oppression of the devil. Acts 10:38 tells about a woman who was bowed over and was bound by satan for eighteen years. Demon spirits can cause arthritis and deformities, muteness and diseases. They can and do drive people insane. They can cause depression and suicide. They seduce people into sin, drugs, alcohol, and all kinds of sexual sin and perversions.

Ephesians 6:11 & 12 says, "Put on the whole armor of God that you may be able to stand against the wiles (tricks) of the devil. For we do not wrestle against flesh and blood, but against principalities, against powers, against the rulers of darkness, against spiritual hosts of wickedness. You can read what the armor of God is in Ephesians 6:13-18.

Years ago in the 1960s, after the astronauts had made their space journeys, they told of the wonderful spiritual experiences they had while in outer space. I asked the Lord why so many of them had these experiences. He said because they were out of satan's domain. He had no influence over them there.

When I was just beginning my journey of following Jesus, I had a scary experience with satan. I was in bed and just beginning to drift off when satan began trying to put thoughts of blasphemy against the Holy Spirit in my mind. I could feel him trying to make me think those thoughts. I just knew one line of scripture by heart at that time, so I repeated it over and over. I was willing myself **not** to let my mind be open to satan even for an instant.

I kept saying in my mind, my human spirit, the Lord is my Shepherd, I shall not want, over and over and concentrated on focusing on those words. I fell asleep saying them to myself. When I awoke in the morning the first thing I said was, "Oh, Jesus, please do not let the devil get me." I had a Bible lying on a chest in my bedroom. I felt myself being drawn to it. I opened it at random, and the first verse I saw was Romans 6:14. It states, "Sin (the devil) shall not have dominion over you, for you are not under the law, but under grace." I knew that was Jesus telling me He would not let satan have me. My mind was at rest over the matter because I knew Jesus had given me that scripture as a message.

That was my first real lesson about the devil. It must have been the Holy Spirit who revealed to me that it was satan trying to put those thoughts in my mind and what to do to keep them out, because I did not know anything about blaspheming against the Holy Spirit at that time. The devil was laying a trap for me, so when I read that in the Bible, I would think there was no hope for me to go to Heaven, and that I could never be forgiven.

I learned later that the thought would never have been my thoughts. They were the devil's thoughts that he would have put there. I would have believed they were mine and taken the blame and the suffering for them. The devil does anything he can to stop us from reaching the spiritual goals God has for us. The goal is to love God with all our hearts and our neighbors as ourselves. He also has a job for us to do in and for His kingdom. The Holy Spirit told me that everyone in the Kingdom of God has a job. Everyone has something they can do that will help others in some way. The devil does not want us to reach that stage of our spiritual growth nor even know what it is.

One of our biggest battles is having thoughts we do not want to have, but not being able to stop them. That is because some of satan's evil army is fighting against them. We cannot win over them until we learn about our spiritual weapons and how to use them. Then we can keep our minds free of the power of the enemy. When we are in any battle, we need to know our enemy and their tactics. The Bible tells us to learn our spiritual enemy's tactics.

That is the main reason for this book—to help you learn. It is all about learning how to win the battle. We can not only win the battle, but we can learn to know when the enemy is planning an attack and stop it before they can do any harm.

In the name of Jesus, we have the ultimate power over them. Also, faith stops all the fiery darts of the wicked one (Ephesians 6:16). We need to read, read, read, our instruction book to learn all we can learn. We need to learn God's rules so we will know when the enemy is trying to get us to break them.

So stand your ground. Do not give in to the devil. Use your spiritual weapons to protect yourself and others. Look up satan, the devil, the wicked one, the adversary and appolyon. Learn all you can about your worst enemy who wants to destroy us all. But remember, we do not need to fear him because Jesus has given us the power over him. We just need to learn to use it.

For years, on Sunday morning, when I awoke I would be filled with anger and other sinful emotions. My thoughts would immediately be, "I do not want to go to church today. I hate going to church." I fought against this until I got to church. I always went even in that condition.

That went on for YEARS. Finally one morning, I was forcing myself to get ready for church, still thinking angry thoughts when the Holy Spirit said to me, "Don't you know an attack of satan when you see one?"

He also instantly gave me the understanding that satan was controlling my thoughts AND emotions. He tried it the next morning but I was ready for him. I got rid of him immediately. It never happened again. Now I get up, get ready and go to church in peace.

The Holy Spirit told me, "If you really, REALLY know God, then satan and sin have no more power over you." We get to know God by studying His instruction book, by seeking to follow His instructions, by talking to Him and asking Him questions.

In my early years of following Jesus, I would hear people say never question God. I learned that we should not "question" why are you letting this happen to poor little me, but it is absolutely permitted to ask Him what am I doing thinking or desiring that is causing me problems or suffering.

Jesus gave us the Holy Spirit as our helper, teacher, counselor, healer and every other spiritual need we may have. He wants us to learn about Him and about spiritual growth. We can ask anything we want to.

He wants us to learn all about satan and his way of doing things to defeat and/or destroy us. He also wants us to learn all the sinful thoughts, attitudes, desires, and so forth, that control us.

The devil does his best to blind us to our faults and sins. The Holy Spirit does His best to reveal these to us so we can be freed from them. There is a spiritual battle going on every day for our spiritual growth and freedom. Every day we think thoughts, all day long. We make the choice. God's way of thinking or the devil's way. We must tune to the spiritual source that is influencing our spirit. Evil or Holy. Is it God's way or satan's? We make the choice.

I wonder how many families the devil's army either uses the anger trick to keep or try to keep from going to church on Sundays. The book of the Revelation 12:12 states, "Woe to the inhabitants of the earth and the sea! For the devil is come down, having great wrath because he knows that he has but a short time."

Can you imagine what someone would do to a person if they hate with pure hate and great wrath toward someone? That is what the devil's motivations are toward destroying us. We need to learn all about him and be on guard to protect ourselves and others.

I have heard many preachers say that the devil can't know what we are thinking, but they are 100% wrong. As I wrote elsewhere, an assistant pastor silently cast out a spirit of fear from my six year old grandson. He did not speak the words to the spirit. He, with his human spirit that lives inside our head, the real us, spoke spiritually, not physically to the evil spirit of fear and commanded it in the name of Jesus to leave, and it received the order and left.

Many times since, I have done that very same thing. It is spirit-to-spirit communication. The devil does know what we are thinking. When we leave this body we are enclosed in, there is no physical mouth or ears to communicate with others. It is all spirit-to-spirit.

As I wrote elsewhere, someone asked how I could hear the Lord speak to me. He told me to tell her that He has no physical mouth to speak to my physical ears. He speaks to my (not just me but to other followers of Jesus also) spirit inside my head.

At my first lesson about spiritual battles, the devil was at my left speaking to me (spirit) inside my head. I didn't know at the time that it was the devil. I thought it was me thinking those thoughts.

The Holy Spirit was on my right side telling me what God's instructions were that were written in the Bible. I thought I was just remembering what I had read. It went back and forth for some time.

When I made the decision to obey the Lord's words, the conversation on the left (evil spirit) stopped instantly. How did it know I had decided against it if it didn't know what I was thinking? I never said one word out loud.

In my spirit, not out loud, I commanded the spirit that was putting critical thoughts about others in my mind in church one evening that I wrote about earlier to leave and it did.

One evening a lady I know was talking to her husband with very abusive words. I saw satan telling her what to say. I commanded him to leave (silently) and instantly he disappeared. The lady's words, attitude, and facial expressions changed immediately, and a look of shame came on her face. I know the Lord allowed me to see satan because I was trying to think of something to say to stop the way she was talking. There was no way satan would shut up and leave just because of any words I might have said.

Once I saw him, I knew I had to use the name of Jesus to get rid of him. I did that and he left. I just THOUGHT it. I did not say it out loud. He KNEW WHAT I WAS THINKING TOWARD HIM. HE KNEW MY THOUGHTS.

People have battles with him every day. Thoughts and/or actions we do not want but cannot stop. We cannot win against the spirits in our own power. We cannot win any arguments against them in our power. We cannot change anyone's mind no matter what wisdom we may use if they are being controlled by an evil spirit. We cannot reason with an evil spirit.

You do not reason with evil spirits because they will never obey us in our own power. When Paul wrote in Ephesians 6 that we do not fight against flesh and blood, that is exactly what he meant. When we are fighting another person, we are not fighting them, but we are fighting evil spirits. We think we are fighting the person, but they are only the tools the evil spirit is using to fight us. They want to make us angry, hurt, hate and anything else destructive.

The Revelation verse that the devil has great wrath and woe to us, because he works all the time to do us damage.

The devil is the one who tempts people to eat the wrong food, because he knows it will harm our health. Then, we feel bad all the time. Our enjoyment of life is gone. We begin praying for healing. Our minds are centered on self, not on God. We just focus on Him long enough to ask for what we want. The devil has gotten us focused on our flesh, not our spiritual growth and relationship with the Lord. When we feel bad and/or tired all the time, we tend to be verbally abusive to those around us. So you see, even our eating habits are a spiritual battle.

It has taken me years to learn all this. The devil put me through much suffering. He almost succeeded in destroying me completely, and would have if I had not turned my life over to Jesus. The devil is the one who causes all these wars. The book of Revelation tells us the devil will be chained for the 1,000 years of Jesus' ruling earth, and he will deceive the nations no more. Thank God He sent Jesus to save us from the devil and his evil army.

It tells us in Isaiah 26:3 that we will have perfect peace if our mind is kept on Him. We need to get our minds off of self and onto seeking God's righteousness, God's nature to be created in us.

I have given many different ways satan can deceive and control us. He has others. They are greed, and the fear of taking control of our own life. He makes us believe that (women) we cannot take care of ourselves, so we will stay with a man who abuses us and/or our children. My mother stayed married to my father even though he was committing adultery all the time. He beat her with his fists many times, but she still stayed because of the fear she could not make it on her own. The devil used this to destroy our whole family. It drove Mom out of her right mind. She did many destructive things to my brothers and me, especially me because I was a female. I dreamed one time that someone had cut off her right hand. It hurt her so badly that she cut off mine. She needed to make someone suffer to pay for her suffering, so she made me suffer.

As I have written elsewhere, as a child I asked Jesus to save me and I loved him very much. That was when satan took over my life with the intentions of destroying me. He made many terrible things happen to me. He persecuted me all my life, even after I turned my life over to Jesus. He tried many ways to get me to lose faith and turn against God. As the Bible tells us he tried to get Job to curse God and die spiritually. I almost did give up many times, but Jesus always helped me keep going.

I asked Him many times why He let satan take over my life and cause all the things in my life that he did. I could not understand why, when I loved Jesus so much and was working so hard to get other people to accept Him as Savior that He let that happen. Finally, I was sitting in church one morning and asked Him again. This time He answered me. He said, "Because I want you to write a book about satan." I was to expose his ways of deceiving, entrapping and controlling people, and, to help people be set free of his evil ways of destruction. To know all the things he was causing in their lives that they were helpless to change or help themselves; and, to learn that help and freedom are available in the name and power of Jesus.

We can be free of satan's power by accepting Jesus as our Savior and letting Him rid our lives of the power of satan and sin.

This is a promise if we meet the requirements. Humble ourselves, confess our sins, ask forgiveness, and trust Jesus to cleanse the sins that were confessed. Then leave it in His hands.

Sometimes it is gone immediately. Sometimes in days. Sometimes a little longer, but He keeps His promises.

As each sin is cleansed, that area is filled with some of God's righteousness. The devil has lost more and more control. We are giving more of ourselves to let the Holy Spirit have His way in our lives instead of satan.

Gradually or quickly (it depends on us) we are set free of all the devils's control in our lives. We will be FILLED with the Holy Spirit. The battle is over. We are free.

When I was about eight years old, a girl down the road asked me to go with her to a revival. She and her brothers and sisters went to this little country church and since we were friends she wanted me to go with her. The man who was preaching was a small man, maybe 5 feet 6 inches and he had white hair.

He wore a black suit with a white shirt and a black tie. He had all the lights in the church turned off. He had a lighted candle so he could see to read his Bible.

The church was so crowded that some people had to stand. They were standing against three of the four walls in the church. I was sitting about midway on the middle isle in the first seat on my row.

The preacher told of Jesus' birth, life, death and the resurrection. As he told about this I was seeing pictures of it in my mind. It was almost as if I were watching it unfold. When he told of Jesus being hung on the cross, and why, I fell in love with Jesus. When he gave the altar call and told us that Jesus wanted us to accept Him as our Savior, I wanted very much to go to the altar but I was very shy. I wanted to go forward. I had a love in my heart for the Lord and wanted to do what He wanted me to. But I wouldn't do it because of the shyness. I could hear people around the building sniffling and weeping. They wanted to go also, but they wouldn't go either. I felt sorry for them and wished they could go forward.

The altar call continued but no one went forward. I knew they were like me. They wanted to go but were too shy. Then I heard a voice speak to me and say, "If you will go, they will go." That gave me the courage to go forward so I stood up and went down the aisle. As soon as I started down the aisle, people came from all directions and packed the altar.

The next night I went, it was the same thing. I had already gone and been saved so I knew I didn't have to go again, but when he gave the invitation people would be weeping but no one would go forward. Again, I heard the voice say, "If you will go, they will go." So I got up and went down the aisle again and as soon as I started down the aisle, people came from all directions and packed the altar. It happened again the next night.

The fourth night I went in and sat down in a pew. My Sunday school teacher Naomi sat down beside me. When it came time for the invitation she put her knees against the pew in front of us. I knew she didn't want me to get up and go to the altar. The preacher gave the invitation. I sat there and fidgeted and wanted to go forward. I could hear the people weeping all around the church but no one would go. The invitation just went on and on. Finally Naomi leaned over and whispered in my ear and told me to go on. I stepped in front of her, then out into the aisle and started toward the altar. People came from all directions and packed the altar again. I never knew until years later that Naomi wanted to see if the Lord was using me, which He was, or if I was just doing that.

I think some of the adults had discussed it, because the little old preacher walked two miles the next day to ask Mom is he could baptize me, but she refused.

As I said, I really loved Jesus. He was very real to me. I wanted to do everything He wanted me to and I was telling my family and friends about Him and trying to get them to go to church and be saved. I was so happy to know Him that I wanted everyone else to know this wonderful person. My father was home for a while so I talked to him about it. He got a Bible out and began reading it. My Mother, in her hurt and pain, made fun of him for it. He put it away and did not read it again for twenty years.

I would have my brothers line up on their knees by the bed at night before we went to bed and say prayers. One night my little brother Mike said his prayer and he said, "Please Jesus, don't let me wake up in the morning and find myself dead." He was trying to say," If I should die before I wake." One night when we were all kneeling beside the bed I went into the kitchen and asked Mom if she would come and pray with us. She refused and said she didn't have time to be doing any praying. So we prayed by ourselves.

I don't know how long it was after I accepted Christ (it wasn't very long) but I was really witnessing for the Lord. One night, my cousins wanted me to stay all night at their house. It was summer. There were no streetlights where we lived. My aunt had left the window open. It was one of those small four pane windows. We went to bed and I woke up sometime in the night. Everyone was asleep. It was pitch dark. I was wide awake and alert. In my mind I realized something was happening. What it was I didn't know. I sat up in bed and leaned against the head of the bed and stared intently into the darkness trying to see what was happening. As I peered into the darkness, it felt as though a force turned my head to the left. As I turned my head I was looking at the open bedroom window. Framed in that window was satan! I could just see him from mid-chest up. He glowed like a red-hot burning ember.

Since then, after I've grown up and seen pictures of him, he's always dressed in a red suit. But I understood it was not a red suit. It was his body. I have seen embers in the fire that looked as though they were on fire all the way through, inside out; the inside was on fire and glowed to the outside. That was what his body looked like, a burning coal that glowed with the fire from the inside out. His eyes were an ugly yellow color. His pupils weren't like ours but pupils of a serpent.

He had two little horns on his head. He was looking straight into my eyes with a look of absolute pure hate on his face, projecting hate from his mind to my mind. His face was contorted with hate for me. Not using his lips or his voice and with spiritual telepathy he said to my spirit, "I'm going to take over your life and I'm going to destroy you." Years later in my adult life, I read the Book of Job and understood why Job went through what he did. The devil wanted Job to curse God and die. He wanted to destroy Job spiritually. Of course I didn't know that then, but that's what satan told me. He was going to destroy me. Then he disappeared. I don't remember having much fear at the time, but I do remember feeling shame. I felt ashamed that satan had come to see me. I never told anyone about that until I was in my thirties. I don't know how I knew who he was. We didn't have horror movies or TV when this happened. I don't remember even hearing about him.

Not long after that happened, my Mother let her friend and her pedophile husband move into our home. I know that was the devil at work, because the guy molested me. When that happened the shame and guilt was overwhelming for a little girl.

The evil spirit of shame was doing its work well. After that, as I grew up, I was kidnapped and raped a number of times. I won't go into all that I endured in my growing up and young adulthood years. I'll just tell you that satan kept his word. After two divorces and a third marriage, I lived in guilt, shame and depression. I had lived in those for twenty-one years. I couldn't stand it any more so I planned to kill myself.

I could not cope with what these things caused me to feel, so I closed down. I had to turn off the emotions to not lose my mind completely.

My spirit was broken. I withdrew and let the soul take over.

I had hidden away inside. I wouldn't come out and express myself through the body. I wouldn't come out and I would not let anyone in, or see in.

My spirit was broken and just gave up the fight. The soul took over and consequently, the devil took over the soul. I had no control. He had told me he would take over my life and destroy me the night he appeared to me and that is just what he did.

I did many things I did not want to do. The real me would never have done any of them, but I had no control. I was under the devil's power and he controlled me.

I had four daughters through the years. My life was so miserable and full of mental and emotional pain that I couldn't cope with it any more. I planned to kill all of my daughters before I killed myself. I believed I would be saving them from living in the terrible world and suffering the mental and emotional pain that I had lived with. I thought I would be doing something good for them.

At the last though I could not hurt them, so I was going to just kill myself. I had started going to church a few weeks earlier hoping it would help me but it was only worse because my husband did not want me to go. I had to listen to him berate me before I left and again when I got home.

I was in deep despair so I went to bed one night and waited for everyone to go to sleep. Then I planned to cut my wrists and let my life drain away in the tub.

As I waited I was talking to Jesus. I was, in a round about way, asking Him to forgive me for what I was going to do. I told Him I was sorry but I couldn't stand to live any longer in this mental and emotional pain I was in. I said, "I can't help it. I have to do it."

When I said that, Jesus appeared to me. He stood beside my bed and said, giving me the choice, either that or turn your life over to Me. Inside myself it seemed that I opened my heart and very intently said it is all yours! I give you my children, husband, home, health, myself, my whole life! It seemed instantly that I went to sleep and instantly it was morning. That is what it felt like to me. When I opened my eyes, Jesus was still there. He said, "Take up your cross and follow me." Then he disappeared. I knew what he said was in the Bible and knew there was more to it.

I looked it up and it said, "Deny thyself, take up your cross and follow me." That is just what I began doing. The cross is where we die to the flesh. My soul flesh had to be put to death, praise God, and the process had begun.

I had gone to bed that night depressed and suicidal. I awoke the next morning full of the joy of the Lord. Then I began following Jesus to Golgotha.

At times I wanted to quit but He always helped me keep going. I thought all of my troubles were over and I would never be hurt again. But satan was not going to let that happen. He began right away trying to stop me.

It was like the Book of Job. God had let satan have me for a while but he didn't let him take my life. Now satan was trying to defeat me. God used him to bring me to the place where I would surrender all to Jesus. Now He used satan to set me free of past sins, hurts and wrong thinking. Satan would attack me in an area that he had programmed me.

I would pray for help. Jesus would show me what satan was using—anger, fear, guilt, shame, pride, selfishness and so forth against me. Jesus would bring it out for me to have a good look at. Then I would repent and He would set me free.

I was full of sin I was not aware of. Jesus let satan work on me to bring it out in the open. The devil meant it to damage me more, but Jesus used it for my spiritual growth. Praise Him!

The morning after I surrendered my life to Jesus, I awoke filled with the joy of the Lord. I lived in that for about eighteen months. Nothing upset me. I had no fear.

When I surrendered everything to Him I thought I would never be hurt again. That was not the case.

People in the church were envious of my relationship with Jesus. Some ladies were just jealous of me. The pastor hurt my feelings terribly and my whole family did too.

I lost some trust in Jesus because of that. I thought He would always protect me from any hurt or upset. When He didn't I was so hurt about that, I tried to take back the control of my life.

The joy left and the depression returned. Jesus had told me to take up my cross and follow Him. The cross became very heavy. I had to begin looking at my sinful self and let Jesus crucify it.

It was very painful at times. At times He had to pry my fingers loose from the control. When I thought I couldn't trust Him, the fear came back. Gradually He set me free of that and I learned that everything happens for a reason: our spiritual growth. I learned to not look at circumstances but keep my mind focused on Jesus and He would get me through it.

Psalms 34:19 states, "Many are the afflictions of the righteous but God delivers them out of them all." It is always safer and more peaceful if we just let Jesus have the control.

When I had been following Jesus for a while and began to have to fight some spiritual battles, I didn't like or want that, so one night in bed I told Him, "You take over and just work all this out for me. Just take all the bad stuff out. I don't want all of this struggle." That night I dreamed a very vivid and realistic dream in color. I dreamed I was looking at some country folks playing and singing an old gospel song. They were singing, "You gotta walk this lonesome valley, you gotta walk it by yourself. Nobody else can walk it for you. You gotta walk it by yourself."

When I awoke I knew I wasn't going to get out of the battle that easily. Remember I wrote of the vivid dream of seeing a battle being fought till the death. Meaning the death of sin in me.

The war is not completely over yet but I have (with God's help) won many battles. The battles become easier as we go because we learn more and more about the enemies tactics and he loses more and more ground.

Slowly the devil lost more and more ground in my life and Jesus gained it. So as I write this chapter on satan you will know that I know from experience.

In Matthew 5:10 it is written, "Blessed are those who are persecuted for righteousness' sake, for theirs is the kingdom of heaven."

In that little country church I had fallen in love with Jesus. I accepted Him as my Savior and King. All I wanted to do was love and serve Him. The devil could not stand that. The night I saw him he began his campaign of persecution against me because of my love for and desire to serve Jesus.

I've heard many people say that after they were saved bad things began to happen to them. That is because they were being persecuted for righteousness' sake.

Years later when I was at the "end of my rope," I decided to begin attending church. I worked on myself for months to quit using swear words. I had not used a swear word for a few weeks so I felt it was okay to start church. I went to church and went to the altar. The next day at work I used swear words all day.

I began to think that Jesus had rejected me. I worked with a lady who went to church and told her what I thought. She told me that the devil was causing that to make me believe Jesus had rejected me.

Jeremiah 1:5 tells us that before we were born God knew us. A few years ago I dreamed I was in a higher place than Earth. I was in a great library. A man with glowing, golden hair and dressed in white, was teaching me from a book in this library. Then he told me I was going to Earth to teach and write a book about Jesus.

I became so enthused to get there; I hurried toward a large open door that opened at the top of a large stairway, the stairway to Earth. When I was almost to the stairs an invisible force stopped me. I strained to proceed but the force held me back. I looked toward the door and saw people coming through it and proceeding down the stairs.

There were four in a row. Row after row four people. They were all naked. I realized that meant they were all naked spirits going to be born into a physical body on Earth. All the time I was straining against the force. Finally a row came along that had only three people. The space closest to me was empty. The force released me. I stepped into the empty space and the next thing I knew I was here on Earth.

I know now that I was sent here to write this book but satan did not, and does not, want it written. That is why he tried so hard and long and had so many things happen to me to destroy me before I could write it. While clearly very powerful and clever, he is not an independent rival of God, but is definitely subordinate, able to go only as far as God permits.

God allowed him to do that so I would learn about him and his evil ways. In 2nd Corinthians he is called the god of this age. People are ignorant of him and his ways. He works to keep them that way.

He likes to have people blame God and/or Jesus for the bad things he causes. If you have or can obtain a good Bible dictionary, look him up and read all the scriptures about him. The more we know about our enemy, the more of his tactics we can protect ourselves and counteract against. KNOW YOUR ENEMY! KNOW YOUR SPIRITUAL WEAPONS! KNOW JESUS WHO GAVE US POWER OVER OUR ENEMY! READ YOUR BIBLE EVERY DAY TO LEARN THESE THINGS!

God allowed satan to break my spirit so I would surrender my life to Jesus. After I did this, then Jesus and the Holy Spirit went to work to break the hold satan and my sinful soul had over me, the human spirit me. As the old song goes, "He's still working on me." Thank God!

After I finished the chapter on satan I still felt something was missing about why Jesus let satan take over my life when I loved Jesus so much and was working to serve Him.

I was wondering about this one day when suddenly the Holy Spirit told me that I was given the EXPERIENCE to sustain me through all the years satan worked to destroy me by using other people, circumstances and my own mind to accomplish that. Many, many times I went back to the time in the little country church where I experienced the love of Jesus for me and my love for Him, and it did help me through those years of persecution.

As I wrote elsewhere, God has a reason for everything He does and/or allows and it is always for an ultimate good.

A family member that I care very much for got into a relationship with a young man from Florida who had come to our small town.

She fell in love with him. He soon met a group of young men. There were four of them. They were all into drugs and drinking.

One morning just before I awoke I dreamed that there was a spirit of Baal over our town. I dreamed that he had evil spirits under him. That all of these five young men were being controlled by evil spirits working under the spirit of Baal.

I looked Baal up in my Bible dictionary and found that the spirit of Baal was a real spirit. (I had thought it was just a statue that people prayed to.) The dictionary stated that he was a lord spirit who commanded lesser spirits to do his bidding.

He is a spirit of debauchery and that is what these young men were being controlled by.

The Holy Spirit told me that He wanted to free the young man my relative was living with. I told Him I didn't know what to do about the spirit of Baal.

He gave me the scripture where Jesus told the people that you first bind the strong man, and then you can clean out the house.

So I knew I had to bind the power of Baal, then cast out the spirits controlling the young man.

I got up my nerve and went to do that. As I was driving to their house, the Holy Spirit told me that the devil was going to try to stop me but would do it through my relative, not the young man.

When I arrived, I explained this all to him. He was nice about it, but my relative began calling me names and saying all kinds of terrible things to me. She told me to get out of her house and that she hated me.

I said I knew it was the devil talking through her. The young man said he would think about letting me cast out the spirits later. So I left.

The next morning I got a call telling me that the young man had beaten my relative so badly that the doctor said he had never seen anyone beaten that bad who had lived.

Both arms were broken. All of her ribs were broken. Her lungs were punctured. The doctor had put tubes into her lungs to keep her alive until she could be air lifted to the Methodist Hospital in Indianapolis.

Her head was so swollen that her nose was almost covered by the rest of her face.

She told me later that at the time he beat her she had left her body. She said it was the most awful, dark, empty depressing experience that she thought anyone could have.

She had been living a life of debauchery herself. When she was out of her body she thought about the welfare of her children and didn't want to leave them. She said then she was put back into her body.

I had prayed for her many times before this happened. About three months before this happened the Holy Spirit told me while I was praying for her that something very drastic would have to happen for her to WANT to give up that lifestyle.

A number of our family members went to the hospital. We were all VERY upset over it. While I was sitting there listening to them talk and trying to deal with it myself, I became aware of a song being sung to me inside my head. I was so upset that it took me a few seconds to focus on the song.

When I did focus I realized someone (the Holy spirit) was singing, "This is the day that the Lord has made. I will rejoice and be glad in it." Knowing Romans 8:28, that all things are for our good, I thanked Jesus for the good he was going to bring out of this.

When I said this (in my spirit) to Him, I felt peace begin at the top of my head and flow all through my body. Jesus spoke to me and said, "I am going to answer your prayers for her now, but I'm going to do it My way." If He had done it my way, it would have been instant healing and spiritual growth.

He didn't do it my way. He did it slowly but He did it. It was a few years but gradually she changed and gave up the bad lifestyle she had lived before. Now she leads a women's survival group.

The young man who beat up my relative let me cast out the spirits controlling him before he went to prison for four years. He asked me for a Bible, which I sent him. He wrote to me often those four years about what he was learning from it. When he was released he went back home to Florida.

The devil meant to kill her, but Jesus didn't let him. What the devil meant for bad, Jesus brought good.

I know many will take offense at the rest of this chapter, but my reasons for going ahead with it are: #1 I believe it is God's will, and #2 I believe it will help many.

I debated with myself and the Holy Spirit over it. Part of me wanted to write it to help others, but the other part did not want to face the wrath of those who took offense.

Finally, the Holy Spirit reminded me of the scripture in my story of the bear chasing me. The scripture that tells us that perfect love casts our fear. By that I took courage and focused on the side of those who might be helped and set free.

So here goes. Many years ago, when I was young, I was intolerant of others' sins. When I became an adult and learned about homosexuality, I had contempt (my pride) for them. Then, I began seeing them on TV telling the audience that they were all right in what they were doing.

Well, my righteous indignation popped its ugly head up right then. When I would see them on TV, I would become angry. This went on for some time.

Then, one day I was at my kitchen stove cooking lunch and listening to the TV at the same time. A program about one of those people came on and so did my anger. But, in the twinkle of an eye, the anger was gone and in its place was compassion.

"THIS IS HOW I WANT YOU TO THINK AND FEEL ABOUT THEM," said the Lord to me.

I had been having satan's thoughts and attitudes about them. Now, I had the Lord's thoughts and attitudes.

Later, I was told to leave a church by the pastor because I expressed these thoughts and feelings in Sunday school one morning.

All of that said, I now come to the real reason I am writing this chapter.

I had a relative that I was very close to. She had told her family (me included) that she was a lesbian. It did not change my feelings for her. I also felt compassion for her.

She had a "special friend." One day she asked me if I would take her and her friend to an out of town theater to see a play. I did and consequently I spent the evening with them.

I arrived home late and went right to bed.

When I awoke in the morning, I had been having a lesbian dream. I then had lesbian thoughts and feelings. I did not like nor want to have them, so I knew it was not me but an evil spirit putting them in my mind.

I immediately bound its power in the name of Jesus and commanded it in the name of Jesus to leave and never come back. It had to obey me in the name of Jesus.

It left and after these ten years has never come back.

I know it has been told to the public that homosexuals are born with a certain thing in their brains. Maybe some are. But, they have the power to not act on this. Just like the heterosexual has the power to not act on their sexual desires.

I believe somewhere along the way, an evil spirit has taken over and they yielded the control to it, because they don't know they are being controlled. It could also be because they either don't know Jesus or if they do, they don't know about the spiritual battle we are all in. Or it could be that they don't want to use the name of Jesus to free themselves of it.

I do not believe that all homosexual persons are born with the homosexual gene, or whatever it is. I believe that, just like my experiences, some pass on the evil spirits to others.

I believe that is why the homosexual population has grown so much, so rapidly.

This information should be good news for them. If they really want to be freed of it, they can be, if they have accepted Jesus as their Saviour, use his name to bind the power of the spirit/spirits and command them to leave.

They will probably try to get control again, but you must take every thought into captivity and guard your hearts and minds from them, in the name of JESUS.

I know when homosexuals read this, the spirits will fight against this information. They always fight against being cast out, but if this is kept in mind, the person can catch on to this and act quickly to counteract against the spirit or spirits.

I have written all of this in hopes that many can be freed. That is my desire and purpose for writing.

If you become angry at me or feel hatred toward me, be assured that is an evil spirit fighting not to lose its control over you.

Unless it is your heart's desire to remain the way you are, remember if we don't like the thoughts and/or feelings we have, they are not ours. They are put there in our brains by the enemy.

If we like and want them, they are ours. It is very important to look inside, know and be honest with yourself and God.

Proverbs 3:5-8: Trust in the Lord with all your heart, lean not to your own understanding. In all your ways acknowledge Him and He shall direct your steps.

Be not wise in your own eyes: fear the Lord and depart from evil.

It shall be health to you and marrow to your bones.

May you seek God and His will with all your heart.

CHAPTER 9

Self

What do you want most in life? What do you pray for the most often? What do you think will make you happy? Is it to be free, to have a very loving relationship, to be healed, to be beautiful, to have your children healthy and happy, to have more money, a nice home, people to love you, lose weight?

All of these prayers and desires are for self. Matthew 6:33 says to seek first the kingdom of God and His good qualities (His righteousness) and he will supply all of our needs. Hebrews 11:6 says, "God is a rewarder of those who diligently seek HIM."

One of the major hindrances to our prayers is that we are focused on and seeking for self. We spend much of our prayer time asking our Heavenly Father to fix everything and everyone for our sake. We ask Him to change this or that person so they will do and/or be what we want them to so they will not do or say things that hurt or make us angry. Reality here is that no one can enter our head and turn on the hurt or angry buttons. We are the only ones who are in there.

Our mind is usually centered on our self. What we want. We consider our feelings only. Other people's feelings do not matter that much to us. Sometimes our mind is so centered on ourselves that we do not care that we are hurting and/or humiliating someone else. Our feelings are all that matter to us. We try to control others to make them be and do what we want. We want to take away their right to make their own choices.

I asked the Lord one day what was the wrong thing in a lady's life that He did not grant her prayer requests. He said, "Her mind is on herself. She prays for herself. She is centered on the flesh, seeking for the flesh. She ignores My instructions to seek My will first. She prays and seeks for her will to be done. Even though she prays for spiritual qualities, it is just to make her happy and have peace. Again, it is all for self. She needs to set self aside and do things to help others be happy. She needs to give of herself not want to take from others."

I understand all of this because I was just like that in the past. I always wanted everyone to please me, to do, say, and be what I wanted. I tried to change (control) everyone to make my life easier. I made my family feel helpless. Because of that, they became angry and that led to rebellion. They did just the opposite of what I wanted them to do.

Many people, though, let themselves be intimidated and let themselves be controlled. They then become angry with the controller and with themselves for yielding the control to someone else. They may begin feeling helpless when others try to control them, as I did. So to protect my self, I began to control others. It became a battle of wills and a vicious circle. They gradually wore me down until I began desiring to commit suicide. If I had not turned my life over to Jesus when He came to save me, I would not be writing this now.

It took me years and many, many experiences to learn that as long as we try to control others, we will feel helpless and angry because God will not let us go on our merry way hurting others. We will go through experience after experience until we repent. We all pay the consequences for the wrong that we do. Everyone is not going to let us control him or her all the time.

One of my daughters tried to control all the time. One day she told me she was tired most of the time. The Holy Spirit told me it was because she put so much effort into trying to change and control others, without success, that she was feeling more and more helpless. These efforts and emotions were draining her energy.

So many people get into these battles of wills over who is in control that all enjoyment of life dwindles away. They have no room for love or happiness. We rob ourselves of happiness by seeking to protect and satisfy SELF.

Who do you think is behind all of this? Right. It is satan working to destroy. He works on our selfish sinful nature to try to destroy as many as he can.

Our Heavenly Father, though, wants to create His Holy nature in us. Matthew 6:33, again. Seek FIRST the kingdom of God. Seek to let Him create instead of letting satan destroy. Let God be in control. He does not want to hurt or shame us, which is what we all fear. That is our motive for trying to control. He wants to free us of the hurt and shame that satan has used to poison our lives. He wants to give us an abundant life.

Oh, how we hurt others and ourselves by believing satan and his lies instead of believing and trusting God and His promises. In Genesis 15:1, God tells us He is our exceeding great reward. How many poor souls miss this great reward by allowing themselves to be controlled by satan's evil spirits?

We can be freed of them if we will humble ourselves, admit to God that we are guilty of focusing on ourselves and trying to control others for ourselves. We have the power in the name of Jesus to bind the power of the evil spirits controlling us, command them to leave and never come back.

Others may try to take their place, but if we watch our minds closely we can catch them before they can do any harm, and we can harm them by binding their power. Pretty soon they will not bother us. We can get the victory over this—helplessness, fear, control and anger—after we get rid of the spirits.

All of this I know because I have been through it. God has put me through this and taught me this so I can tell others how to be set free.

As I touched on earlier, we will go through difficult situations that are there for us to see what sin is controlling us and to repent of it. If we do not repent and let the Lord cleanse us of it, we will soon go through another dealing. It will be worse than the first one, and then another and another until or unless we quit resisting the Holy Spirit and yield to Him.

As long as we insist on being in control and living for self, we will suffer helplessness, frustration, anger and the rest of the negative emotions that go with the self-life.

I did not learn, repent and yield to the Holy Spirit when I raised my four daughters, so the Lord sent me a grandson to raise. Raising him was harder than the four girls! I thought I would give up following Jesus because it seemed more than I could deal with. I would tell Him I could not do it anymore. He would tell me to keep on keeping on. Well, I struggled through. That was a big part of His breaking my sinful soul's desire to be in control.

I learned that there would not be peace in my life until I yielded the control to Him. When I first turned my life over to Jesus I yielded everything. I thought there would be no more hurt, sorrow, troubles or unhappiness. When all of those came along, I was disillusioned and lost my trust in Jesus. I then tried to take back the control because the fear of all these returned. Here came the feeling of helplessness, which frightened me very much, so I began trying to protect myself by being in control again. The suffering began because I became centered on myself again instead of Jesus.

"They are kept in perfect peace whose mind is staid on God." Isaiah 26:3

CHAPTER 10

Self Esteem

Matthew 5:10 tells us, "Blessed are those who are persecuted for righteousness sake, for theirs is the kingdom of heaven." In the book of Job, the devil tells God if He will let him have Job, he will make Job curse God to His face.

When God puts us in our human body, the devil is ready to attack. He can only do what God allows him to do, though. He assigns one or more of his evil spirits to do their best to influence and program us to reject God and our Savior, Jesus.

Jesus told us that in this world we would have trials and tribulations. When we have them, an evil spirit is there to give us the devil's thoughts and attitudes about them. Jesus also said that our foes are the members of our household. We sometimes get more persecution from evil spirits through our family than anyone else.

Our parents may not know how to be a good parent. They may have already been programmed to be angry, verbally and/or physically abusive. A parent can love their children but still be abusive to them. They are yielded at the time to satan's spirits or God's Holy Spirit.

If they are yielding to their sinful programming, they will handle situations abusively. When this happens, they will say or do things that cause low self-esteem. The spirit will put the thought in our mind that our parents do not love us.

We become fearful of them. We feel helpless and alone. We believe there is something wrong with us that even our parents cannot love us. The low self-esteem has begun.

The sins of the parents are visited on the children. The children learn to handle problems as the parents set the example.

Feelings of inferiority and worthlessness are controlling the majority of humanity today. Countless people possess little or no sense of self-worth. They are oppressed with poor self-esteem. It is one of the basic problems affecting mankind.

This destructive condition is so prevalent that it affects many Christians who quietly struggle under this heavy burden of poor self-esteem. They have deep feelings of inadequacy and uselessness. They fear any new experience or job for fear of failing.

Many people fear facing a problem concerning others because of fear of rejection. They feel that others can see their worthlessness so they expect to be rejected. I know from experience that it is very hard to live with someone you do not like, and believe no one else likes you either.

Some people believe they are dumb when they are really very intelligent, or they think they are ugly when they are pretty or handsome. They think they are failures when they have succeeded.

Poor self-esteem is a cancerous condition, which corrupts our emotions, actions, attitudes, thoughts and values. This is the root of many destructive symptoms.

Poor self-esteem causes us to criticize, hate and reject ourselves so we expect others to think of us that way, too. We will always feel unwanted, unneeded and unloved. It destroys self-acceptance.

We will have no self-confidence. It causes us to withdraw from people and isolate ourselves both physically and emotionally. This is the cause of feeling alone when we are in a group of people. We never feel we belong. It sometimes causes negative, complaining and an argumentative spirit.

It makes us jealous and envious of others. It causes unforgiveness, resentment, intolerance and suspicion toward others. We will be overly sensitive, moody, introverted. It is a major cause of depression.

So many young people kill themselves because of the depression low self-esteem causes. To outward appearances they seem like everything is going for them. When they kill themselves people cannot understand why. They could not see the undertow of the low self-esteem.

I believe satan oppresses us with a spirit of shame. Shame and fear are very destructive to our human spirits. They are two major emotions that satan uses against us. Shame destroys all enjoyment of life.

There will be no joy of the Lord when we live with shame. It is extremely painful emotionally. When satan instilled that in me, it was so painful that I tried very hard to suppress it, but it was in the back of my mind all the time.

At times it would surface and I would want to die to get rid of it. The devil told me as a child that I would feel that way all of my life. I felt hopeless and trapped (helpless) and wanted to kill myself. That is when the depression in my life started. The Holy Spirit told me some years after I turned my life over to Jesus, that I had been given a strong will to survive, and that is what kept me from killing myself.

I lived in depression for a little over forty years. I called that my forty years in the wilderness. Back then no one ever heard of depression. I just thought I was extremely unhappy.

In Revelations 12:10, it tells us that satan is the accuser of the brethren. He or his evil spirits are always there accusing, criticizing and discouraging us.

He also uses us to do these things to each other, also. One of his greatest lies is that we are useless, inadequate, and of little value, if any, to God. He even uses scripture in his clever attempt to make us believe his lies. He wants to bring us to a state of despair, which is where he had brought me the night I was going to kill myself.

He tries to cause all the things of low self-esteem I have written about so he can prevent any of our participation in the kingdom, and prevent the work of God in our lives.

He uses unresolved guilt from our past to torment us. Guilt is very painful. It is our way, also, of punishing ourselves. Many followers of Jesus cannot forgive themselves for past sins.

Low self-esteem will cause a person to stay in an abusive relationship. They may feel inadequate to take care of themselves in the world. They may believe that they are so inferior that no one else would ever want or love them. They may take any kind of abuse to feel that they have someone to take care of them.

They keep hoping the abusive person will change and they can get back the happiness and feelings of love they had at the beginning of the relationship.

They refuse to see the future destruction and pain for fear of being alone and helpless. The person doing the abusing has the same feelings of low self-esteem. They are afraid the abused person will find someone else, and they would suffer hurt and shame.

The abuser feels they have to abuse the other person to maintain control over them. The devil gives them this reasoning. "I will make them stay faithful to me even if I have to beat them into submission to protect myself from hurt and shame." The irony of this is that they are ashamed of abusing the other person and suffer the hurt of the loss of the abused person's love.

What horrible damage satan does to human beings by instilling a low self-esteem in their soul and spirit. Guilt is another facet of low self-esteem. Guilt causes a strong sense of remorse, regret, self-condemnation, and a deep-seated disappointment in us. This only magnifies our feelings of inferiority.

If we grew up in a household of criticism, rejection and disapproval, we probably acquired a negative self-image. Such an environment creates a sense of insecurity (fear), inadequacy and inferiority. Lack of love, support and encouragement brings an attitude of self-contempt and self-rejection. The child will grow up with a sense of poor self-esteem.

I've talked to others who thought a good self-esteem was pride. Pride is exalting self; feeling superior to others, having contempt for others and being intolerant of others' sins and mistakes; and boasting of our achievements, qualities, possessions, actions, etc.

When I turned my life over to Jesus, I had much self-hatred. After He freed me of the things I have written here and created some of His qualities (fruits of the Spirit) in me, I began to like what He (emphasis on He) was doing with my life. I like myself now, but I realize it is all of God's doing so I can take no pride in it at all. I am grateful to Him. He can and will do the same for others if they will humble themselves and yield their lives to Him. To acquire a good self-image we must look squarely in the face of low self-esteem.

The devil hides this knowledge from us. We do not realize what is causing our depression. The Holy Spirit began revealing this to me a little at a time.

First, I had to look at the sin in my life and admit it to myself and to God. Then He began taking me back to my childhood and showing me the destructive effect that circumstances had on my spirit, and the many times I was sinned against had caused me to do the things I was ashamed of.

The devil causes people to sin against each other as part of the destructive plan he has for our lives. He persecutes us continually one way or another. He uses others and he also uses our own mind against us.

We are all born with a sinful nature, but God does not want us to be destroyed because of it. He wants us to know that we can make a choice to let us be controlled by it or let Him have our life so He can free us of the sin and replace it with God-like qualities (Fruit of the Spirit).

We must reject the lie that we are worthless, and believe what scripture tells us concerning our self-worth. Second Corinthians 6:18, "We are sons and daughters of God." Ephesians 2:10, "We are His workmanship, created in Christ Jesus for good works." Matthew 5:13, "We are joint heirs with Christ." Psalm 8:5, "We are crowned with glory and honor." Romans 8: 29 & 30, "We are people of dignity and destiny."

Second Corinthians tells us that in Christ we have been forever changed. We are now a new creation in Christ. When satan tells us his old lies about us, we are to resist him and turn our thoughts to the scriptures that prove satan wrong and expose him for the liar that he is.

We must guard our mind and bring every thought into captivity to the obedience of Christ (Second Corinthians 10:5). We must use our reasoning power instead of accepting the old way of thinking and believing. Change your mind! Philippians 4:8 tells us what kind of thoughts we should think. Obey scripture.

Our mind can be our worst enemy, or it can be our best friend. It depends on how we use it. Remember it is satan who wants us to have low self-esteem. Stay alert; watch what is taking place in your mind. You can be in control of what goes on in it. We must have a Godly self-love (Ephesians 5:28 & 29). Without a Godly self-love, we are vulnerable to low self-esteem thoughts.

Self-love simply means that we see ourselves as worthwhile creatures in Christ. If we are blessed enough to feel Godly love for ourselves, in reality we are allowing ourselves to receive God's love for us. We are really feeling His love expressed in our spirit.

It is not selfish self-love or self-centered egotistical love. That goes with pride. That is what we create in ourselves to cover the low self-esteem. This is what satan uses to keep us from letting ourselves see the low self-esteem. We must repent of and give up this pride to work through and be freed of the low self-esteem.

We are born sinful creatures, but so is everyone else. None are inferior, none are superior. We are all alike. God only wants us to learn of this and decide whether we want to stay this way or turn to Him and let Him, through Jesus, cleanse us of the sin and make us new creatures with His nature. That is why we are here—to choose sin or God's righteousness.

First John 1:9, "If we confess our sin He is faithful and just to forgive us our sin and to cleanse us of ALL unrighteousness." We must accept God's forgiveness. If we do not, satan will keep tormenting us with guilt. This blocks our freedom from low self-esteem.

We must believe that God wants us to receive His forgiveness. We must remember, though, that we must forgive others. We must realize that they have suffered the same persecution from satan that we have, the same low self-esteem, and the same distortion of their spirit and soul.

They, as we, have been crippled mentally and emotionally by satan's destructive influence and programming. We are not fighting flesh and blood, people, but evil spirits.

They, as we, suffer from their choices that satan influences. We are all here for the same reason and in the same battles. Some people win. Some lose. Those who win, will have good self-esteem, and those who lose live with poor self-esteem the rest of their lives.

A person can be "saved" but still live with low self-esteem, because they will not allow themselves to give up the pride and acknowledge the sin in their lives. We must accept our life situations as being for our spiritual growth. Romans 8:28, "And we KNOW that all things work together for our good to those who love God, to those who are called according to His purpose."

When satan does his evil work in us to give us low self-esteem, he means for it to destroy us, keep us from loving God and being what God wants us to be. He wants to take us to Hell and the lake of fire with him.

But God lets this happen to humble and try us, as He did the Israelites in the wilderness for forty years. It was to humble and try them.

Also, the Holy Spirit told me that if I had not gone through what I did, I never would have turned to God. He also told me that He lets people go through suffering so they will see their helplessness and their need for Him.

Much of life is beyond our control, i.e., where, when, to whom, which race we are born, whether rich, poor, healthy or physically handicapped. However, if we fail to see all this from a Biblical perspective, we will fail to accept ourselves.

We must realize that God created us the way we are for a divine purpose. He does not see our situations as liabilities. He often uses the very things we consider to be hindrances for our ETERNAL BENEFIT, spiritual growth. When we accept our circumstances, we can accept ourselves and gradually let Him build a Godly self-esteem.

In conclusion, we must embrace a Biblical perspective. Respond to the clarity of God's Word. Discipline our thoughts. Have a Godly self-love. Accept God's forgiveness. Accept our life situation. Always thank God for the good He will bring from all the things we go through. It IS all for our good!

CHAPTER 11

Focus

When my husband died, I was getting ready to go to the funeral parlor for the calling hours. Suddenly the Holy Spirit said to me, "You can focus on the suffering and the grief and you can suffer, or you can focus on showing love and comfort to those who are suffering." I made the choice and focused on giving the love and comfort to others. From that moment on, for weeks I walked in the love and joy of God. It was so strong that I could not get close to anyone without that love flowing from me to him or her.

People would come into the funeral parlor looking very sad and not knowing what to say to me. I would go to them and give them some of the love and comfort of God. Their whole countenance would change. When they left it was with hugs and smiles.

I missed my husband but it was not what I focused on. For example, it was like talking on the phone to someone and something is going on in the room at the same time. You know that something is happening but your attention is on the phone conversation. That is how I felt. I knew my husband was not coming back. I missed him but the love I was experiencing was so strong I paid little attention to his death. When I think of his death and funeral, I think of the love, joy and peace I was given. All I did was make the choice and the Holy Spirit did the rest.

When we encounter someone, do we focus on finding fault with him or her? Something we can criticize and feel superior to, or look for good that we can compliment and help them feel good about themselves. Where is our focus??

Many people become depressed around the holidays. They may focus their thoughts on how much they miss a loved one who has passed on, or a divorce, or just being alone. They are focused on themselves. Some commit suicide at that time. Instead we can focus on helping someone else. Just about everyone knows someone in need. Volunteer at a soup kitchen, have an old or alone person for dinner or call and encourage someone. If we really want to help others instead of feeling sorry for ourselves, Jesus will give us directions. Self-pity causes depression. Believe me, I know.

Instead of focusing on our spouse's faults, we should focus on our own and ask Jesus to forgive us and to cleanse us of all unrighteousness. First John 1:7 through 9 tells us if we confess our sins, He is faithful and just to forgive our sins and to cleanse us of them. But if we do not confess (admit) them to Him, we have to live with them and the suffering they bring to others and us.

We need to focus on how we can help, teach, encourage and comfort others, especially our family. I had a dream one time in which there was a group of women. They were complaining about how badly their husbands treated them. Someone spoke up and said, "If you women treated your husbands the way you want them to treat you, your marriage would be much happier." The same with our children. Focus on treating them with the love and respect that you want from them instead of trying to control them with anger and criticism and they would have much better attitudes.

I knew a couple that had a son. The son did not do too well in school. The parents criticized him all the time and he felt like they did not love him because of the way they talked to him and made him feel worthless. The Holy Spirit told me to tell him that his parents loved him. They criticized him thinking it would motivate him to do better. They did not know how to motivate him any other way but it just made him feel unloved and worthless.

I went to their house and asked to speak to the boy alone (he was in his teens), and I told him what the Holy Spirit said. He cried. His parents wanted to know what I was saying to him so the dad came out asking me what I had said to his son. I told him the same thing and they should show their son love and praise him for what he did right. Try to help him but never criticize him. Focus on helping and teaching him with love and encouragement. The Holy Spirit also told me to tell the son to do little good deeds for others and that would help his self-esteem to grow.

They did what the Lord, through me, told them to do. Their lives changed and the father became a good father. He taught his son many things that helped him grow into a good husband, father and nice giving person. The parents changed their focus from anger and criticism to love and encouragement.

I have seen from experience, people will shame a person who is overweight thinking they will shame them into losing weight, but it makes that person feel hurt and shame, which makes them eat more to feel some pleasure (feel good for a few moments) which makes them feel more shame and guilt. The wrong attitudes and actions destroy God's creation. We should look inside ourselves and see what is going on there.

When sickness or problems come into our lives our minds usually instantly focus on ourselves. How can I solve this? What can I do to fix this? O, woe is me, I am in trouble now. How can I control things?

When someone says or does something that hurts and/or embarrasses us, we focus on self and begin to defend ourselves by trying to hurt or embarrass back. One of the reasons our prayers are not granted is because of our focus on self. We focus on trying to control people to do, be or give what we want them to do. If they do not we will be hurt and/or angry. We will say or think unkind things. These things always bring unpleasant consequence, BUT, if, when bad or hurtful things happen we focus on God and his instructions, we will deal with them His way. Things always go better with doing God's will.

I was listening to a person one day, but my mind was on myself and how what they were saying pertained to or affected me. The Holy Spirit said to me in a very emphatic way, "Get your mind off of yourself and think about how it pertains to him. He needs help." So I learned to really focus on the other person and see if I could teach, comfort, encourage or help them in any way. The Bible tells us to put the other person first and help them if we can. When we focus on ourselves, we are being self-centered. When we focus on God, we will be God and others-centered.

Are we focused on changing (controlling) others so we can be happy, or are we focused on changing ourselves so we can help others be happy? If we do the latter, we will reap GOOD consequences. The important thing is to focus on God and doing His will so things will go well with you and your children forever. Read Deuteronomy 5:29. God Himself tells us that.

Where is Your Focus?

Good or bad	Love or hate
Happy or sad	Forgiveness or unforgiveness
Self or others	Giving or taking
Trouble	Or God's Promises
Anger or mercy	Self or God?

Have You Checked?

CHAPTER 12

The Brain

We are not physical beings having a spiritual experience. We are a spiritual being having a physical experience. The brain is a physical tool that we use to communicate ourselves (spirit or soul) to the outside world. The brain is the computer of our body. It has to be kept in good running condition so the rest of the body functions like it was meant to function. We all have one, but how do we use it? The brain is not us. It is ours.

It is an amazing machine made of flesh. The brain controls the body, but who controls the brain? We, who live inside this body, and will some day leave it and go back to God, who gave it. The brain is flesh. We are spirit. We are in charge of the brain. Our brain and body are made up of chemicals and electrical systems. Everything we eat or drink is made up of chemicals. Some are healing and restorative. Others are destructive chemicals such as alcohol, cigarettes, drugs, etc. We can and do damage our brain by putting the destructive chemicals into it. We can also damage it by not feeding it enough of the nourishing chemicals.

We can think of our brain as the engine in an automobile. It has to be well maintained in order to run properly or it may begin breaking down. If we put gas, oil and water in it, as we should, it runs okay. If we fail to do this, it may quit running. The brain doesn't think. It is our mind that does the thinking. The brain does what our mind, we ourselves, tells it to.

Do we tell it to create good or bad chemicals? We make this choice by the kind of thoughts we think and the food we eat or don't eat. The brain creates the chemicals that create the emotions that we feel. Emotions are chemicals that make us feel what ever goes with the thoughts we have. When we put destructive chemicals in our body, alcohol, nicotine and all the other destructive chemicals that are put in cigarettes, drugs, etc, we are slowly destroying the health of our brain and our body. This will cause the organs to malfunction. Blood pressure, heart, lungs, liver, kidneys and so forth. This is all about the physical aspect of the brain.

Our physical person is operated and maintained by electrical systems. We have two electrical systems. These are the two nervous systems. For the brain and the nervous systems to function properly, they have to have the proper chemicals taken in. There are healthy and restorative chemicals such as vitamins and minerals. Everything we eat or drink is made up of chemicals.

So now we know about the physical working of the brain. Good food and good thoughts equal good feelings and good health. Destructive chemicals put into our bodies, alcohol, nicotine, etc, and sinful thoughts equal poor health and poor brain function.

I had a friend who had a brother who had to be committed to a mental health facility. After some time, he was better and released. Later my friend called me and asked me to pray for him. She said he was having mental problems again. After we hung up the phone, I began praying for him. The Holy Spirit spoke to my spirit and told me that the man had starved his brain by not eating the things he should so he was starving his brain of what it needed to function properly. He explained that the food we eat or don't eat affects the brain as well as the body. If we don't eat enough of the nourishing foods, the brain becomes unhealthy. When that happens it does not function well. It may begin to break down.

There was a young man who was friends with one of my daughters who had been in and out of mental hospitals for some years. He began calling me to pray for him, or to just talk. The next time he called me, I told him what the Holy Spirit had told me about my friend's brother. He told me his doctors had told him the same thing. He had starved his brain and that was why he had to be committed so many times.

He had shock treatments and had to take strong chemicals to try to help his brain. I taught him about the need for protein, fruits, vegetables, and whole grains to help his brain be healthy. He took my advice and never had to be hospitalized again. He never had to take medicine again, either. He told me I had helped him more than the doctors or medicine had. I told him I had just had given him the information and he was wise enough to use it.

Later a member of my family developed an eating disorder after they graduated school. They began dieting and did not do it in a healthy manner. After a while they began displaying emotional problems such as depression and lack of energy. The parents finally took over and made them go to the doctor for help. They had developed a bipolar disorder because of decreased necessary chemicals in their brain from an unhealthy diet. They also developed schizophrenic characteristics. I prayed for them. The Holy Spirit told me they also had starved their brain. I went to talk to them and told them what the Holy Spirit told me. They said that was true.

Genesis 2:7 tells us that God made man out of the dust of the earth. The earth is made up of chemicals also. It has iron, magnesium, calcium, sodium, potassium, manganese, chromium, and others. Our bodies also have these chemicals. The brain needs the right amount of chemicals to be healthy, and all of the food that God has created has the healthy chemicals in them. Different foods have different chemicals. Carrots have different ones than milk. We are made up of chemicals. We need them to live and function, as we should.

The Bible tells us the life is in the blood. Our blood carries all the chemicals to all parts of our body and brain. If those chemicals are out of balance so will our health and brain be.

I have a theory about so many young people developing schizophrenic tendencies. I believe that when they are not under their parent's supervision, they no longer eat the healthy foods. They live on snack foods and drinks. They do not maintain a healthy diet for the brain. Mom is not with them to insist on them doing this, so they just eat their pleasure foods. This damages their brain. It depletes the brain of the nourishing chemicals. Their brain is depleted of the healthy chemicals such as serotonin. A low count of this is one of the major causes of clinical depression.

The Holy Spirit told me in a dream that corn and tomatoes eaten together produce this chemical. I try to eat this combo in some form every day, i.e., chili with corn on the side, diced tomatoes and corn, Italian tomato sauce with corn. You get the idea. Brazil nuts also have serotonin.

How tragic that we let satan control us and don't even realize what is going on. In the fourth chapter of Hosea, God says, "My people perish for lack of knowledge because they have rejected that knowledge."

I told a member of my family who dieted a lot the importance of eating at lease 60 grams of protein each day. The word protein in Latin means number one, most important. I also told her how to eat a healthy diet. She ignored me and now she is on a walker and has many health problems. She is about thirty-five years younger than I am. A number of others are now diabetic and have high blood pressure and other problems. They all said I was a health food nut.

As I wrote earlier, we make the choices. I pray all who read this make the right ones. The brain can be made healthier. I know I messed mine up when I was young going on unhealthy diets.

Jesus forgave me and restored my health, but I had to follow good health rules. We must determine to do what is best for ourselves and follow through.

The devil knows that if he can control us into unhealthy eating habits, he can cause us to be unhealthy. When this happens he knows our mind will be centered on self and desiring to FEEL good.

We then become centered on self and not God. We are centered on the creature and not the creator, but we are instructed to seek to know God and His will. His way of caring for His temple, the body, first. He gave us all these instructions for our good so we can feel good and enjoy life. He wants the best for His children.

We listen to the lies of satan and let him control us instead of God. We are so afraid of being helpless that we fight against letting God have control, but all the time we are being controlled by satan.

He is the one who gave us the feelings of helplessness, fear, anger and the desire to hang on to, stay in control. We are helpless in many situations but God is not helpless. If we put our trust in Him, He can protect and/or help us through anything. He longs to develop our potential so that we can be, obtain, and live the life of love, joy, peace, and righteousness in the Holy Spirit.

God wants us to see our helplessness but only to realize our need for Him. We work overtime trying to stay in control because we don't believe His word. The devil wants us to feel helpless because he knows we will begin trying to have the control instead of trusting God to protect us.

Our body has a system of glands. When a thought is put into the brain, it sends a message through the nervous systems to the glands telling them to produce the chemicals that will produce the feeling or emotion that corresponds to that thought, healing or destructive.

This is why we were instructed in God's instruction book (the Bible) to take every thought into captivity according to Jesus, the Christ. We are to closely guard our brain from sin and satan's destructive thoughts. Why? For our own good!

So you see, we are in a spiritual battle even over our eating habits and thoughts. The devil and his army work all the time in every area of our lives to hinder and destroy us. The Holy Spirit is with us all the time, trying to protect and help us.

Which do we respond to the most? If we sin, we suffer. If we obey, we are rewarded. God's word is true. Our lives are affected by our choices. We reap the natural consequences of our thoughts and actions. God set those laws in motion when He created the Universe. We defile the temple of God (our body) when we put destructive chemicals and/or thoughts into it. We must guard our brain very diligently. It is the only one we have to get us through this life. Lets try to make it last in good shape as long as our body does.

The devil will cause people to hurt or embarrass us and then give us hurt, angry, self-pitying, vengeful, selfish, hateful, unforgiving thoughts. These are all VERY destructive to the well being of the body, soul and spirit. He can cause us to fear, feel inferior, shame, self-hate, or other thoughts along this line.

He can, if we let him, keep us thinking these things most of the time. These will cause depression, which is VERY destructive to the health of our body, brain, soul and spirit. The brain is just a member of us. Paul wrote in Romans 6:16 that whoever we yield our members to we are their servant. If we yield our brain to the devil, he uses it for his purposes and he rules our thoughts and emotions. They are always destructive.

If we yield it to the Holy Spirit He will use it for God's purpose. So now we know that the emotions can be used by the Holy Spirit or the devil. We make the choice by the thoughts that we choose to allow or disallow into our brain.

The devil or one of his evil spirits will put a negative thought in our minds. If we accept that thought the brain takes over and sends a message through the nerves to the glands to produce chemicals that go with that thought. Fear thoughts, feelings of fear, self-pity thoughts, which by the way lead to depression, angry thoughts, chemicals producing angry feelings.

The brain doesn't care what is put in it. Just like an auto, it doesn't care what is put in it. They are both only machines, one metal and bolts, the other flesh.

Here is one of satan's tricks he played on me. I had never really focused on my weight. I always ate what I wanted but when I turned my life over to Jesus, I quit smoking. I gained twenty pounds before I knew it.

I became obsessed with losing that twenty pounds. I went on unhealthy diets. I destroyed my health. I had hypoglycemia, hypothyroidism, allergies, and gallstones. I had always had a lot of energy but now I felt exhausted all the time. I awoke exhausted every morning. I also had arthritis in my hip.

I became a semi-invalid because of the exhaustion. I was also very depressed. I began to pray for healing. I prayed for years. I think it was over fifteen years.

Finally the Lord gave me a dream. In the dream, people took their Bibles and went to church. They sincerely desired to know God and to learn what was in the Bible and what it meant so they could worship and serve Him and become what He willed for them.

While they were in the church, some very large and very black men, not African-Americans, but coal black, set up tables with many pleasure foods. When the people came from the church these black men tempted them to eat the pleasure foods—sweets, unhealthy foods.

The people ate them, as I had done in my waking hours. They became unhealthy, began to feel tired and bad. Then they began seeking to feel good.

When I awoke, I was given the understanding of the dream. Matthew 6:33 tells us to seek the kingdom of God above everything else. I had begun doing this after I turned my life over to Jesus.

When I gained weight, went on unhealthy diets and became tired all the time, my mind zeroed in on myself instead of God or Jesus. The Holy Spirit showed me that I had been focused on and seeking for the FLESH above all else.

As I write this, I am seventy-eight years old and am not on any medication at all, and I have not been for years. So I know that what I have written is true. We need to be in obedience to God's instructions. We can save ourselves so much suffering if we will do that. Self-control! It is harder to say no to ourselves than to anyone else.

I read the question in a newspaper once that asked, "Do you have an inquiring mind?" I thought about it and realized I did not. I began to look into myself. I called it spying on my own mind. I began to watch what I was thinking and feeling. I learned I was not really in touch with my feelings. I would ask the Lord what I was feeling. After He revealed that to me, I would ask why I was feeling that. I was amazed at all I learned about myself that I had not been aware of.

If the Holy Spirit wants to express love for someone through us, He gives that message to the brain. The brain sends the message to the glands through the nervous system to produce the love chemicals. If we yield to satan, he will give the brain the message to express hate in some way, such as anger, hurtful, humiliating words, or even a violent act.

I was seeking for the flesh first, not obeying Matthew 6:33 in seeking to know God and seek to be a righteous person. That was why He allowed me to suffer all those years.

In Hebrews 12:1 we are told that we suffer so that we might be partakers of His Holiness. He chastens those He loves. Hebrews 12:16.

So you see, we must be on guard all the time. The devil is deceiving and sly.

To take very good care of our health we must use self-discipline and self-awareness. Just remember our brain is like a computer. We are the ones who put or allow to be put everything that goes into it.

So guard your brain and thoughts very carefully. The enemy is at the door all the time.

We know that our emotions are just feelings produced by chemicals. They are a physical attribute of the body. They can be used by us, the devil or the Holy Spirit, whomever we yield our brains to.

Matthew 6:33: Seek first the kingdom of God and His righteousness and He will take care of us and supply all that we need. TRUST HIM!

"Walk in the Spirit and we will not fulfill the lust of the flesh," Galatians 5:16. This means as long as we are yielded to the Holy Spirit, satan and sin cannot be in control us. God's instruction book was given so we can learn to live, eat, think, speak, feel and so on, everything as God wills, so we will not have the suffering in our lives that disobedience causes. The brain is affected by all or the lack of these. We live in the temple of God.

I hope you are taking very good care of it for Him and for yourself.

CHAPTER 13

Suffering

I believe the most asked question today is why does God allow suffering. Romans 8:28 tells us that all things work together for good to those who love God and are called according to His purpose. This means that everything that happens is for our spiritual growth.

Many people need to be broken before they will surrender to God, and that is just what happened to me. First, my spirit was broken so I would turn my life over to Jesus. The second breaking was of my sinful soul. Jesus did that after I gave my life to Him, giving Him the right to do with it as He pleased.

My spirit and soul were both filled with sin which caused me terrible mental and emotional suffering. Jesus went to work to cleanse me of sin, heal me of hurt and shame of the past and teach me how to let myself be used by Him and the Holy Spirit to help others. This is His will for us all. Most people do not understand why, after we are saved, He lets what we consider bad things happen to us. He is really working all of these for our good.

The book of Job is His example of this. Job was upright and perfect. The devil comes along and says to God, "Let me have him and he will curse you to your face." The devil attacked Job where he attacks humanity—in our family, marriage, financial welfare, our physical health, our mental and emotional health, and hurt from friends.

Job knew about God. God had put a hedge around to protect him. Seemingly, he had no big problems, but he feared them. When God removed the hedge and let the devil cause all the problems he did, Job got depressed, cursed the day he was born, grieved, wished for death, complained, despaired, had sleepless nights, experienced hopelessness, helplessness and fear.

These are what we all experience at one time or another when we are suffering something that we have no power to change and do not understand why God is letting it happen to us. We must remember that it was the devil who was causing these things to happen to Job. He hates God and he hates all who love God.

To get back to Job, in all these troubles and suffering, Job submitted to God (Chapter 1:21). He resigned himself to the situations (Chapter 2:9 and 10). In the end, after Job had suffered all this but had not done what the devil wanted him to do — curse God — God put a stop to it all and revealed Himself to Job. He showed Job His greatness. Then Job, instead of knowing about God, knew Him personally. Job had held on to his faith in God. God rewarded Job with much more than he had in the beginning.

The basic meaning of the book of Job is that the devil attacks and persecutes everyone who comes into this world. We are tested. Will we curse God and die spiritually, or will we choose to trust God no matter what?

So a lot of our suffering comes from satan's persecution, i.e., being molested, raped or abused in different ways, or the murder of loved ones. These things we have not done to others, so it is not a reaping of what we sowed.

I was talking to a friend one time. She was telling me about the bad things happening in and to her and her family. I wanted very much to say something to help her, but I could not think of anything that I knew would help her. That night I dreamed of her. In the dream, Jesus told me she was living in a traumatic situation, and all I could do was pray for her, which I did. Things did get much better for her. The dream told me that God was the only one who could help her, and He did.

That made me think about how much suffering there was in this world. I asked Jesus why. Why do people have to suffer? He said, "So they will see their helplessness and their need for Me." So, a lot of it is to bring us to our knees before Him. A lot of it also is because we, in our sinful state, hurt and make others suffer. That is where we get done to us as we do to others. That is why Jesus said to do unto others, as you want others to do unto you, because He knew it would be done to us. He loves us. He does not want us to hurt others, because He does not want us to have to get it back, and He does not want the others to suffer either.

Another reason we suffer is because we do not nourish and care for the temple of God, as we should. We put destructive chemicals into it. We smoke, drink alcohol, take drugs, etc. Everything we put into our system goes to the brain, also. We destroy brain cells. We under nourish the brain and body because we do not like a lot of foods that God provides for us. Instead we like to eat the pleasure foods. When we under nourish the temple, we begin to feel bad. We will be tired a lot. We will not feel as cheerful. We will not enjoy life.

When we begin feeling bad, we become focused on self. We become focused on what we can do to feel better. We pray for healing but go on eating, drinking and smoking things that are causing the trouble in the first place. Believe me, I learned this by experience. In these things we cause our own suffering. We may go on unhealthy diets so we will look good even though they make us feel bad. Pride and self-will are very destructive and cause much suffering.

Another reason for suffering is the fact that we are being pruned. God cuts away dead and destructive things in our lives so the good fruit can flourish.

In John 15: 1&2, Jesus said, "I am the true vine and my Father is the gardener." He cuts off every branch that does not bear fruit, while every branch that does bear fruit, He prunes so it will be even more fruitful. The fruitless branches are cut off, but the fruitful branches are cut back. The ones that do not bear fruit are burned. The ones cut back are being prepared for more growth. Our suffering is a form of spiritual pruning. It improves the spiritual growth of those who hang on to Jesus.

Some pruning comes from being persecuted by satan through other people such as being rejected, talked bad to, or about, ostracized, hated or even killed. Jesus said in Matthew 5, " Blessed are those who are persecuted for righteousness sake, for theirs is the kingdom of heaven."

If we look at suffering from our point of view or understanding, we cannot make sense of it. We will be angry with God, sorry for self, depressed, or despair of trying. That is looking at it according to the natural man. The Bible tells us that according to the natural man it is all foolishness (1st Corinthians 2:14). It has to be looked at in the spiritual to be able to understand and accept that God has a good reason for everything we go through.

Revelation 3:19 states that God chastises those He loves. It is as we do with our children. We know if they are not chastised for their wrong doing, they will never learn right from wrong or self-control. Proverbs 13:24 says, "If a man spares the rod he hates his son," which means that he does not care that he grows up and suffers from his sin.

So many people ask why children suffer cancer or other devastating illnesses or afflictions. The Lord told me one time that their spirits are one of God's jewels, and that they chose to come here and suffer that for their family's spiritual growth. Everything that happens is for our spiritual growth. They come here, suffer, only God knows how much, then die and go back to live with their Heavenly Father again.

God has a reason for everything He does or allows. It is up to us to spiritually discern that, and as Job said, "We receive good from God, shouldn't we accept the bad also?"

My oldest daughter could not get along with my husband, her stepfather. She began asking me to let her go live with her biological father. I did not want her to go. I also knew if I did, my whole family would turn against me, so I refused over and over. She kept badgering me about it, so I finally asked Jesus if I should let her go. He said to let her go for her own spiritual growth, so I did.

I was right. My whole family except one brother turned against me. Life with my daughter's father was not what she thought it would be. The Lord would wake me from sleep and tell me to pray for her. I would and the next day or so she would call and tell me what had been happening at the time the Lord woke me.

I would ask the Lord if I could bring her home now. He would always say no. She stayed there for about a year. Finally she came to visit and was bruised up from her boy friend hitting her because she went out with another boy. She was seventeen at the time. After she left, I was very upset about it. I thought if I asked Jesus to bring her home, He would say no, so I told Him I could not take it. I was going to close my mind to the whole thing and just not think about it anymore. He said to me, "No, you bring her home now, she is ready to accept Me." I brought her home. Two weeks later she went to church with me and accepted Jesus as her Savior.

She told me that before she went to her father's to live, she thought the kids that drank and did all the things they should not do were the really cool kids. I was very strict with her. She did not go out with any of them, but when she lived with her father, she was allowed to do as she pleased. She learned the hard way that she wanted nothing to do with that type of people.

Jesus put her where she could learn what they were really like. She was a different person when she came home. Jesus knows what we need to grow spiritually. Sometimes growth is very hard to attain. She suffered but she learned what Jesus wanted her to learn. Sin brings suffering. Sin is not pretty.

The church I attend periodically has home Bible classes. A number of people will open their homes for these classes. I would always ask the Lord where He wanted me to go, which home group to attend. He always revealed it to me some way. It was always out in the boonies or maybe ten miles from my home. Well, this certain time there happened to be one three blocks from my home. Oh, boy, I will go to that one, I said to myself, and I did.

The couple who owned the house are very nice people. Their house had one of those sunken living rooms. I had never been in their home. I did not know about the sunken living room. On the very first night I went and did not see that it was sunken. When I stepped "into" their living room, I fell and broke two bones in my left foot.

I suffered pain from that and also suffered having to pay a few dollars less than $1000 for x-rays and doctor fees. I asked Jesus why He had let that happen to me. Instantly I saw a picture in my mind of a shepherd carrying a lamb on his shoulders and Jesus brought to my memory something I had read thirty years earlier. Back in Biblical days, when a lamb strayed from the flock, the shepherd broke the lamb's leg. He then carried the lamb on his shoulders until its leg healed, teaching it to never stray again.

I got the message. I had not asked Jesus which home group He wanted me to attend. I just went where I wanted to go. I had strayed from Jesus and gone where I chose. I had done my will and not His will. It was a hard but lasting lesson.

Another time I caught a virus and asked why. I had a friend who went to another church. His pastor was a woman. He would tell me things she would say. I would tell him something to the effect of, "Oh, yeah, well, this is what I believe about that." When I asked Jesus why I got so sick, he told me it was because I was competing with my friend's pastor. He has His ways of getting our attention. He works to correct our wrong attitudes and actions.

When I was a relatively new follower of Jesus, I did something in church one evening that caused me to be ashamed of myself. I dreamed that night I was a little child showing off while riding a child's tricycle and fell into a hole. That was the true picture of what had happened in church. I was so humiliated, and that lesson stayed with me also.

There are times we can make ourselves suffer because we feel guilty about something. I said something hurtful to my husband one day. I felt very guilty for it. I came down with some internal problem that put me in the hospital. The family thought I was dying. The Lord showed me that the guilt had caused my digestive system to be messed up. He brought me out of it.

Another cause for suffering I was shown is some people substitute sympathy for love. I knew a lady who as a child thought (wrongly) that no one loved her. When she was ill as a child she got much attention and sympathy. The devil told her child's mind to substitute sympathy for love. She accepted this. Her whole life has been nothing but sickness and circumstances that draw sympathy from others.

In fact I have known more than one person who was programmed to live this kind of life. Remember satan programs our subconscious mind as children and then controls us with that as adults. The people do not consciously realize what they are doing. They create situations in their lives to manipulate others to feel sorry for them. They usually eat unhealthy diets that cause health problems.

One evening I visited my grandson and his family. Their three-year-old daughter had fallen and scratched her face a little. When I arrived, the first thing they did was tell me about her accident. I stooped down in front of her and started to say, "Oh, you poor little thing." Before I could get the words out, the Holy Spirit said, "Do not do that or she will feel sorry for herself all of her life." So I just told her it would get better. As she got older and started learning about Jesus, when she got hurt, I would pray for Jesus to make it better then tell her He would. Now I do that with all the children that tell me about a hurt or are with me when it happens.

Another reason for suffering is based on Matthew 20:16, "they who want to be first shall be last." Many people, when children, will become jealous of a sibling. The devil puts it in their mind that the sibling is loved more, or loved and they are not.

They will begin competing with the sibling. They will hurt and or embarrass them because they are angry with them. Their spirit may love them, but the sinful soul may even hate them. The competing will become so ingrained, programmed in their mind that they eventually become controlled by it. It becomes part of them. This is how an evil spirit can take over a person's way of living.

They automatically begin competing with everyone. They probably do not realize what they are doing. But if they are not always first in everything, if they do not always win, they will become hurt and angry with themselves and others. They become hurt because of the old message whether true or false, that they are not loved or loved as much. They spend their whole life suffering the hurt and emotional upset of anger.

Always putting themselves first, always trying to be the one favored, praised, the winner or loved one, is what causes much suffering in their life. In Philippians 2:3, "Let nothing be done through selfish ambition or conceit (the great I should come first) but in lowliness of mind, let each esteem others better than self."

In Philippians 2:4, "Let each of you look out not only for his own interests, but also for the interests of others. So you see that the striving to always be first is against God's will, so it is sin. If we sin, we suffer. In this, we suffer many humbling experiences. When we strive to be first, we usually come out last. We always want to, and try to look good or better than others.

Matthew 23:12 tells us if we exalt, show off, strive for praise, we will be abased, embarrassed or humiliated. This is being humbled. If we do not humble ourselves and put the other person first, we will be humbled. This is one of satan's favorite tricks to use against us because he gets much pleasure and glee from humbling us. He knows if he can get us to exalt ourselves, he can have his pleasure party at our expense.

My mother was caught in this terrible trap. She became envious of her twin brother because her mother favored him. She lived most of her life being humbled. She had a terrible life. I did the same. I was envious of my older brother because Mom favored him. I lived a miserable life before I turned it over to Jesus. One of my daughters was envious of her younger sister. She also lived a very bad life.

The Lord taught me all of this. At first it was very hard, but when He showed me what I had to suffer every time I exalted myself (shame and hurt), I let Him clean it out of my subconscious mind. He freed me of satan's evil attitudes and emotions. It took Him time but he kept on working on it for me. Thank you, Jesus!

Another reason we suffer is if we, in our heart and/or mind want others to suffer, we shall suffer also. When we say something to hurt and/or embarrass someone, we have made an appointment for some time in the near future to be hurt and/or embarrassed just as much as we wanted our victim to suffer.

We reap what we sow. Even in our thoughts and desires. Proverbs 23:7, "As a man (or person) thinks in his heart, so is he."

Ecclesiastes 12:13 & 14, "Fear God and keep His commandments, for this is man's all. For God will bring every work into judgment, including every secret thing, whether good or evil." Matthew 12:25, "Jesus knew their thoughts."

Hebrews 4:12, "For the word of God is living and powerful, and sharper than a two-edged sword, piercing even to the division of the soul and spirit, and or joints and marrow, and is a discerner of the THOUGHTS and INTENTS of the heart." Hebrews 4:13, "All things are open to the eyes of God to whom we must give an account."

So, if we wish bad on others or rejoice at their suffering, we shall suffer also. When we go to stand before God and have not repented of these sins, we shall be judged for them. Jeremiah 5:25, "Your sins have withheld good from you." James 4:11, "Do not speak evil of one another but speak blessing that you may receive a blessing."

All suffering is for our spiritual growth. It is to prepare us for when we stand before God on judgment day. He wants us to stand before Him with nothing to be judged for. He wants to be able to say, "Well done, my good and faithful servant, enter into my rest."

Habakkuk 3:17 & 18, "Though the fig tree may not blossom, nor fruit be on the vines; though the labor or the olive may fail and the fields yield no food; though the flock may be cut off from the fold and there be no herd in the stalls—yet I will rejoice in the Lord, I will joy in the God of my SALVATION."

When we respond to suffering well, it brings a deepening relationship with God. When we can trust that He is working everything for our spiritual good, it helps us to accept everything in peace. We can deal with it in thanksgiving that He will surely bring good out of it. It may seem terrible in the flesh, but it is a blessing for our spirit.

We can, as Job said, "My ears have heard of you, but now my eyes have seen you." We can rest in the knowledge that He is our loving Heavenly Father who is working everything out for His child's best welfare. This life is just temporary but when we leave here, it is forever. He wants us to have a wonderful, joyous life forever. He is trying to bring us to that.

Here is an epitaph in an English churchyard: "Who plucked the flower?" asked the gardener. "The Master," someone said. And the gardener held his peace.

After I first turned my life over to Jesus, I thought I would never be hurt or have problems again. Boy, was I wrong. They started immediately. My family and friends began saying hurtful things to me. Even my pastor did that from the pulpit. I began to see that he did that to others, also. I used to say he hid behind the pulpit and threw spiritual stones at his congregation. That first time he did that to me I went home and cried until 2:00 in the morning. I prayed about these things, but they still happened.

After a long while I saw what was going on. The devil would have something happen to me. I would ask God why. He would show me something destructive the devil had programmed in my subconscious—a sin, fear or destructive way of reacting to people and/or circumstances. The devil knew all of my sins, weaknesses, fears and psychological hang-ups. He began attacking me in these areas and trying to get me to quit going to church and turn away from God.

This is what Jesus told us about in the book of Job and also in the parable of the sower in Matthew 13. This is when, where and how satan gets people to turn back from following Jesus. He used them on me. I would ask Jesus why this or that was happening. He would tell me what the devil had in me that he could attack me with.

I would ask His forgiveness and ask Him to cleanse or heal me of whatever it was. I eventually learned that Jesus allowed satan to do this so I would look to Jesus and into myself and see the truth of what I had allowed satan to do to me. He was using it to help me face these things, bring them out to my conscious mind and deal with them as an adult.

As a child growing up when bad, hurtful, fearful or whatever satan had happen to me, I dealt with it as a child, of course, because I was a child. As Paul said in 1 Corinthians 13:11, “When I was a child, I thought as a child, I understood as a child; when I became a man (adult) I put away childish things.”

Jesus helped me bring out the way I dealt with things as a child and taught me how to deal with them as an adult. As a child, I let myself be controlled by the thoughts and feelings the devil put in my mind when things happened to me and/or those around me. My child mind did not have enough information and knowledge to reason things out or to realize I was being controlled by the devil, so I accepted what the devil knew a child would receive.

These things were too much for a child to deal with, so I put them away someplace inside so I did not have to look at them or feel the devastating feelings that went with them. Although they were hidden from my conscious mind, they still ruled my life, my attitude about myself and other people in the world. To me it was all bad. After I gave my life to Jesus, He began to bring these hidden things out as I could deal with them. He taught me to deal with them, not as a child, but as an adult.

Even though it brought out very hurting emotions, I would face it, work through it and get over it. I found that talking about things to someone lessened the pain. The more I talked about it, the less and less power it had over me. Soon I could look at it, talk about it without the emotion of hurt, hate, self-hate or whatever it had caused in the past, and I was healed and freed of it. I had dealt with it as an adult, not as I had as a child. Shame, fear and hurt were the predominate feelings that caused me to suppress so many things.

I believe the devil works the very same way in most people. He is out to make us suffer so much that we will either curse God, kill ourselves or lose our mind. He comes to kill, steal and destroy.

Jesus came to give life and that more abundantly. He wants us to live lives of love and happiness. It is not His desire for us to suffer. We never want someone we love to suffer. Neither does He. He loves us!

Jealousy is another reason we suffer. Jealousy breeds hate. Hate creates poison in our system and brain. It causes us to desire terrible things to happen to those we are jealous of. The devil can use jealousy to destroy us and use us to destroy others. Jealousy is a sin. God does not reward sin.

We will suffer the consequences of all of this. We will suffer them as long as we hold on to the jealousy.

If we sin, we suffer. We need to ask ourselves why am I jealous. What does satan have in me that he can use to make me jealous of others? Then humble ourselves and admit what the Holy Spirit shows about ourselves.

First John again. If we confess, He will forgive and cleanse us of all unrighteousness, but we have to really want to give it up. If we don't want to give it up or want to and can't, then we need to bind the power of the evil spirit that is controlling us in this. Then command it to loose us, to leave and never come back.

Then ask Jesus to clean out all the darkness the evil spirit has put in our subconscious mind and replace it with what He wants to put in it's place.

People often ask why God lets bad things happen to good people. In reality there are no good people. There are only people through whom God shows His goodness. We are all born completely sinful. God cleans us up and creates His good qualities in us. Any good we see in any human being, God put it there or it wouldn't be there.

If He removed His goodness from us we would be left with our own sinful nature again.

No matter how good we seem, we all have room to grow and every thing God allows in our life is for our spiritual growth.

Jesus Himself said there are none good but God.

As I grew up, my mother was abusive to me and my father was abusive to my older brother, John. He was also abusive to my mother. He wasn't abusive to me, only once until I was about ten. After that, he was abusive to me also.

But during the years until I was ten, I felt guilty because Dad was kind to me but not to Mom and John. The devil put in my mind that if it weren't for me, he would be good to them.

I always felt sorry for John and felt guilty when he was abused. Finally the Lord gave me a dream about it. He told me in the dream that John's suffering was not my fault. He said if John had not suffered as he did, he would have lived a life of crime. God has a reason for everything He allows.

When Rob was about three years old, he decided he wanted to empty my refrigerator. He began to take things out of it and put them on the floor.

I told him to stop but he wouldn't. I finally gently slapped his hand. He cried because it hurt his feelings more than it hurt his hand.

I felt awful, so I asked Jesus if I couldn't just pick him up, love on him and tell him about doing wrong. "Can't I teach with love instead of punishment?" I asked.

Instantly, He said to me, "I didn't love you out of your sin, did I?" Then He gave me the scripture, if you spare the rod you hate your child.

Pain and suffering is always for a reason — our growth.

When one of my daughters was in the first grade, her teacher sent a note to me telling me she as not going to pass her on to the second grade.

She wrote that even if her grades came up, she still would not pass her.

This was when I was a relatively new follower of Jesus, and did not have much understanding yet.

I began praying very fervently that the Lord would see that my daughter would not be held back. I prayed it very often.

One day when I prayed it, He told me that because I had prayed it for so long and so hard that He was going to grant my petition, but she would have to suffer some other way.

My reason for wanting her to pass so she would not have to endure the ridicule from the other children.

As it turned out, she had to endure it for another reason.

I was given the understanding later that it was for her humbling. God rules in the affairs of humans. Daniel 4 again.

CHAPTER 14

Healing

My husband and I adopted one of our grandsons when he was seven months old. His name is Robert, but I call him Robbie. When he was five years old, he became ill with strep throat. He was very ill for about three weeks. When he got over the strep throat he complained of stomach and lower abdominal pain.

He would keep me awake nights crying. I would pray for him but the pain continued. I took him to our family doctor a number of times. He finally admitted he did not know what the problem was and recommended a pediatrician. I took Robby to her as soon as I could get an appointment. She said she thought he had parasites in his intestines and put him on a medicine for that. He seemed to get worse.

I took him to a specialist in another town who has a very good reputation. He asked what medication Robby was on and I told him Velosef, a medication our family doctor had prescribed for him since he became ill with the strep throat. He gave him all kinds of tests and then told me he'd had hepatitis some time in the past because his liver was not normal. Robby had told me that he was tired all the time. The specialist told me the medicine for the parasites often messed up the liver.

The pain did not go away. I had to take him to the hospital emergency room one night. They tested and probed. They gave me a prescription but it didn't stop the pain.

Rob would cry at night with the pain. I would call our doctor in the morning as soon as he was in and sometimes I would be crying in sympathy and frustration. He would give me another prescription that didn't work.

The pain had started in June. Robby started kindergarten in August. Then one day in December the school called me to come get the little guy because he was doubled over in pain.

I picked him up at school and took him straight to our doctor's office. He was crying and vomiting. The doctor gave him a shot and kept him there until closing time.

I took him home and put him on the couch in the TV room. I sat down on the floor beside him and put my hands on him. I began to pray. I had prayed many, many times before but this time I sat beside him for five hours praying.

Please, Lord. Please, please heal him. Please, please! For five hours I prayed this.

Finally a little after ten o'clock the Holy Spirit spoke to me and said, "Why don't you stop begging Him and start thanking Him?" I did this at once and while I was doing this I realized that all the time Robby had been sick and I had been praying for him, I did not really believe God would heal him.

I felt in the back of my mind that He didn't love me so I had to beg and beg Him to get Him to do anything for me. I really didn't believe God loved me! Therefore, he didn't want to do anything for me.

I thanked Him and praised Him anyway for healing Robby as the Holy Spirit had told me to do, then I got us ready for bed. As I settled down for sleep the Holy Spirit spoke to me again and said, "Rob will be better in the morning." He didn't say healed or well, but better.

I awoke about five a.m. and instantly knew in my heart that he was better. Rob woke up a minute or two after I did and said, "I feel better, Grandma." I thanked the Lord and we went back to sleep.

We awoke again at nine o'clock. As I awoke the Holy Spirit spoke to me the third time. This time he said, "Rob's problem is the Velosef!" I immediately called our doctor and asked what the side effects were for the Velosef. He said a slight diarrhea. I hung up and called my pharmacist and asked him if someone who was on Velosef for months could it do harm to the stomach and colon. He told me most definitely. I had a prescription for it that the doctor had given me the night before. I threw it away.

I had told every doctor the name of the medicine Rob had been taking all along and none of them realized this could be the problem. I decided not to take him back but I would pray for him from now on. Knowing God does love me and He does want Rob well.

He has answered many, many prayers for us since this. When Robby would get sick or hurt, he came to me and said, "Pray for me, Grandma."

There are many questions asked about why some are healed and others are not. God has a reason for everything He does, and everything He does not do.

He sort of treats us like we do our children. They can have a reward if they clean their rooms, or eat their veggies. Maybe they get to go to the zoo if they clean their rooms. If they don't they will be upset because they didn't get to go.

Whether they go or not is in reality, their choice. Do they choose to clean their rooms or not? This choice determines the outcome.

This little example tells us that many of the sicknesses we have are caused by the choices we make. Do we smoke, drink alcohol, take drugs, eat many sweets, and do other things that are detrimental to our health?

Our body is the temple of God. Are we making it as healthy, peaceful and comfortable for Him as possible? Are we using it to do His will or our selfish, self-centered will?

Many years ago the devil got my mind centered on my weight. He gave me the desire to lose weight so I would look good. This is all the sinful soul, which the ego controls, as the brain controls our body.

Now the devil knows all about the ego and how to manipulate it. If our purpose for eating a certain diet is to sincerely keep the body healthy to please our Heavenly Father, it is a good purpose, but if it is for our ego it is for our sinful self.

I have learned through the years that if I eat the right things for the right reasons, I feel cheerful and have energy and my brain works better.

When I dieted for self, I ruined my health. I lived in fatigue and depression. This was the devil's plan to keep my mind on myself. About the only time it was on God was when I was praying to be healed.

Instead of seeking God's righteousness FIRST, I was seeking to FEEL GOOD FIRST. I was seeking for the flesh.

That went on for years until God got all of this through to me.

Why don't you heal me, God? I go to church every Sunday. I read my Bible every day. I tell people about You. I help people when I can. Why don't you heal me?

I was doing all of that, but I was also in rebellion because I was trying to be in control instead of yielding to Him.

If we sin, we suffer. If we obey, we are rewarded.

All sickness is not because of our self-will. Some sickness is for our spiritual growth. In fact everything is for our spiritual growth.

I explained it in the chapter on Suffering about that.

This chapter is more about why we are not healed at times because you see after I learned what I have just written I repented and God slowly, as I obeyed, healed me. I did grow from it.

I learned very much from the sickness years.

Another reason we are not healed is unforgiveness. Unforgiveness causes other sins in our lives. It causes, first of all, rebellion because we are rebelling against Jesus' command to forgive. It also causes anger, resentment, bitterness and hatred. All of these are sins.

By these we prevent ourselves from being healed.

Another reason that prevents healing is control. Most people in this world want to and try to be in control. This, and pride, are satan's major crimes against God and humanity.

God withholds many things in our lives, including healing at times, because we refuse to yield the control to Him. We fear what would happen if we give the control up.

Much, much worse happens to those who refuse than those who yield to God. He wants to give us lives we can enjoy and in which we can be happy.

That's what we want also, but prevent that by letting the devil deceive us into believing we are in control when in reality, he is controlling us.

God tells us in His Word that He is a jealous God. He is jealous for our sake. He knows the outcome of those who refuse to yield to Him.

God does not reward us for sin although He is merciful. He healed me of a number of things during the years. But He did not heal the fatigue and depression until I finally learned that I was seeking for my flesh first and God second. When I confessed this, asked forgiveness and focused on seeking Him first, He not only healed me but also taught me how to maintain my health.

Some people use sickness for attention. Some use sympathy as a substitute for love. Some have the will to die so the brain brings sickness.

We can pray for healing for years but the subconscious mind obeys our will. God does not force us to be healed if we refuse to receive it because of these orders that have been given to the subconscious mind.

Of course the devil gave these thoughts to them some where in the past. They accepted them so the devil controls them by them.

They may, on the conscious level, want to be well, but they, on the subconscious level, are obeying the programming to seek attention, sympathy, love or even death.

Jesus said that some people suffer sickness or affliction so the works of God should be made manifest in them. John 9:3.

I asked the Lord one time why I couldn't heal everyone I wanted. He told me I had the power to do what HE WANTED ME TO.

God has a reason for everything He does or does not do. He does what's best for each one of us, even though we can't understand why. It is not His perfect will for us to suffer, but He knows for some reason known only to Him, that it is for our spiritual growth.

We know when we are doing wrong. We know we should drink water instead of all the soft drinks we consume. We know we shouldn't eat so many sweets, but we desire the pleasure of the good taste of these.

We know we shouldn't smoke but don't want to face the battle of giving it up. We do so many things that are harmful to our health and then we ask God why He let us have bad health.

Many people tell us that God does not put sickness on anyone, but if you read Leviticus 26:15 & 16, or Psalms 107:17, Micah 6:13, Acts 12:23, and there are many others, you will see they are wrong.

Sin brings suffering. It is for chastisement, correction, to bring a person to repentance. Our heavenly Father will go very far to keep us from having to be judged for sin when we stand before Him. He wants to be able to say, "Well done, my good and faithful servant."

He knows that what we don't repent of here, we will be judged, meaning we will suffer for them someplace else. Even their good works will be burned up. First Corinthians 3:13-17. (13) "Every man's work shall be made manifest: for the day shall declare it, because it shall be revealed by fire; and the fire shall test each one's work of what sort it is." (14) "If anyone's work which he has built on endures, he will receive a reward." (15) "If anyone's work is burned, he will suffer loss but he himself will be saved yet so as through fire." (16) Do you not know that you are the temple of God and that the Spirit of God dwells in you?" (17) "If anyone defiles the temple of God, then God will destroy him. For the temple of God is holy, which temple you are."

Through the years people have imagined and tried to create God in the image of man. They will be greatly shocked and remorseful when they stand before Him and see how wrong they were.

God does want us to be healed but sometimes He will not grant it until we realize why He has allowed it. The devil is always there, trying to destroy us. He knows all of this. He knows the Bible. He uses that as a guide in what to tempt us with every day.

If God says don't, the devil tempts us to do. If God says do, the devil tempts us to don't. We are making choices constantly. Do we obey God or the devil? We pretty well make our own state of health by the choices that we make.

God loves us and wants the best for us. Let us yield to Him and receive the rewards He has in store for those who obey Him.

Matthew 13:58. "Many are not healed because of their non-belief. Now He did not many mighty works there because of their unbelief."

In John 5:14, Jesus said to a man he had healed, "See, you have been made well. Sin no more lest a worse thing come upon you."

In Jeremiah 5:25, "Your sins have withheld good from you."

But in Jeremiah 3:22, it tells us God will heal our backslidings.

God loves us and wants us to be healed. He begs us to repent of sin and live for Him and by His words. Then He will heal our children and us. He will make things go well for us and our children.

He wants us to be happy but He can't make us that way if we are living for self and not Him. He knows living for Him and by His word is the only way we can have His peace and His joy.

He wants that for all of us.

CHAPTER 15

Doubt and Discouragement

Many times through the years in counseling others, I have seen many have problems with discouragement. Not knowing God and His ways as well as they should, they had no understanding of why He allowed different circumstances to take place in theirs and other's lives.

This comes from not reading and studying the Bible, and praying as they should, asking God to give them knowledge, understanding and wisdom. He wants us to have all of these.

He tells us in the book of Proverbs that these are all more valuable than gold and silver. They will help us understand why God does and allows the circumstance that occur in our lives.

I have learned that if we don't understand, we become fearful and/or angry at God. We begin feeling helpless, which causes us to be discouraged. If this continues we may fall into despair, as I did.

I also learned that if I understood how God works, I knew everything that He allowed to happen was for my, or others ultimate good. I knew He was working for our spiritual growth and He would ultimately bring good out of it.

Knowing this (knowledge) I could live with it without being discouraged. Hebrews 12:1-15:

(1) "Let us lay aside every weight and sin that so easily ensnares us, and let us run with endurance the race that is set before us.

(2) "Looking to Jesus, the author and FINISHER of our faith, who for the joy that was set before Him endured the cross, despising the shame and has sat down at the right hand of the throne of God."

(3) "For consider Him who endured such hostility from sinners against Himself, lest you become weary and DISCOURAGED in your souls."

(4) "You have not yet resisted to bloodshed, striving against sin."

(5) "And you have forgotten the exhortation which speaks to us as children. My child, do not despise the chastening (discipline, punishment) of the Lord, nor be DISCOURAGED when you are rebuked by Him."

(6) "For whom He loves He chastens, and scourges every one of His children whom He receives."

(7) "If you ENDURE chastening, God will deal with you as sons and daughters. For what son or daughter is there whom a father does not chasten?"

(8) "But if you are without chastening, of which ALL have become partakers, then you are illegitimate and not sons or daughters."

(9) "Furthermore, we have had human fathers who corrected us, and we paid them respect. Shall we not much more be in subjection to the Father of spirits and live?"

(10) "For they indeed, for a few days, chastened us as seemed best for them, but HE for our PROFIT, that we may be partakers of HIS HOLINESS."

(11) "Now no chastening seems joyful for the present, but painful, nevertheless, afterward it yields the PEACEABLE FRUIT of RIGHTEOUSNESS to those who have been trained by it.

(12) "Therefore strengthen the hands which hang down and the feeble knees."

(13) "And make straight paths for your feet, so what is lame may not be dislocated, but rather be healed."

(14) "Pursue peace with all people and holiness without which no one will see the Lord."

(15) "Looking carefully lest anyone fall short of the grace of God, lest any root of bitterness spring up, cause trouble and by this many become defiled."

So you understand that everything that happens to us is for OUR GOOD.

We tend to see things in the natural. But God wants us to see them in the spiritual. If we see them in the natural we will respond in the natural. We may feel angry, bitter, resentful, vengeful, or self-pitying, unloved by God, all alone in our troubles, think God has rejected us, be fearful and anxious, and think God has forsaken us.

These are our natural (sinful) ways of coping with them. Doubt and unbelief come to the forefront. They are what rob us of faith and courage. We become DIScouraged.

Jesus went through much suffering and temptation in the wilderness. The Bible tells us He learned obedience through suffering.

We all have our suffering and temptation to learn obedience so that He may establish our hearts blameless in holiness before our God and Father at the coming of our Lord Jesus Christ with all His saints. First Thessalonians 5:13.

Abraham didn't know where God would lead him. Just as we don't know when we first begin our journey with Him, but if we will keep seeking and following His instructions, He will lead us THROUGH the wilderness to the promised land.

Because of doubt and unbelief the Israelites wanted to return to Egypt and bondage. Today many have turned away from God when they encountered hardship, sorrow or any troubles, and forfeited forever many blessings. God would have bestowed blessings upon them and theirs, but they returned to the bondage of satan.

Please do not let doubt and unbelief cause you to be discouraged and defeated and robbed of future blessings.

The devil is working all the time to get you to turn from God. Remember he asked God for Job so he could make Job curse God and die spiritually. Job resisted the devil and trusted God. I pray that you will do the same.

We do things for our children's good but they don't understand that. They think we don't love them and are just being mean to them, but we know it is needful for their mental, physical or spiritual good health.

The same is with God and us. His children. If we can keep this in mind we won't become discouraged.

First Peter 1: 6 & 7, "In this you greatly rejoice though now for a little while, if need be, you have been grieved by various trials that the genuineness of your faith, being much more precious than gold that perishes, though it is tested by fire, may be found to praise, honor, and glory at the revelation of Jesus Christ."

Second Chronicles 20:15, "This is what the Lord says: do not be afraid! Don't be discouraged."

Psalms 34:17, "The Lord hears His people when they call to Him for help. He rescues them from all their troubles."

The Lord is close to the broken-hearted. He rescues those whose spirits are crushed.

Isaiah 43:2, "When you go through deep waters, I will be with you. When you go through rivers of difficulty, you will not drown. When you walk through the fire of oppression, you will not be burned up; the flames will not consume you."

When we go through deep waters, when we go through the fires, they are to cleanse and purify us. We usually do not understand this. We may become discouraged, which can and does many times, lead to depression. Depression can cause physical problems, trouble sleeping, and loss of appetite, loss of weight, loss of interest in sex, complaints about the body, lack of energy. Thinking patterns—problems with concentration, poor memory, trouble making decisions, excessive self-criticism, and thoughts of death or suicide. Emotions — hopelessness, guilt, irritability, crying, fear, gloomy outlook (sometimes covered by the opposite behavior such as giddy, inappropriate laughing or being very quiet and sweet). Activity—slowing of most activity, withdrawal from social contacts, deterioration of work and personal appearance. If you are depressed you may display irresponsible behavior and attitudes and be increasingly dependent on feelings.

A poor diet can cause us to have the lack of important chemicals in our brain that can cause depression.

Discouraging, wrong thoughts and attitudes bring on depressing feelings. Sin in our lives will cause guilt, shame, and self-hate, low self-esteem, which causes both discouragement and depression.

There is a physical depression, mental and emotional depression, caused by traumatic experiences of the past, abuse, and neglect and such as that. Then there is spiritual depression caused by consequences of our sinful thoughts, words or actions.

These can all lead to not only discouragement but also to despair, a feeling of absolutely no hope of life getting any better. A decision of giving up.

I believe when this happens a person's health breaks down, they commit physic suicide by the will to die. The devil and sin have power to destroy. In Second Corinthians 4:4, he is described "as the god of this world." John 8:44. In John 12:31 "the prince of this world,"

In Ephesians 2:2, "The prince and the power of the air." In Matthew 4:5, "The tempter." He can only go as far as God permits though, although God won't go against our will.

The important thing is to learn satan's wiles; these are his ways of deceiving us and making us believe lies about others and ourselves. How he distorts our outlook on the world, other people and ourselves.

If we are not looking at others with love, understanding, and looking for good in them, for ways to help them learn and grow, then we may be letting satan be ruling our outlook and emotions.

I learned that the emotion of discouragement was a feeling of "what's the use" or "I give up" or "I just don't care any more." I would have these feelings often but did not realize it was discouragement until the Lord, through a visiting speaker, gave me the understanding.

After that I could bind the spirit giving me these thoughts and feelings and in the name of Jesus, get rid of them. When I quit letting them enter my mind, I quit being discouraged.

I learned to handle discouraging situations by always being on the Lord's side. I remind myself that He loves me and everything that happens is because He loves me and is trying to teach and help me grow. Then I thank Him for the good He is going to bring out of this no matter what it is.

Once I do this, I have peace over the situation, even though the situation may not change. I got through it by looking at myself, admitting the wrongful reason I've had to experience it, repenting of the wrong (sin) what ever it is, asking and receiving His forgiveness.

I have then been freed of another of satan's deceptions in my mind. This is how the Lord has freed me of many things satan and sin had controlled me with for many years. It took the Holy Spirit many years to free me because I did not know the things I have written for you, so you may be freed much, much sooner.

These are the last days (before Jesus returns) and God said He would do a quick work in the last days. I can see Him doing this in many peoples lives.

I pray that, if you haven't already turned your life over to Jesus, and given Him the right to do as He wishes, to set you free of the power of satan and sin, that you will do that now.

You will NEVER make a better choice in this world, and you will NEVER be sorry.

Here are a few of His promises. Deuteronomy 31:8: "Do not be afraid or discouraged, for the Lord is the one who goes before you. He will be with you; He will neither fail nor forsake you."

Joshua 1:9: " I command you—be strong and be of good courage. Do not be afraid or discouraged. For the Lord, your God, is with you where ever you go."

Joshua 10:19: "The Lord, your God, has given you victory over the enemy. Don't be afraid or discouraged. Be strong and courageous, for the Lord will defeat all of your enemies."

First Chronicles 28:20: "Be strong and courageous and do the work. Don't be afraid or discouraged by the size of the task, for the Lord, my God is with you. He will not fail you or forsake you."

Psalms 37:4: "Delight yourself also in the Lord and He shall give you the desires of your heart."

If we seek to have Jesus' thoughts and attitudes in all things, we will never be discouraged because there is no discouragement in Him. It is written in the Bible that we have the mind of Christ.

He gave us the Holy Spirit. He and the Holy Spirit are at one with each other. The Holy Spirit has all of the thoughts and attitudes that Jesus has. The Holy Spirit was given to us to give us the thoughts and attitudes that are in the mind of Jesus.

This is how we have the mind of Christ. We have the Holy Spirit. It is His pleasure to instill Jesus' thoughts and attitudes into our minds so our minds are transformed from the darkness of the thoughts and attitudes of satan, and our sinful nature into the light of the thoughts and attitudes of the Father, Son and the Holy Spirit.

This is how we can be partakers of the Divine Nature that is written in Peter 1:4. May we all be partakers!

Some of the promises I have written were from the Old Testament, but in Second Timothy 3:16, it tells us that ALL scripture is given by inspiration of God, and profitable for doctrine, for reproof, for correction, for instruction in righteousness that the child of God may become complete (spiritually mature) thoroughly equipped for every good work. If I may, I will add that it is given also for our encouragement.

CHAPTER 16

Fear

I've heard many people say and teach that fear is the opposite of faith. Actually, it is unbelief that is the opposite of faith. The unbelief causes fear because if we cannot or will not believe what God told us in His instruction book, we believe we have no one to help us through troubles or protect us from hurt and/or harm.

We know in our spirit that we cannot protect ourselves in most things that happen in life whether sickness, earthquakes, criminals, other people sinning against us. You get my meaning. When we know we are helpless to protect ourselves and those we care about, and we believe God will not help us, we feel helpless, alone and afraid. We have anxiety.

The scripture tells us that fear has torment. We can never have real peace as long as we fear. Faith in God and His promises bring peace. If we really believe, we trust God to supply all of our needs, as Matthew 6:33 and Philippians 4:19 tell us, we will have no fear of ever being without what we need. Jesus said in this world we will have trials and tribulations, but be happy because He has overcome the world. So He can help us through and overcome anything.

I used to fear someone close to me dying. I feared I would grieve so much I would lose my mind. I thought this often. One day I was standing at a grocery checkout line having this fear again. Suddenly the Lord spoke to my spirit and said, "You keep your faith in Me and I can get you through anything." That was years ago. Since then, I have had a number of close family members and close friends die. I have been amazed at how easily He did take me through each one.

Sometimes in our lives we see our helplessness. Unbelief and a feeling of helplessness are the two major causes of fear. We are all helpless in many cases, but God is not.

My older brother lived in fear. He did not believe the Bible was true. He told me one day that he feared driving to work. He feared being car-jacked or worse. He said he carried a gun in his car to protect himself. I told him I did not have to be afraid because I had the most powerful being in the universe for my bodyguard—God. He smiled but said nothing. I felt sorry for him and wanted him to know he could feel safe if he would only believe.

Fear is an emotion that every person experiences. It is a feeling that we have when we feel threatened in any way. We can feel fear in physical, emotional, social, or spiritual areas. We may have fear of speaking before an audience. We fear being hurt or humiliated. Fear of failure or fear of a broken heart can keep us from ever falling in love.

If we have low self-esteem, we are afraid to let anyone see how we really feel about anything. We do not want them to see the "real" us. We fear others will see us as we see ourselves. We fear making decisions. We are afraid of making a mistake.

We fear losing a spouse to someone else. If someone else wants them, we feel we cannot win because we are inferior. We (especially women) fear we cannot take care of ourselves, so we marry for security, never really being happy. We fear losing a spouse, so we dominate and try to control them. We feel if we can control them, they will not do anything that will hurt us.

Second Timothy tells us, "God did not give us the spirit of fear, but of love, power and a sound mind." When we are living in fear, we do not have a sound mind. Most of our fears are not based on a real danger, but they are planted and cultivated by satan and/or his evil soldiers. Some fears even develop into phobias. Fears rob us of the enjoyment of life and the peace that God wants us to have.

When we fear, we become centered on self. We will always be ready to defend ourselves. We will take everything personally against ourselves and be ready to fight back verbally or sometimes even physically.

Most people fear death. Remember Howard Hughes? He was a millionaire, but he lived cooped up in his apartment. He was afraid to go out or let people visit. He wore gloves all the time. He began being this way after his father died. I believe he became afraid of dying. He felt helpless to stop it but he began doing everything he could to try to stop it. He was helpless to stop it no matter what he did. He lived in a prison of torment because of the fear satan instilled in his mind. The devil instills all kinds of fears in our subconscious mind. Anytime anything causes us suffering in any way, we fear going through that again.

Fear of speaking before an audience is caused by being humiliated in front of a group of people (no matter how small the group) some time in the past. We will not take a chance on going through that again. If we make a wrong decision that causes us suffering in any way, we may become afraid to make decisions again. When faced with an important decision, we may become conflicted on which way to go until we become so agitated by it that we become depressed.

The devil sets out to destroy us and our usefulness to God. He will make us afraid to witness for Him to others. God gives everyone in His kingdom a job to do to help others in some way, but satan does all he can do to prevent that. Two of his main tools to do this are fear and pride. They are both meant to protect SELF from any hurt or shame.

As children, our parents may have a fear of having no control over us, so they cover or compensate for the fear with controlling with anger or even hitting. When either of these happens, satan puts into the child's mind, "If they loved me they would not hurt me like this." This will cause fear and low self esteem in the child. They fear that anything bad can happen to them, and they will not be able to protect themselves.

They believe the parent will not protect them because they do not care about them. They also become afraid of the parent. They will tell the parent they love them in an effort to coerce the parent to love them to try to get back in the parent's good graces so they might not hurt them. The child becomes an adult FEELING like they are helpless, and then uses anger and maybe hitting their children to try to control them. Generation to generation! The Bible tells us that the sins of the parents are visited on their children.

Fear causes a person to want to have power. This causes wars. Fear causes us to lose the ability to love. If we are hurt in a love relationship, we may fear that hurt for the rest of our lives and never be able to fall in love again.

The Bible tell us that in the last days, because of the things that happen upon the earth, the love of many will grow cold. I believe we are in the last days. I also believe many, many people have lost the ability to love. I believe there are so many divorces because of the fear of being hurt, so they get in the "I'm in control mode" and they begin hurting each other to keep SELF safe. It all goes back to SELF.

The devil tells us we are in a dangerous world full of dangerous people, and we have to do anything we can to protect ourselves. These are satan's thoughts and attitudes that he wants to control us with. He is still trying to and does rule over many of God's creatures. He rules with hatred and cruelty.

But God is the SOVEREIGN ruler, and the wonderful thing is that God can and will free us of all the things satan has and does to control us. Second Timothy 1:7 states that God did not give us the spirit of fear. The first thing we need to do is bind the power of the spirit of fear that the devil has given us. We need to bind its power in the name of Jesus. Remember, the power is in the name of Jesus, not us. In the name of Jesus they have to obey, so we have the authority to use His name (If we belong to Him) to fight our spiritual battles.

Bind the power of the spirit of fear, in the name of Jesus. Then, command that it has no more power over you or anyone else (so it does not go from you to someone else) ever again in this world, in the name of Jesus. Command in the name of Jesus that it loose you now, get away from you, and never come back.

The Holy Spirit told me a long time ago that as long as we have an evil spirit controlling something in us, we can never get the victory over it, but, once it's gone, then we can get the victory. After you command it to leave, then pray for Jesus to cleanse all the fear that the spirit has programmed your subconscious mind with. Ask Him to cleanse it out and replace it with faith.

We cannot just quit doing the sin, but we have to replace it with some of God's righteousness. Faith is that. As we gain more and more ground in this battle we are in, as we get rid of more and more enemies, we can replace them with God's righteousness, and we have more and more peace and enjoyment of life. It is a battle, a battle to the death. It is a battle to the death of the sinful nature and the creation of Jesus' divine nature replacing it (2 Peter 1:4). What could be better?

Here are some scriptures that helped me get the victory. In Ephesians 6:17, Paul tells us the sword of the Spirit, which is the word of God, is our weapon we use against the enemy.

Also the shield of faith is what we will be able to quench all the fiery darts of the devil. So, we must use scripture to fight the enemy and gain the victory over them.

The first one I will give you is the first one God gave me when I was new at this which is Isaiah 41:10, "Fear thou not, for I am with you: be not dismayed (means do not look to the future disheartened, with apprehension, fear, downheartedness or depression) for I am your God: I will strengthen you; yes, I will help you: yes, I will hold you up with the right hand of my righteousness."

Psalm 56:3, "When I am afraid, I will trust in you (change my mind from fear to God's help). Psalm 27:1, "The Lord is my light and my salvation whom shall I fear?" Psalm 37:1, "The angel of the Lord encamps around about them that fear Him and delivers them."

Psalm 91:1 & 7, (1) "He that dwells in the secret place of the most High shall abide under the shadow of the Almighty." (7) "A thousand shall fall at your side and ten thousand at your right hand, but it shall not come near you." Genesis 15:1, "God is a shield against fear." Exodus 14:13 & 14, "God fights our battles." Joshua 1:9, "God is always present." Luke 8:50, "Faith dispels fear." Psalm 23:4, "God delivers from fear."

Fear is something we feel and do that God commanded us not to do. It is sin. Focus on affirming your faith in God. Focus on faith and not the fear. We have the ability to change our thinking when fear comes up, nip it in the bud. Say, "Watch out fear, here comes faith," or "I choose faith not fear."

Proverbs 3:5, "Trust in the Lord with all your heart and lean not unto your own understanding." Our understanding tells us we have reasons to be afraid. If a loved one is ill or money is tight, we look at that with fear when we should look at it with faith and trusting God.

Let's see. First we get rid of the spirit, then we pray for God to free and cleanse us of the sin of unbelief and fear. We read scripture every day, especially faith scriptures. We quote them over and over to ourselves.

I, myself, when I have any thought I know is not of God (and I know fear thoughts are not of God), I remember that the Holy Spirit told me that any thought I have that I do not like and do not want is not me, but the enemy is putting those thoughts in my mind. So, I direct my thought to binding the spirit putting those thoughts in my mind and command it to leave. Then I focus on Jesus and praise Him. Problem solved!

It took some time for me to be able to come to this place, but I kept doing the things I have written in this chapter. God's word is true. He will do what He promised if we do what He instructed us to do. He wants to set us free from the power of satan and sin. He wants us to walk in His light, not satan's darkness. Jesus came and suffered unimaginable torture. He suffered for us so we can be freed of the power of satan and sin.

We need to saturate our mind with His instructions and promises. That will eventually renew our mind and transform our soul and spirit. The more we know of and know about Him, the more we will understand why things happen as they do.

We will understand there is a battle being waged for our spirit. Ephesians 6 tells us we do not wrestle against flesh and blood but against evil spirits. We think we are fighting ourselves to stop the fear, but we are fighting against evil spirits. The only way we can win the victory is to use our spiritual weapons in a spiritual battle. First, we have to realize that it is a spiritual battle when we cannot control what is going on in our thoughts and/or feelings. Then we need to use our spiritual weapons, the name of Jesus, faith and the scriptures.

The secret of living a righteous life is to surrender everything and everyone to Jesus, and He will set you free of everything that is not of Him!

CHAPTER 17

Faith

The greatest gift we are given after our salvation is the Gift of the Holy Spirit. It is He who uses His power to do what is helpful in our spiritual growth. It is all His power and abilities used in, through, and for us and others. Jesus said He would send us a helper. That Helper is the Holy Spirit.

All the fruit and the gifts we receive are in the Holy Spirit, and He gives and uses any of them He chooses for the good of us and others. He produces them. They are His to use in whomever He chooses and for whatever He chooses.

First Corinthians 13:13 says, "And now abides faith, hope and love, these three: but the greatest of these is love." The most important gift of all is to have the Love of God planted in or put into our heart so that God's love will be manifested through us to others by the Holy Spirit. The next greatest is to have faith planted or put into our heart, our human spirit. By faith mountains, or obstacles can and will be removed from our life and ourselves.

"Without faith it is impossible to please God, for he who comes to God must believe that He is, and that He is a rewarder of those who diligently seek Him." (Hebrews 11:6) By faith Noah built the ark, by faith Abraham obeyed when God told him to sacrifice his son Isaac; although God had no intention of letting Abraham do that, because He had promised Abraham that he would bring forth nations from Isaac's descendents. God also had already prepared a sacrificial lamb at the altar for Abraham to sacrifice.

Abraham was going to do it because he believed that God would raise Isaac from the dead. (Hebrews 11:19)

By faith Abraham obeyed when God told him to leave his home and family even though he did not know where God would lead him. By faith Noah built the ark. By faith Sarah received strength to have a child even though she was past childbearing age.

Romans 4:17 states, "God calls those things that be not as though they were." God spoke of things that were not as though they already existed. He told Abraham that Isaac would be born twenty-five years before it happened. Faith calls it done before it can happen.

They Holy Spirit gave me this example to help me understand this. A child wants a bicycle so he asks his father for one. The father tells him he will get a bicycle for Christmas. The boy is happy because he trusts and believes his father. To him he already owns a bicycle. He just has to wait for its delivery. At Christmas it is delivered. The boy had faith in his father's promise.

Our Heavenly Father has given us many promises in His Word. Do we have faith in these, or do we doubt? Faith calls it as done before it can be seen. Faith is acting as though God told us the truth. We do not have to see it to know we shall have it. By faith we accept it as done. First Peter 2:24 tells us, "by His stripes WE WERE healed," not are healed; by faith it is already done. We just need to receive it as done by faith.

This next scripture has been proven to me for many, many years. It is Philippians 4:29. It states that, "God shall supply all of your needs according to His riches in glory by Christ Jesus." He knows what we need before we do. He already has it ready for us. We are His children. He is our Father. It is His obligation to care for us and supply our needs.

God has given us many promises in His instruction book. We must read, read, read and then read it some more. The more we read it the more it is imbedded in our spirit, soul and subconscious mind.

The more we read His promises, the more we can accept them as true and have faith in them. After I gave Jesus my life, I read the Bible every spare moment I had. I believed them. I would pray for people and they would be healed. After a while though, when I prayed, I would begin to doubt. I would fear that what I was praying would not happen.

One morning I awoke from a dream. I dreamed I stepped into a small room. I turned and closed the door, but I saw that there was a tiny door set in the door. There was a monkey looking through this tiny door.

I leaned over to look at the cute little monkey, but when I got close to it I saw that it wasn't cute at all. It had an evil look on its face.

I began trying to close the tiny door and it began fighting to keep it open and come through the door. I was fighting to keep it out.

I was given the understanding of the dream. It meant when I prayed for someone, an evil spirit of doubt and unbelief would try to control my mind.

The Holy Spirit showed me that by fighting to keep the door closed in my mind as I prayed, I was fighting to keep out the evil spirit of doubt. He told me that I was in a spiritual battle with an evil spirit. I was trying to win the battle with my mind (my fleshy weapon). In Second Corinthians 10:3, Paul tells us, "For the weapons of our warfare are not of our flesh." Then in Ephesians 6:10, "Finally my brothers (and sisters) be strong in the Lord and in the power of His might." Then following that chapter he tells us that we must use our spiritual weapons to fight spiritual battles.

The Holy Spirit told me I needed to fight spiritual battles with spiritual weapons, the name of Jesus, the words of God and faith. I can use these to protect myself and keep my mind free from the influence of evil spirits. Our fleshly weapons are useless against the devil and his army.

Ephesians 6:12 says, "We do not wrestle against flesh and blood (ourselves or others) but against evil spirits." Therefore, we must prepare ourselves for battle because they will come against everyone.

Ephesians 6:10-17 tells us how to prepare ourselves for battle. We must learn the truth of God's Words, seek and find His righteousness, and saturate our mind, soul and spirit with the gospel. Above all, we must put on the shield of faith, then we will be able to protect ourselves from all the fiery darts of the wicked one. We will be able to protect ourselves from everything the devil and his evil army throw at us.

Faith is our protection. Faith is our spiritual weapon to fight our spiritual battle with. This is why the devil sends one of his spirits of doubt. He wants to be sure he can have an opening to destroy our weapon against him: FAITH. He does not want to lose control of us.

When we pray we must first ask Jesus if it is His will to pray for what we desire. We may pray amiss. For about five years I appeared on our local TV station. The name of my program was "Seeking the Kingdom." It was based on Matthew 6:33 in which Jesus tells us to seek the Kingdom of God and his righteousness above everything else.

One day an article in our local newspaper stated that our property tax might be raised quite a bit. I began asking Jesus, Oh, what will I do because I cannot pay that much." I asked it over and over. Finally, He asked me, "What did you tell the people on your TV program?" I answered, "To seek God's Kingdom and His righteousness." I suddenly knew that was what He was telling me to do.

"What is your righteousness in this situation?" I asked. Instantly, the song "Have Faith In God" was being sung to my spirit, inside my head. It is a wonderful song of faith that God is on His throne, that He watches over His own, that He will not fail to take care of us, that we are not to fear, and that He shall prevail. So I chose to receive the faith He told me of (or sang to my spirit). I received it with joy having faith that all would be well, and it surely was because my property tax was lowered and not raised. Thank you, Jesus.

So, faith is an aspect of God's righteousness and it is given to us. Romans 12:3 tells us that God gives each one of us a measure of faith, and as we use that faith, He gives us more. Romans 1:17 says, "The righteousness of God is revealed from faith to faith." As we use the measure of faith we have, God will increase our faith as we follow Him.

Remember the parable of the talents (Matthew 25:14-29). The master gave some servants money to use while he was gone. He told them to use it in such a way that it would increase. That tells us we are to do the same with the faith we are given. I have learned through the years that whatever we use we will be given more. Many times we must step out in faith to use the gifts and/or talents He has given us. In doing this, we grow spiritually and in faith.

My grandmother used to tell me that practice makes perfect. The more you do anything the better you get at it. I have learned this is true. I now tell my grandchildren and great-grandchildren the same thing. Another way to grow in faith is to attend church to hear the gospel preached, to listen to

Christian radio and watch Christian TV. Put as much about it in your mind as you can. Romans 10:17 says, "Faith comes by hearing the Word of God."

My late mother-in-law had to be put in the hospital for a while. She thought she was going to die. She had nightmares about it. I did not know how scared she was, but on Sunday morning in church, the Holy Spirit told me to take my Bible and go visit her after church.

As I went, He explained about her fears. He said she was terrified of dying because she thought she would go to Hell. I took my Bible and asked her questions. Had she ever asked Jesus to save her soul? She replied, "Yes." I read scriptures to her. I asked more questions and read more of God's promises to her. She accepted by faith then what I had read and told her. She knew then she would not go to Hell.

Later, her granddaughter asked her if she was afraid to die. She answered, "I used to be but Esther talked to me about it and I'm no longer afraid." It is wonderful what having faith can do for us.

Years ago I heard a preacher say we had to build our faith. I thought I was in deep trouble, because I did not know how to do that. I worried about it a lot. One day a friend brought me a book. He said the devil will try to keep you from reading this because he does not want people to know its contents. I was skeptical about that, but curious, so I read it. He was right, and as I read some of it a strong fear came over me, and I wanted to put the book down. What he had told me motivated me to get past the fear and read it anyway.

When I finished that book, I knew I did not have to manufacture faith. I knew that God gives faith. The next morning my grandson said, "You kept me awake half the night." "How did I do that," I asked. "I slept all night." "You did not," he replied. "You sang "I Am Bound For The Promised Land." That was how much the book and knowledge that God would supply the faith that I need affected me. My spirit sang that song while my body slept.

Please do not ask the name of the book. I returned it to my friend who later died and, alas, I have forgotten the name of the author and the book. The point is that as we use what faith we have, God gives us more.

Romans 1:17 tells us to live by faith. When I was a new follower of Jesus, I thought the flesh thoughts. I thought it meant you could quit work, pray and trust Jesus to take care of you. I knew a young husband and father who believed that, too. He quit his job and went on a missionary journey, expecting God to support him. His motive was to not have to work a regular job. He and his family returned very soon. He learned the hard way. I learned watching him. I learned as time went along that to live by faith means to believe, trust and obey God's Word as best I could. I learned if I did not obey, I suffered some unpleasant consequences. I live by faith not my fleshly understanding. Proverbs 3:5 tells us, "Trust in the Lord with all our heart and lean not on our own understanding."

I learned to have faith in His instruction that if you sin you suffer. We can quit all the sins of the flesh but still sin in our thoughts, words and attitudes. We sin in pride, selfishness, self-centeredness, anger and so forth. I learned to have faith in His Word that He knows every thought we think, every feeling we have, everything we do and why we do it.

I also learned to have faith that He is with me (and you) every second of every day and night, twenty-four-seven. After awhile, I not only had faith that He was with me, I knew and still know that He is with me all the time. He tells us in the Bible that He will never leave us nor forsake us. When we know that He is standing, watching and listening to us all the time, we try harder to please Him.

I have known people who went on trips and did things that were not right, thinking no one from the church would know about. What they did not realize was Jesus went on the trip with them; someone from church did see them.

If we know God's Word and have faith that it is true, then we know God watches and tries to correct us when we stray or disobey. His instructions were given for our benefit, which is to help us learn to live our lives so we can avoid the pains of chastisement. Thus, we can live in peace. We all want that for our children, and God wants that for His children.

First Peter 1:5-7 tells us, "We are kept through the power of God through faith for salvation ready to be revealed in the last time. In this you greatly rejoice though now for a little while, if need be, you have been grieved by various trials, that the genuineness of your FAITH being much more

PRECIOUS than gold that perishes, though it is tested by fire, may be found to praise, honor, and glory at the revelation of Jesus Christ."

When we stand before Him we can have joy in knowing we will be rewarded for living by faith. James 1:1-2 says, "My brothers, consider it all joy when you encounter various trials, knowing that the testing of your faith produces patience." When we have trials we can lose faith or we can use faith. Our faith tells us that God has a good reason for allowing this. Everything that happens is for us to use that to grow in faith and maturity. It is all for our spirit to grow into God's character.

Having faith in God and His Word is wonderful in the fact that it makes sense of the whys and wherefores of the world. It gives us peace because if we can accept everything in faith we are not upset when trials or tribulations come along. We can trust God that He has a good reason for this happening, and we can trust Jesus to get us through anything in peace.

In John 16:33 He tells us that all through life trials and tribulations will occur, but be of good cheer because He has overcome everything (the world). Therefore, if we leave it to Him, He will over come the things we go through in, for or through us, in good cheer. I interpret good cheer as joy. He has taken me through things like that, in the past. I would have gone to pieces, but I had His joy even when things looked very bad, because I trusted Him.

God told the Israelites, when He took them through the wilderness forty years, it was to humble them and test their faith. Faith is one of the gifts of the Holy Spirit. Pray for that gift, but as I wrote earlier, love comes first in the list of gifts. Pray for that above all else. Romans 54:1, "Therefore being justified by faith, we have peace with God through our Lord Jesus Christ."

Here is some homework for you:

- Galatians 2:16—Faith brings righteousness
- James 1:3—Faith brings endurance
- First Peter 1:5—Faith brings blessings
- John 5:24—Faith assures eternal life
- John 12:46—Faith dispels darkness

Before we pray for the gift of love and the gift of faith, we must first bind and cast out anything that can prevent us from receiving them. Get rid of the spirits of doubt and unbelief and the spirit of unforgiveness. We have to learn to spy on our own mind, humble ourselves and look at what is in there that should not be, ask for forgiveness, accept the forgiveness and get rid of it in the name of Jesus.

We have to get rid of all darkness. First, turn on the light of righteousness. The devil is darkness—God is light. Turn on the light by reading God's instructions, praying for faith in what you read and praying for God's help to apply that to your life. Then, every day, look for an opportunity to use it for God's glory. By turning on the light, we remove the darkness.

Faith helps us to accept the trials and tribulations that befall us as we live our lives out on Earth. We must trust and believe. Romans 8:28 says that God will bring good out of everything which He allows for our spiritual growth and/or our loved ones spiritual growth.

If we hold on to our faith in that, and focus on that when trials and/or tribulations come, we can get through them with the peace that passes understanding. People will marvel at your attitude during these times. How can they have such peace, they ask. It is past the understanding of unbelievers. It was past my understanding at first. I thought there was something wrong with me until the Holy Spirit showed me that I was experiencing the peace that passes understanding.

Some years back I heard a preacher say you can have anything you pray for if you have faith. From what I had learned about repenting of sins, asking amiss and the consequences of disobeying God, I could not believe that. I prayed quite fervently about this a few times. I believed we had to meet some requirements.

One morning when I awoke, Jesus was sitting on the side of my bed. The first thing I did was ask Him about that. (The reason He manifested Himself to me was to answer that question.) "Can we really pray for anything and receive it if we have faith?" I asked. He said, "If you meet the requirements." "What are the requirements?" "That you love one another as I have loved you." And then He disappeared. I asked myself, "How did He love us?" He loved us so much. He sacrificed His life for us. We must forget self and focus on helping others learn and grow. We can give our lives for others by living it for them. The Bible tells husbands to give their lives for their wives. This means to live for their wives sake and not be centered on self, to put her first, after Jesus of course.

In the past I tried to control others by praying for God to do in and for their lives what I thought was best. I had faith, but it did not often happen. The Holy Spirit told me that we do not control God with faith. He also told me we cannot control others through God. I was praying amiss—Big Time!

I have learned to pray, "Father, thank You for doing what is best for me or them," or "Thank You for the good You are going to bring out of this. Thank You for letting Your will be done." There have been times when He told me to pray for someone or something. What He told me to pray for came to pass. If we do pray for something, we must pray for it with thanksgiving. Paul told us to let our requests be made known with thanksgiving in Philippians 4.

The song the Holy Spirit sang to me when I was afraid about my property tax also says, be not afraid, be not dismayed, have faith in God. Faith is trust in the person of Jesus, the truth of His teaching and the redemptive work He accomplished at Calvary. Faith is not to be confused with a mere intellectual assent to the doctrinal teachings of Christ. Faith is knowing in our spirit that the teachings of Jesus are true and right for our well being. It is knowing, accepting and acting on His words.

Faith is living according to His will no matter what our circumstances. It is knowing in our heart that it is all for our spiritual good. Romans 8:28 says, "And we know that all things work together for good to them that love God, to them who are the called according to His purpose." As Job said, "Even though He slay me, I will trust Him (God)." (Job 15:13)

Jesus told us that He said what His Father told Him to say (John 14:10). So, when we have faith in Jesus' words, we are having faith in God the Father, also.

We will all have trials and tribulations in this world, but Paul told us in Hebrews 10:35-38, "Cast not away therefore your confidence, which hath great recompense of reward. For you have need of endurance, so after you have done the will of God, you may receive the promise. The just shall live by faith; but if anyone draws back, My soul has no pleasure in him."

In Hebrews 11:6 Paul says, "But without faith it is impossible to please Him: for he that cometh to God must believe (have faith) that He is, and that He is a rewarder of them that diligently seek Him." God rewards those who hold on to their faith and trust in Him, and keep seeking to know Him better, and grow in submission and obedience.

He helps us along when things get tough. He will comfort and encourage us to keep on, keeping on. He told me that many times through the years when I wanted to just quit, or when I would become discouraged, disappointed or just spiritually fatigued.

Desiring to please Him, I would struggle on. One day during one of these struggles, I felt overwhelmed. I turned on the TV. The very first words I heard from a preacher were, "You will have the victory." That encouraged me to focus on that and not on the hopeless state I was in. Hopelessness is one of the very damaging tools satan uses to defeat a follower of Jesus. Hopelessness and helplessness equals depression. These things rob us of our faith. It is what causes (I believe) most suicides.

Without faith, when trouble, sickness, a loved ones death or other things we have no control over happen, and we have no one to help, are the perfect times for the devil to move in and take over our thoughts and emotions. He especially does this to the followers of Jesus.

If we focus on our faith, which is our shield, we block the devil's fiery darts he shoots at us as it tells us in Ephesians 6:16. But without our shield of faith, he hits his target, our thoughts and emotions, and causes our spirit (us) to fall into his trap. Oh, what evil pleasure he gets from that.

If we keep our faith in Jesus' love for us, He can and will get us through everything the devil and the world throws at us. He can get us through anything, and Jesus said that He could get us through it in good cheer and/or the peace that passes understanding. Now isn't that a great reward? (Hebrews 10:35) I know these promises are true because I have experienced them many times through the years, especially when a loved one died, and there have been many of those times.

By faith He helps us forgive all the unforgivable things of the past. I know this from experience, also. If someone was tortured as Jesus was, had the hide torn from His back, thorns buried in His head, His beard pulled out, His hands and feet nailed to a tree, beaten in the face by soldiers, had to endure the pain of all our sins, and only God knows how much He suffered for us.

How can we not believe He loves us enough to keep all of his promises to help us through the hardships of this life? When I first turned my life over to Him I thought there would be no more hardships, troubles, sorrows, hurts or humiliations. For a while, during the brand new baby stage, there were not, but when I began learning to walk (by faith) some of these things began to happen.

I lost my trust in Jesus for a while. He finally got through to me about the cleansing and healing process. These are the times of suffering. The devil would attack me. Jesus would show me what was in me that the devil could use to cause me suffering. If we sin, we suffer. I was full of sin.

The sinful nature (soul) that I was born with (as is everyone) had to be exposed. The devil and I had done a very good job at deceiving me. Jesus told us He would give us the Holy Spirit to help us. One of His jobs is to convict us of sin. Boy, did I get a lot of that.

I gradually learned that Jesus was cleaning me up (the suffering time), healing me from the past, and teaching me His word and ways, to use me to teach others what I am writing in this book.

This is His will for us all; to be saved from the power of satan and sin; to be healed and freed from the past; and, to win souls and teach others the things He teaches us about the kingdom of darkness and the Kingdom of Light (God).

To reach His goal for us, we must cling to and use the faith that He gives us. "Eye has not seen, nor ear heard, nor have entered into the heart of man the things which God has prepared for those who love Him." (First Corinthians 2:9)

How many poor souls let go of their faith when some kind of suffering or temptation comes along? They will give up unimaginable wonderful blessings because of unbelief. The devil came to steal, kill and destroy. These poor souls do not realize that the devil has done all of that to them.

In the 11th chapter of Hebrews, it tells of so many people who went through terrible suffering and death, but they held onto their belief (faith) in the promises of Jesus. They judged God faithful who had promised. They all died in faith, not having received the promises, but having seen them in the future, assured them of a heavenly homeland that God prepared for them. Faith in God's promises helped them endure the torture to the end.

Always remember that we must ask the Lord what He wants us to pray for in any situation. Still our mind and wait on Him. He usually puts a thought or an understanding in our mind. If we know what His will is that we are to pray for, we can then pray in faith. "If we pray according to His will we know that he hears us. If we know that He hears us then we know that we have our petition." (First John 5:14-15)

Faith purifies the heart of fear, doubt and unbelief. It fills the heart with peace and joy. It takes away the torment of fear and doubt. If we can focus on Jesus, not ourselves, we can do much better in rejecting fear.

Fearing to witness for the Lord is being centered on self. This is fear of being hurt by being rejected, mocked, or humiliated. These things are fears we acquired in the past when these things happened to us. We reacted with hurt and embarrassment. This is the way satan wanted and programmed us to. But now with the Holy Spirit with us, we can let Him deal with these His way.

I know if we let Him, He will deal with them. Someone in past Bible classes would always do these things to me, so I wanted to quit going. The Holy Spirit told me to keep going and He would defend me. When someone came against me after that (not just that person), in my spirit, inside my head, the Holy Spirit gave me the thoughts, attitudes and words that He wanted me to have and use. He will do that for those who will yield to Him. He will not do that if we are in the wrong, but He will try to correct us.

To live by faith, we are to live by believing, yielding our thoughts to Him and obeying what we are given by the Holy Spirit. We live by His faith that He gives us. Faith is a gift and a fruit of the Holy Spirit. The Holy Spirit offers faith continually. It is up to us to choose to receive or reject it, or choose to live in the fear satan puts in our mind.

I have learned to watch my thoughts and feelings. Taking every thought into captivity means to watch the thoughts we have, and to judge whether they are the thoughts that Jesus would have us think. If they are not, we are to reject them immediately before they can cause the brain to create the emotion that goes with them.

Someone came to Jesus and told Him that a man called Lazarus had died. Now Lazarus had two sisters, Martha and Mary. When Mary saw Jesus she said, "If You had been here my brother would not have died." When Jesus saw her and those who were with her weeping, He groaned in His spirit and was troubled. He asked, "Where have you laid him?" They said to Him, "Lord, come and see." Jesus wept.

Then the Jews said, "See how He loved him! (Lazarus) Some of them said, "Could not this Man, who opened eyes of the blind, also have kept this man from dying?" Then Jesus, again groaning in Himself, came to the tomb where he brought Lazarus back to life.

JESUS DID NOT WEEP BECAUSE LAZARUS DIED. HE WEPT BECAUSE THE PEOPLE DID NOT BELIEVE HIM WHEN HE TOLD THEM THAT HE WAS THE RESURRECTION AND THE LIFE.

He knew He would raise Lazarus back to life. He had no reason to be sad that Lazarus was dead. He wept because the people did not have FAITH in what He had told them about Himself.

I wonder, does He still weep when we don't have faith in His words to us? The blessing now is that we have the Holy Spirit to help us grow in faith. We first must admit our doubts. Then ask for Him to increase our faith. We can't manufacture it. We will be given more as we use what measure we do have.

He will help us grow in faith. In fact, that is the Holy Spirit's will and job. He longs to help us grow in all areas of our lives.

I will close this chapter with Matthew 11:28-30 and First John 5:3&4, "Come unto me all you who labor and are heavy laden and I will give you rest. Take my yoke upon you and learn of me, for I am gentle and lowly of heart and you will find rest for your souls. For my yoke is easy and my burden is light." We labor so much under the heavy yoke of fear, doubt and unbelief. These burdens make our lives heavy and weary.

Jesus wants us to have faith in Him and His word, so He can give us rest and peace. That is why He died for us. That is His will for us. He is telling us He loves us and wants to teach us that he is trustworthy. He is faithful to us,

He is kind, His whole desire is to set us free from the power of satan and sin, and give us a wonderful life of abundance.

First John 5:3&4, "For this is the love of God, that we keep His commandments; and His commandments are not burdensome. For whatever is born of God overcomes the world, and this is the victory that overcomes the world—OUR FAITH."

Pray for God to increase your faith and use what He gives you. Do not let satan steal it from you.

Remember the song that tells us, "Only believe, only believe all things are possible, only believe."

The more we use our faith, the more it grows. Faith is made perfect by our works. James 2:22.

CHAPTER 18

The Fear of God

One day a friend brought a book to me. She asked if I would read it and tell her what I thought of it. I read the book and realized it was all the new age thoughts, beliefs and attitudes that were flooding the media.

When I took it back to her and told her what it was, she asked me to explain the new age beliefs to her. In my mind, I realized it would take to much time to go into a long explanation about it, so in my spirit, inside my head, I asked Jesus to please give me that information in a "nut shell." I meant the shortest version that He could.

Immediately, He gave me the following explanation. No savior, no satan, no sin, no Bible, no rules, no Hell, no authority, always in control, and they have created God IN THE IMAGE OF MAN.

This, my reader, is what satan is using to take over the souls and spirits of the poor people who are ignorant of what God teaches in the Bible. The author of the book wrote that Jesus had gone, as a child, to Italy, France and England to be taught of "wise men" there. The Holy Spirit told me that the author had written what he believed was good logic. The trouble is that he was absolutely wrong.

Luke 2:4 tells us, "Jesus grew strong in Spirit and was filled with the wisdom and the Grace of God was upon him." In John 7:14, "now about the middle of the feast Jesus went up into the temple and taught." John 7:15, "And the Jews marveled saying, how does this man know letters, having

NEVER STUDIED." John 7:16, "My doctrine is not Mine but His who sent Me." That clearly explains that Jesus was given everything He knew from His Father, God.

It seems silly to me that the Son of God would be taught by sinful man. It is written in God's Word, the Bible, that man's wisdom is foolishness with God (1st Corinthians 3:19).

Many, many young people's lives were destroyed and some were killed because of all the wrong things the devil put in their subconscious mind. The person is controlled by what the subconscious mind believes.

When we have no fear of God, we have no fear of committing sin. They do not consider there is a reaction to every action. There is a consequence to everything we say or do. Good or bad. Good for the good we do. Bad for the bad we do.

Proverbs 1:7, "The fear of the Lord is the beginning of wisdom, but fools despise wisdom and instruction." Proverbs 3:7 &8, "Fear God and depart from evil. It will be health to your flesh and strength to your bones." Proverbs 8:13, "The fear of the Lord is to HATE EVIL."

Proverbs 9:10 & 11: "The fear of the Lord is the beginning of wisdom and the knowledge of the Holy One is understanding. For by Me your days will be multiplied and years of life added to you." Proverbs 10:27, "The fear of the Lord prolongs days, but the years of the wicked will be shortened." Proverbs 13:13, "He who fears the commandments will be rewarded."

Now let's take the new age beliefs: 1. They say that Jesus was a teacher and/or a prophet, not the Son of God. 2. The devil does not exist. He is a bogeyman made up to frighten people into being good. 3. There is no sin. If it feels good, it is okay. 4. The Bible is not God's Word. It is just things men made up and wrote to try to control others. 4. There are no rules. We all have a right to be and express ourselves. No one has the right to say another person is wrong in what they say, believe or do. 6. No Hell. There is no Heaven or Hell. We make one or the other for ourselves here on earth. When we die, that is the end of life (denial, fear of Hell). 7. No authority. No one has the right to tell me what to do. Not even God. 8. I am the master of my fate. God has nothing to do with it (always in control). 9. They create God in the image of man. They attribute to God their own ideas of what He should be. Poor,

poor people. When they stand before the Real God, they will be overcome with shame and regrets.

All of these ideas and attitudes were given to them by satan. He lies, deceives, deludes and destroys. These people have fallen victim to him. They have believed his propaganda, and they teach it to others. They believe, in their pride, that they have superior knowledge that the rest of humanity does not have.

They have no fear of God. Years ago when the young people were taking over the colleges, I thought they were mentally ill. Some years before this, some psychologists had written books on rearing children. They advocated that a child should not be punished. When I thought that these young people were mentally ill, the Holy Spirit told me that they had never been punished for their sins, so they had no fear of suffering.

They did not realize that there would be consequences of their actions. They were shocked when they were punished for the wrong that they were doing. They believed that they could make the authorities bow to their demands, as they had done to their parents. They had been programmed by the devil to think, feel and believe all of this.

Proverbs 14:26 & 27, "In the fear of the Lord there is strong confidence and His children will have a place of refuge and safety. The fear of the Lord is a fountain of life, to run one away from the snares of death!"

Proverbs 15:16, "Better is a little with the fear of the Lord, than great treasure with trouble."

Proverbs 15:33, "The fear of the Lord is the instruction of wisdom and before honor is HUMILITY." Proverbs 19:23, "The fear of the Lord leads to life, and he who has it will abide in satisfaction. He will not be visited by evil."

If we have wisdom, we will understand that the way to a peaceful life is to fear doing anything against God's will, because we will know that if we sin, we will suffer for it. But if we obey Him, we will be rewarded. The fear of God, the way I understood it, was if our worldly father loves us, he will punish us for our wrong doing, because he wants us to grow up to have a good, happy, healthy, productive life.

Our worldly father knows if we do not suffer for our wrong doing, we will continue in that. We will get worse and worse as years go by. Consequently, our life will become more and more unhappy. If he punishes us, hopefully we will learn that we will suffer for wrongdoing and strive to overcome that and begin to do better in life.

Gradually we become a better and better person. We have been programmed to live a good life. Through all of this, we love our fathers and know he loves us, but we fear the punishment he gives, and we understand it is because he loves us that he wants to train us to be a good person so we can have a good life. What loving father does not want good for his children?

So, this was a word picture of our Heavenly Father. To fear God is the beginning of wisdom. If we have no fear, we have no wisdom. We go on our own way doing what we feel like doing regardless who we hurt or humiliate. Every time we hurt and/or humiliate someone, we have just written on our spiritual record I deserve and will receive hurt and humiliation sometime in the future.

If we fear God, if we know these things are true and we know that if we break God's laws, go against His will, that we are going to suffer for it, isn't it pretty unwise to go ahead and do it anyway?

All through the Bible it tells us, if we fear Him and keep His commandments, we shall have peace prosperity, happiness and good health. We will have no fear of man or the world, because we will know that God will always provide for us. We will know that He will help us THROUGH anything that comes our way.

Those who have no fear of God will do as they please, what they desire to do, live by their feelings, and sin against God with no fear of suffering. But the suffering will come. Then the sorrow, regrets, mental and emotional pain begins. The devil blinds people to the FACT that the instruction book (the Bible) from God telling us how to live our lives so we do not have to suffer is TRUE!

If we have the mind of Christ, which the Bible tells us we do in First Corinthians 2:16, then we can learn to think as He does, because He told us how. He tells us how in Matthew chapters 5 (the Sermon on the Mount) through 7, and in Matthew 5:43-48. He also gave us the Holy Spirit to give us the thoughts, attitudes and will of Jesus as we follow Him.

If we learn, accept and practice His thoughts, attitudes, and will on everything, then we will not have to suffer as we go through trials and tribulations, as Jesus said we would go through in John 16:33. This is because we will not be thinking sinful selfish, self-centered, prideful, hurtful, damaging thoughts that cause us to be unhappy and cause harm to us and to others.

We can go through everything in peace, even joy in circumstances that others could not even understand why we were not suffering because of them.

We are subject to all of God's rules and our lives are ruled by them whether we believe or not. The Bible tells us that God rules in the affairs of men. Daniel 4:35, "All the inhabitants of the earth are reputed as nothing. He does according to His will in the army of Heaven, and among the inhabitants of the earth. No one can restrain His hand."

Second Corinthians 7:1 says, "Therefore having these promises beloved, let us cleanse ourselves from all filthiness of the FLESH AND SPIRIT, PERFECTING HOLINESS IN THE FEAR OF GOD."

The good news in all of this is that Jesus died for our sins, so we can and will be forgiven if we give up our sin, confess it to God and ask for His forgiveness. Again, 1st John 1:7-9 tells us He is faithful to forgive and cleanse us of the sin we repent of, confess and ask His forgiveness. He always forgives us under these circumstances, and He will cleanse us of them. Sometimes we will still go through the consequences, but He can get us through them in peace. Praise His Holy Name!

Some people think God is up there just waiting for us to do something wrong so He can gleefully punish us. This is absolutely not true. We suffer for our sins by the natural consequences of them. God told us what not to do, because He does not want us to suffer. What loving father wants his child to sin so he can hurt him? None, and neither does God.

He is loving, kind, gentle, merciful, forgiving, compassionate, understanding and faithful to His Word. He is also just in His treatment of the wrong doer. He warns and pleads with us to live right so we do not have to be judged for our sin. We, as earthly parents, tell our children to be good so we do not have to punish them, because we love them and do not want to see them hurt or unhappy. It is the same with our Heavenly Father.

Psalm 103:11-19, "For as the heavens are high above the earth, so great is His mercy toward those who fear Him; (12) As far as the east is from the west, so far has He removed our transgressions from us. (13) As a father pities his children, so the Lord pities those who fear Him. (14) For He knows our frame that we are dust. (15) For a man's days are as grass: as a flower of the field, so he flourishes. (16) For the wind passes over it, and is gone; and its place is remembered no more. (17) But the mercy of the Lord is from everlasting to everlasting to those who fear Him, and His righteousness to children's children; (18) to such as keep His covenant, and to those that remember His commandments to do them. (19) The Lord has established His throne in Heaven and His kingdom rules over all." Fear God and be happy.

Many years ago I knew a young man who would betray his wife and commit adultery with other women.

He had been doing this for some years. I had prayed for him in the past that he would surrender his life to Jesus.

Jesus said that was a choice he had to make. Sometime later, I prayed for him again. I asked Jesus to please work with him in some way.

Jesus said He would, but if this young man did not repent this time, he would have to reap the judgment.

About three weeks later, he called his wife from work and he was weeping. He told her that the Lord had told him he must repent.

He said he did repent and he has proven to be true to his word.

CHAPTER 19

Forgiveness

Forgiveness is something Jesus told us to do. He told us the greatest commandment is to love. If we love Him, we forgive. If we love Him, we keep His commandments. We do not hurt others and we do not want others to be hurt.

In unforgiveness we desire for the person we do not forgive to suffer. There are always consequences to our thoughts, attitudes, words and actions. So, if we desire that someone else suffers, the consequences will be that we suffer.

Jesus said if we do not forgive, we would be turned over to the tormentors. These are evil spirits. They will torment us with the frustrated desire for the unforgiven person to suffer. Unforgiveness causes anger, resentment, and bitterness and even hate and possibly murder. All these things cause suffering.

Forgiving someone is for us. He wants us to live in peace. We cannot do that if we are walking in anger, resentment and bitterness. He revealed to me once that I was blocking blessings in my life by not forgiving. He also told me that forgiveness was a healing to the soul. We block love, peace and joy from our own heart.

We feel that we have a right to punish the person who offended us. We feel they deserve to suffer because they offended the great ME.

When someone hurts us, it is usually because we are reaping the consequences of hurting someone in the past. We do not understand this, though, because our ego does not see us doing wrong.

Unforgiveness can cause stress. Stress causes damage to our body, soul and spirit. Sin causes stress and stress causes sickness. For example, it tells in the Bible (Mark 2:3—12) that four men removed a portion of a roof to let down a crippled man on a bed so Jesus could heal him. Jesus told him his sins were forgiven. Jesus forgave his sins and the man took up his bed and walked. Unforgiveness is sin.

My mother did some very cruel things to me. As I was growing up, I began to have this feeling against her. I did not let myself admit what it was but I would say and do things to hurt and humiliate her. After I turned my life over to Jesus, He began to deal with me about my feelings for her. He showed me that I really hated her. We had a big argument and we would not speak to each other for over two years. If we happened to come face-to-face in one of the stores in town, we gave each other a hateful look and went on our way.

Every time someone mentioned her name I began telling him or her some of the things she had done. The hate spewed out of me. The Lord began to convict me of it. I prayed for Him to free me of it because I knew He wanted me to quit hating her. I asked Him to take the hate away. He told me He could not answer that prayer. I asked why and He said because in my heart I really did not want to give it up. I then asked Him to help me want to give it up and He said He would work on that. This happened a short time after we had the argument.

After I prayed to want to give it up, every time her name was mentioned I went into my list of things she had done to me. One of them was she had sex with my first boyfriend when I was thirteen and he was fifteen. She did this in such a way that I would see her do it.

Every time she was mentioned I would spew some of the hate out by telling the person how bad she was. The Holy Spirit told me one time that when we have a strong emotion and hold it in, it turns against us and puts pressure on our nervous system. Our nervous system goes all through our body.

The pressure from the negative, strong emotions turns against us and begins destroying our health. So, sin does cause sickness and unforgiveness is a sin.

My unforgiveness had caused me to hate my mother. As I wrote earlier every time she came to my mind, I relived the offenses and would feel the same anger and hate. Finally, one evening I was driving a missionary to Indianapolis to a church, and on the way she asked me about my family. I started to tell her about Mom, but instead I thought to myself, "I am sick of even thinking about that." The hate was gone.

All of my growing up years I had held in the strong emotion of hate. In fact I never admitted to myself that I hated her. She was my security. I needed her so I did not dare admit it to myself. God knew I needed to get rid of it to relieve the pressure on my nervous system. I had stored up a lot of it through the years. Every time I talked bad about her I was releasing some of that pressure. So, as time went by, I was getting rid of more and more of the stored up hate until finally it was all gone.

The night I realized it was gone I dreamed of seeing Mom walking along a road. I stopped my car, ran back and threw my arms around her and said, "After all these years I still love you." The Holy Spirit gave me the understanding that the love had always been in me (the human spirit in me) but the hate that my sinful soul (the proud ego) had buried the love. The sinful soul was in control of me—the spiritual me.

It took the Holy Spirit two years to clean out the hate. He did the work for, and in me. I would never have seen and understood that if He had not shown it to me.

Jesus came to set the captives free. I was a captive to unforgiveness; therefore, I was also a captive to hate. In reality I was a captive of the devil because he was the one who controlled Mom to do what she did and then gave my sinful soul (ego) the thoughts and attitudes he wanted it to have.

After I had the dream, I loved her, so I naturally forgave her. I was so happy that I went to the phone to tell her I forgave her. I wanted her to be happy too. Jesus said to forgive from the heart and that is what I did. All the past things she had done had no effect on me any more. When I put my hand on the phone to call and tell her I forgave her, the Holy Spirit told me not to do that. Of course I asked why. He said, "You call her and ask her to forgive you for how you responded to her and how you treated her." It took me a second to mentally digest that, but I understood. I called her and asked her to forgive me and she said she did.

My mother was not a forgiving person. She may never have forgiven me if Jesus had not instructed me to ask her to forgive me. So, by having me ask her, He was giving her the opportunity to receive a blessing. Isn't He so wise and kind?

Years later Mom developed lung problems and, as time passed, they became worse. I went to visit one day to talk to her about life after death. I explained to her that anything we repented of here on earth we would not have to be judged for when we left here and stood before God. I told her to be sure she had forgiven everyone before she left here.

She still had unforgiveness and all that went with it for her late twin brother's wife who had been very cruel to him when he was dying from cancer. Mom said she had tried and prayed but just could not forgive her. The Lord revealed to me that at the time he died, Mom was so angry with her that she let a spirit of hate and unforgiveness take control of her thoughts and emotions concerning this. He also revealed when we have something we do not like, know we should not, do not want, cannot get rid of, then it is a spirit controlling us.

I explained this to Mom and asked her if in the name of Jesus I could bind the spirit's power and command it/or them to leave. She said yes so that is what I did. She told me later that she had seen her ex sister-in-law in the post office and when she saw her she forgave her. She was very happy about it.

What a wonderful release and what peace we have when we really forgive someone from the heart as Jesus told us to do. We may also feel the joy in the Lord. I believe this is our reward for obeying Jesus. The key is forgiving from the heart. We may say I forgive them but I will never forget it. That is not forgiveness from the heart. If we are honest with ourselves, we will realize we still have some animosity toward that person. Where there is someone in our life who has hurt or shamed us, we may not admit it, but we have a fear of being around that person. We are afraid they will do it again. Being human as we are, we all want to avoid these things that cause suffering.

Jesus did not say we have to spend time with the person who has hurt or offended us. He just told us to forgive from the heart. When we do that, the animosity goes away. The anger, resentment and bitterness go. Peace over the problem takes their place.

When we are living in unforgiveness and all that goes with it, we are not in our right mind. Our right mind (free spirit) is kind and forgiving. We can live in our right mind or our wrong mind. We can live in the Spirit or the flesh. If we walk in the Spirit, we will not be controlled by, live in, or fulfill the lusts of the flesh.

When we are in unforgiveness, we wonder why we do not have the joy of the Lord. He does not reward us for disobedience. He does not reward us for hurting or desiring to hurt others. We parents do not reward one child for hurting another child. We love all of our children. We do not want to see one of them suffer or the one doing the hurting being that kind of person because we know that needs to be corrected. That means both children we love will suffer. We do not want one child to hurt another. So it is with God. We are all His creation.

God knows the unforgiving person will suffer as long as they do not forgive. That is why He tells us to forgive. He does not want us to suffer. The Holy Spirit told me that He loves us and does not want us to suffer. That is why He gave us the instruction book (the Bible) to teach us how to live our lives so we do not have to suffer.

The devil wants to program us to be like him. He is hate. God wants us to be like Him. He is love. Hate brings torment. God's love brings joy. Unforgiveness brings torment. Forgiveness brings peace.

Some people will hold on to unforgiveness even after the person who hurt them has been dead for years. How can they hurt the person after the person dies? They are just hurting themselves. One lady kept hating a person who had hurt her even after the person died. She did not see that before she was acquainted with the person who hurt her; she had been very verbally cruel to her family. She had a gift of insight into people. Instead of using it for good she used it to hurt and humiliate others.

One of God's rules in the instruction book is that what we do to others will be done to us. We reap what we sow. Jesus told us to "Do unto others as we would have others do unto us." This was to help us prevent being treated badly. He does not want the other person or <u>us</u> to be treated badly. He told us how to prevent it.

Many things happened to me when I was young for which I felt sorry for my self. I was angry with the offending parties. I wanted to or did hurt back. I felt that I was a victim. After I turned my life over to Jesus and thought of one of those happenings, He would take me back in my memory and show me where and when I had done or said the same thing to someone else. He showed me that I had just gotten back what I had put out.

When I got the message, I began treating others a lot differently. I could forgive many people when I realized that the devil has a right to use other's sins to hurt me after I had hurt someone. When I quit hurting others, then I did not deserve to be hurt; therefore, when someone tried to hurt me, the Holy Spirit would give me His thoughts and attitudes so I did not accept the hurt they were trying to inflict on me. I should say that the devil was trying to inflict hurt on me by using the other person's sins.

Many people have trouble forgiving themselves. I was one of them. The Lord began working on me to forgive others. It was a process. I did not forgive everyone overnight, but I was willing to do so. I wanted to because I love Jesus and I wanted to please Him. Later I looked back and realized that as I forgave others, I was gradually forgiving myself. It is written in the Bible, "If you do not forgive others, you will not be forgiven." Therefore, as I forgave others, I was forgiven and I accepted that forgiveness and was set free of the unforgiveness for myself.

Not everything that happens to us is something we have done to others. As a child I was molested and as a teenager I was raped. I had not done that to others. But in the book of Job it tells of satan asking God for permission to try to get Job to curse God and die spiritually. Well, he does the same to everyone one way or another. He causes suffering in everyone's life for the same purpose.

Because of the things that happened to me in my growing up and younger years, I was a mess when I married my last husband. I could not feel or express love. He was very hurt, disappointed and angry because of this so he set out to make me suffer for not being what he wanted me to be.

He greatly succeeded. He never hit me but he was a mental and emotional bully. He was very cruel in his words and actions. This went on for years. We both lived in depression and anger. He suffered because he was making me suffer but he could not see he was causing his own suffering. I finally turned my life over to Jesus. He began changing me but I remained unhappy for a long time.

One day I was watching a TV program called The 700 club. The host, Pat Robertson, was talking about forgiveness. The thought came to me that was what was wrong with me. I needed to forgive my husband for all the hurts of the past. It took me a couple of days, but I did it. He worked the second shift so one night I wrote him a letter and explained why I could not show love and asked him to forgive me.

I did not wait up for him that night. Neither one of us ever mentioned the letter nor the word forgiveness, but he was a completely different person from then on. Before, he did not want to do anything for me and would not if he could get out of it. After the letter he could not do enough for me. The last year of his life was a very good year. He accepted Jesus before he died.

Forgiveness is a wonderful healer. My grandson that I raised was hurt by someone and began telling me how he would like to get even. I suggested forgiveness. He rejected that. I said, "You always forgive your mother and me, why don't you forgive this person." He said, "It is easy to forgive you two because I love you." God tells us through the Bible that love covers a multitude of sins. Too bad we do not love everyone, as we should. That is the greatest gift—God's love. We should pray for that everyday, then it would be easy to forgive everyone.

We need to remember that the Holy Spirit is the one who does all the work. We make the choice and He carries it out. He said to me years ago when I was feeling helpless, "You do what you can do and I'll do what you cannot do." He is always there to help us in our spiritual walk. We make the choice to forgive and He takes away the unforgiveness, cleanses us of that unrighteousness, and our life becomes easier. In fact, the more we obey and let Him cleanse us, the better our lives will be.

The Holy Spirit told me that when God created the universe (not just our world on this planet), He created it with two major laws; (1) If we sin we suffer, and (2) If we obey, we are rewarded. The Bible tells us that God is no respecter of persons. This means we are all ruled by His laws alike. We do not sin and get away with it. We might believe that we will because we are special or the rules do not apply to us. Even if we have not read the Bible or have read it and do not believe it, God's rules still apply to each of us. So if we do not forgive, we are breaking one of God's rules and WE WILL SUFFER FOR IT.

I hope you who are reading this will understand and forgive others. If you cannot, ask God to help you want to and set you free from the spirit of unforgiveness. Remember that we do not fight against flesh and blood, but we fight against evil spirits. Also remember Jesus gave us all power and authority over the enemy who is the devil and his evil spirits. In the name of Jesus we can AND MUST bind their power and command them to loose us, to get away from us and never come back. In Jesus name they have to go. He revealed to me that the power is in His name.

There are many prayers that God does not hear because we regard iniquity in our hearts (Psalm 66:18). If He does not hear them, then He cannot grant them. Unforgiveness, with its desire for others to suffer, is iniquity—SIN. So, there are prayers He cannot grant because He does not hear them. Our iniquity blocks Him from hearing them.

Hurtful things happen to everyone. Jesus said in John 16:33 that we would all have trials and tribulations but be of good cheer for he has overcome the world. He meant that bad and hurtful things would happen to us. We would encounter many offenses, but if we let Him deal with them through and for us, He can get us through them in peace.

Sadly, I received the devil's thoughts and attitudes and became the angry, bitter, hateful person he wanted me to be and he used me to hurt many people. He uses one person to hurt another. He uses the people around us to try to destroy us. Our families are handy weapons to use against each other.

Jesus taught me to try to understand all of this to see that the devil was controlling the offending person. He had strong holds in their lives just as he had them in mine and used them as he had used me. When Judas betrayed Jesus, it tells us in John 22:3 that the devil entered Judas. He went to the leaders, betrayed Jesus, then left Judas. Judas came to himself and went out and hanged himself. He did not realize that the devil had controlled him. The devil had a strong hold in Judas, which was the love of money. The Bible states that he was a thief.

The devil does things. We think we are doing or thinking them, and then we take the blame and guilt for it. The Bible states that the devil accuses us. He accuses us to one another for what he has done and to God. He hates us with a pure hate. He has no mercy. His great pleasure is to make us sin. He laughs with glee when he can do that.

My point in all this is, we are to try to understand why the person has become the way they are, and why they would do things to hurt and/or humiliate others. If we can empathize with them and get our minds off ourselves and ask Jesus to give us His thoughts and attitudes about the situation, then it is easier for Him to free us of the hurt and help us forgive the person who has hurt us. Then we will be making a righteous judgment. We will be obeying God instead of the devil.

The Holy Spirit took me back in my memory and helped me look at the people that had hurt me. He helped me look at them and see them as He did. He showed me that they were like me in that they were born with a sinful nature. The devil had programmed them to be what he wanted and then used them to help him try to destroy others.

As I wrote before, I was destroyed to the extent that I intended to kill myself. The devil's job would have been completed, but Jesus gave me a choice. I chose to SURRENDER everything to Him. He began repairing the damage the devil and I had done and replacing it with the fruit of the Holy Spirit. He cleaned me up and set me free. Praise His wonderful name!

He helped me see what a terrible life my mother had lived. She had suffered much in her life and had been hurt deeply many times. Jesus helped me understand why she was like she was, and He gave me compassion for her instead of hate. That understanding helped me forgive her.

Jesus came to set the captives free. If we are captive that means we have been captured by someone or something. If we cannot or will not forgive them, we have been captured by a spirit of unforgiveness. Jesus' name and power can and will set us free if we will make the choice. Our lives will be happy or unhappy. It will be determined by the choices that we make. Do we choose to do God's will or the devils?

God's will is written in the Bible. We need to read and obey it if we want to be happy. Remember the old hymn, "Trust and obey, for there is no other way to be happy in Jesus, but to trust and obey." I pray you will do that.

I will close this chapter with the words to a song the Lord gave to a close friend of mine. She has gone on to her next life, but she told me before she left that I could use the song any way I wanted. Here are the words to it.

Lord this is my prayer.

Please give me the grace
to forgive the unforgivable,
as You have forgiven me.

Please give me Your love
so I may love the unlovable
as You have loved me.

Don't you think we all should pray that prayer?

CHAPTER 20

Control

So many parents try to control their children with anger. One angry person can destroy a whole family.

Anger is a reaction. We may automatically become angry if we are opposed. Our children become afraid of us. People tend to dislike or even hate what or who they fear, so people will avoid us if they can.

Our children will be hurt and believe they are unloved. They then become angry and do things they know will upset the parents. Therefore, they believe they have power to control others' emotions. They feel they have some control in their lives. No one wants to feel helpless.

The Holy Spirit taught me that the feeling of or belief that we are helpless is the major cause of fear and worry. Of course, worry is fear. We fear and worry about things we have no control over. If we had control over them, we would have no fear. We would feel confident that we could handle the situation. Helplessness creates fear.

When we are in fear or worry, the basic thing we are really experiencing is a belief and or feeling of helplessness. Most people at some time in their life see their helplessness. As babies, toddlers, children, teens, adults, middle-aged or old people facing their last years on earth, we will experience helpless situations or feelings of it.

We are helpless to control our environment, situations, other people, even ourselves at times. When we feel helpless, we become afraid. We feel and/or think we are unable to protect ourselves. Fear causes us to want to be able to protect ourselves, so we will TRY to control who or what is causing us to feel helpless.

How do most people try to control? With anger, of course. The Holy Spirit taught me that there is a cycle of all of this. First, the feeling of helplessness. This triggers fear. Fear triggers the desire to be in control to protect ourselves. That desire triggers anger in most people. Anger triggers verbal and/or violent abuse.

The Holy Spirit told me that evil spirits controls all these. They all work together to begin and complete the cycle. Helplessness—fear –self-protection (control)—anger. Once the helplessness is experienced, the cycle runs its course. The evil spirits have put all of this into our subconscious mind. It is so programmed to it that once the helplessness is felt or seen, it progresses so fast that we are not consciously aware of what is happening in our brain.

When we are threatened or offended in any way, we instantly go into the anger control mode. Many people live in a state of feeling helpless and afraid. They will then live in a constant desire to be in control.

Years ago the young people called them control freaks. I was one of them. I felt a need to be in control all the time. I had been controlled all of my life by others. So I tried to control others to stop them from controlling me. I felt helpless most of the time, so I lived in a constant state of anger.

If my children asked to do something, it was an automatic no. No thinking about it. I had to do the opposite of what they asked to prove I was in control. If I knew they did not want to do something that is what they had to do. Through the years, I have watched this work out in many families. Father and/or mother dominating or trying to dominate their family.

The Holy Spirit told me that when we try to control our children or spouse, they will become angry at us and do the very opposite of what we want them to do in rebellion of being controlled. We are in a way forcing them to make wrong choices. It is taking away from them their ability to think things out and make their own choice. Possibly a much better one.

They have become programmed to rebel against everything we tell or ask them to do to protect themselves from being helpless and under our constant and complete control.

I was also taught that some children felt so helpless that they quit fighting and gave up. The Holy Spirit told me that if we made all of their decisions for them, they would marry someone who would make all of their decisions for them, also. They would lose the ability to make decisions because we had taught them that they were helpless and incapable of making a right decision themselves. They would live in fear and/or anger all their lives unless they turned to God for help.

All of this can go on for years without people realizing what is happening. I was explaining this to a lady one day. She had four grown children. She said she had been angry with her husband and children for years but did not know why. Now she realized that they were all trying to control her. As it turned out later, she finally let herself see that she had been trying to control all of them to begin with, but she had not realized that either. They were trying to protect themselves from her control.

We think we know what is best for everyone and want him or her to do what we think they should do. We think we are right in what we are doing. After all, we are just trying to help and/or keep them safe, or keep them from making the same mistakes that we made. But, in reality, we are being controlled by evil spirits, and they are using us to destroy others.

This is satan's whole purpose—to steal, kill and destroy. He has destroyed many families in this way. He blinds us to our wrongs and deceives us into believing we are doing the right think in trying to make others do our will.

We teach our children that we solve our problems with anger and control. It is passed down from generation to generation.

I know a couple who live in fear of helplessness. They control their children with angry abuse. The children began life as happy, loving little people. As they began to walk, the parents used anger to try to control them. Before long, they were no longer the happy, loving little things they were as they started out. They realized their helplessness and became afraid of their parents. Because of the parent's example set before their children, they all three became rebellious, angry and controlling children.

When the mother became pregnant with her fourth child, the second child, who was seven at the time, made this prediction. She said, "When this baby is born, it will be alright for a while, but it will get to be mean just like the rest of us." So sad. She was right except for the fact that he was worse because he had parents AND older siblings controlling him.

When parents display anger toward their child, the devil will put in their mind that Mommy and/or Daddy do not love them or they would not treat them like that. The child then not only feels helpless, but they also think and feel that they are all alone in the big, scary world with all the big, mean people and they have no one to help or protect them if their parents do not love them. These children can, and most do, carry this fear all of their lives. They feel both helpless and hopeless, which is the two main symptoms of depression.

One angry person can destroy their whole family or destroy their happiness, and their real personality. The happy, loving, kind person becomes an unhappy, angry, controlling, emotionally depressed person.

They marry and treat their family with anger and control so the problem goes on from generation to generation. The sins of the fathers or parent are visited on their children. We teach them that this is the way to live and deal with others. Anger and control are both just two of the sins we teach them. I wrote "we" because I came from a long line of angry controllers. I was guilty of it, too, but thank God, He has freed me of those.

These are some of the things satan programs into our subconscious mind. It starts in young children and may be there until the day we die. Helplessness, fear, control and anger. How can we become free of these? First of all, we must give our lives to Jesus. It tells us in John that without Him, we can do nothing. (John 15:5)

We then need to look inside to find out what all is in there. Good and bad. We must humble ourselves to be honest enough to admit it is there when Jesus brings it to our attention.

Because of my self-hate and self-punishment, I would be consumed with shame for days when He showed me anything about myself that I did not like. He first showed me selfishness and self-centeredness. Then pride. Then He showed me I was a dominating, controlling person. These were all very hard for me to deal with.

I would be devastated with shame for days, thinking God hated me for this. After three or four days, the shame would lessen. Finally, I had a dream that explained to me that self-punishment caused all of this. The dream told me all I had to do was say to Jesus, "Yes, I see, and admit to you that I have this sin (whatever it was), and I ask You to please forgive me and cleanse me of this sin." Then, accept his forgiveness, and wait for the cleansing. Some of it happened soon. Other times it took Him awhile.

The helplessness, fear, control and anger took awhile, because the anger and control was what I believed in my subconscious mind was the only way I could protect myself or get what I wanted. The Holy Spirit told me that the two main reasons we try to control are fear and selfishness.

The Holy Spirit showed me about the four evil spirits who controlled all of this. This was in the beginning of my education of evil spirits and how they work. As I learned, I used the information I was given. That we, in the name of Jesus, have power and control over them.

During the time I was learning, the Holy Spirit taught me that I had no reason to be afraid because my Heavenly Father loved me and would defend me. I did not have to defend myself. The first time I saw this happen was at a Sunday evening meeting at the church I was attending at the time.

A lady I knew told our pastor that I believed something that he did not. That evening, he attacked me verbally in front of the whole class. Many in the class agreed with him. They began giving me scriptures why I was wrong. I knew I was not wrong, but one man gave me so many, so quickly, that my mind could not keep up with them. I stopped trying, and in my spirit I asked Jesus to deal with it for me. When the man stopped talking, I opened my mouth and the Lord said, "Yes, and you have a right to believe that don't you?"

His mouth fell open with surprise. The pastor's face turned very red, and I know he wanted to hit me. I began saying things to calm him down. I knew he would not hit me, but I felt sorry for him.

The next morning I woke up feeling very happy. As I was doing my dishes, I became aware that a song was running through my mind. It was "What Do You Know, The Lord Accepted Me." However, instead of singing that, the Lord accepted me, I was singing in my spirit, "What Do You Know, The Lord Defended Me."

The pastor came to me a couple of weeks later and told me that he had thought about that meeting a lot, and he realized that we all do have a right to believe what we choose to believe.

As I have written elsewhere in this book, what people become angry at, they think about the longest, and he sure was angry in that meeting. The great thing for me was the Lord did defend me and has done it countless times since then.

He is always true to His Word, Psalms 62:2, "He is my defense." Isaiah 41:10, "Fear not, for I am with you: be not dismayed (look to the future with fear) for I am your God. I will strengthen you. Yes, I will help you, I will uphold you with the right hand of my righteousness."

We do not have to be angry to defend ourselves. God can and will (if we let Him) defend us through His Holy Spirit.

The Lord gave me a dream that helped me understand that He does not want to, nor will He force His control on us. He wants us to yield to Him so He can set us free. We have no reason to fear He will force us into submission. He will break the hold satan and our sinful soul have over us.

Everything He tells us not to do is to prevent suffering in our lives or other lives. Things He tells us to do will help bring happiness and peace to us. He is our loving Father. Everything a loving father does is for the good of His child.

Our earthly fathers chastise, correct, and discipline their child to prepare them to be a happy, healthy, productive loving adult. That is God's will for us. That is what He attempts to do for us. But when any situation comes up that is unpleasant, we take the wrong attitude. Why is God letting this happen or why are you doing this to me, God? We do not see it as an opportunity to learn something or grow in some way. We dig in our heals and refuse to look to ourselves for the reason. God does not want to control, He wants us to yield to Him so He can heal, cleanse us and set us free.

When the grandson I raised was about fourteen years old, I began telling him he was doing this wrong, or he was doing that wrong. I would point out his faults to him. One day I was doing that and the Lord said to me, "You just love him and let the Holy Spirit convict him of his sins."

I realize I was trying to change him, which is just another word for control. When we try to change a person, they see that we do not like the way they are, and they become hurt and then angry. We do more damage than good. We damage the relationship and we damage their self-esteem. We damage their thoughts of us, their attitude toward us, and their feelings for us.

We do not realize it, but many people try to control someone into loving them. I know a lady who, as a teenager, told a young man she had sex with, that she was pregnant. He married her, but in reality she was never pregnant. She always tried controlling him because she was afraid he did not love her, even though he stayed married to her. She lived in fear for years that he would leave her. That fear caused her to become very controlling.

Because of the control, he became angry with her and began drinking and staying away from home to avoid her anger and control. He eventually did have an affair, but that was not the real person he was. He cut off the affair and never strayed again.

So many people destroy their marriage because of their fear and/or selfishness. If we all treated our spouses the way the Bible tells us to treat others and the way we want to be treated, I believe there would be very few divorces.

We demand, or expect them to treat us with love, kindness and unselfishness even though we are not treating them that way. The Holy Spirit has taught me that love does cover a multitude of sin (First Peter 4:8). We are to love people and accept them as they are. We can pray for the Lord to set them free. Let Jesus and the Holy Spirit take care of their spiritual growth.

I have always loved my brothers and children even though I saw many things that needed changed. I put those things aside in my mind and focused on the love I had for them. That love covered any sin or fault I saw in them.

Of course, after I gave my life to Jesus, I would pray for them when the Lord directed, and I would talk to them about it. There is a time and place for these things, and we must let Jesus control these. He knows when a person is ready to look at themselves and acknowledge the thing He wants to free them of, and let Him do the talking.

He will do that if we yield to Him. Many times He has told people things through me that I did not know, and I was grateful to learn it myself. The fear of being helpless keeps us from yielding to Jesus and/or the Holy Spirit. The more we trust Him the easier it becomes to yield to Him.

When we are driving a car and come to a yield sign, we have the power to obey that sign and yield. We also have the power to disobey. It is our choice. God just wants us to yield so He can help us or use us to help others. We have no reason to fear yielding to Him. He only wants to help.

Remember satan was kicked out of Heaven because he tried to take control of God's creation and creatures. We are God's creation and creatures.

When we need to fear is when we are trying to control God's creatures, other people. I believe that is one of the major reasons for suffering in this world, for wars, for divorces, and for children rebelling. Matthew 7:12 says to treat others the way you want to be treated. Wouldn't it be wonderful if we all did that?

How can we be freed of the desire to control? Jesus said He came to set the captives free in Luke 4:18. When we are trying to control someone, we feel that we are in control, but the reality is that we are being controlled by evil spirits. We have been taken captive by evil spirits.

In John 8:31 and 32, Jesus tells us that if we abide in Him, we are His disciples, and we shall know the truth and the truth shall set us free. We first must ask Jesus to save us from the power of satan and sin, and to take over our lives and let His will be done. Abiding in Him means each day determine to live it as He wills. We must read the Bible and obey it the best we can.

This implies that because someone goes to church, they should never do anything wrong. Someone said that to me one day. My response came so quickly that I realized later that the Holy Spirit had given it to me. I said, "We go to church to learn God's will and ways, and to learn to do the right and not the wrong. We are like children starting the first grade. You cannot expect a first grader to graduate the second day of school."

Our spirit is new, but we still have the sinful soul to contend with. The soul has to be cleansed of sin. It has to be restored to live in obedience to God.

Romans 6:14 tells us sin shall not have dominion over us because we are not under the law but now under the grace of God. Jesus died for us so we could be saved from sin. We can be changed and that is what it is all about. To turn our life over to Jesus, let Him have control, and let Him clean us up and set us free. The only drawback is that most people refuse to relinquish the control, so they stay trapped by their own will. They refuse to confess the sin in their life, but those who do are blessed by being freed of them.

As a new follower, I had a hunger to read the Bible and learn God's instructions. I still had trouble looking at myself. I have always liked to read. Now I would begin reading better books. No more fiction, only nonfiction.

It seemed every book I read was on selfishness and being self-centered. Every time I read that, I would say to myself, "Oh, that is not me, I'm not selfish. I gave this person this or that person something else."

Then one day, as this was going on, suddenly I saw the truth. I was selfish and self-centered. I was absolutely shocked by the truth. I saw that I was selfish with my feelings, with my time and with my love. This was all with my family.

I did my duty—the things I was supposed to do to take care of my family and home. But I seemed to have shut off my feelings.

I was dominating to my family. I did not understand the rebellion I was fostering in them. I did not put myself in their place and recognize they had feelings too. To me, I was the only one with feelings. Self-centered. My mind was always on myself. What I wanted should always come first. They should keep their room spotless because I wanted it that way.

I learned later that this was caused mainly by the fear of being helpless. They were all angry with me for being so controlling, so they did the opposite of what I wanted. This made me feel more helpless, because I could not control them. Then I put on more pressure to be in control. It became a terrible cycle that made us all miserable.

There was never any peace in our home, all because of my desire to be in control and have everything and everyone do and be what I wanted.

I know it was the Holy Spirit (He is to convict us of our sins) who gave me the understanding of all this. He also showed me that it was because of things that happened to me in the past that caused the fear and caused me to turn inward toward myself.

He also taught me about the four evil spirits that controlled all this and how to get rid of them and keep them from controlling me anymore.

I had to be completely honest with myself. Watch every thought, and if it was not one that Jesus would want me to have, I immediately bound the power of the spirit in the name of Jesus and commanded it to leave and never come back.

If we do not see what is going on in our own mind, we can be controlled by the evil ones. We will respond and/or react to people or circumstances the same way over and over. The way satan has programmed us to do.

The more control we surrender to Jesus, the less pressure we have on ourselves. He is happy to take it over and relieve our spirits of the burdens. His will is the only thing that will make us truly happy. Why do we fight so hard against that?

Because satan has blinded us to the truth. Jesus said in John 8:31 & 32, "If you abide (live) in my word, you are my disciple indeed. And you shall know the truth and the truth shall set you free."

We are to live for and by the word of God. We are to seek God's will more than anything else and He will take very good care of us, His beloved children. He will defend, protect and provide for us. We can rest in Him.

Years ago, I was not living in peace at all. It was during my controlling years. While reading the Bible one day, I came across Hebrews 4:9, "There remains therefore a rest for the people of God." I became angry when I read that because I did not have that rest. I had hypoglycemia at the time. I was fatigued all the time but I did not know I had hypoglycemia.

I just knew I was a semi-invalid because of the fatigue. So when I read about God's rest, I wanted to know why. Why couldn't I have that rest? When I went to bed that night I thought maybe if I pray to be filled with the Holy Spirit, I would have rest. So, I prayed.

I went to sleep praying to be filled. It was so strange. I went to sleep, but though I was asleep, I was aware somehow that I kept praying even though I was asleep. I woke up in a few hours still praying. When I came fully awake, the Holy Spirit said to me, "That is not the answer."

Then I thought maybe I needed to pray for the baptism of the Holy Spirit. I began praying that. I had the same experience of praying in my sleep and being aware somehow that I was doing that. I awoke in a couple hours, still praying. Again, the Holy Spirit said, "That is not the answer." I was disappointed but I drifted off to sleep. As I awoke in the morning, I was talking to God. I was saying in an I-give-up attitude, "Okay, let your will be done." The Holy Spirit said, "That is the answer."

When we try to stay in control, it is very stressful and tiring. When we let go of the control, and let God do the work, we can rest from all the struggle and stress. Hebrews 4:10, "For he who has entered His rest has himself also ceased from his works as God did from His." God rested on the seventh day (Genesis 2:2).

Do you want that rest? Then let God be in control. You will be safe. It is always safe to trust the Lord.

When the grandson that I raised was in his early teens, he had some friends that visited frequently. They would fool around as teenage boys do. I would get angry and try to control them. They only got worse. It was very upsetting to me. I prayed for Jesus to stop it for me.

That night I dreamed it was going on as usual. I was angry with them and they were angry with me so they continued their destructive actions. Suddenly the dream changed. The scene was exactly the same but I was showing the boys love, and they were being very careful not to mess up my house. It was explained to me that they were being careful not to break anything in gratitude to me for showing them love.

From that time on I showed them love and they responded exactly as the dream had shown me. They were very kind and respectful to me. I had been afraid I would not have control over them so I tried to control them with anger and criticism. It did not work. They became my good friends and I grew to really love them. Anger and control are destructive. Love is creative.

As I was writing this, the Lord gave me the following message for the readers of this book. Please quit trying to control. I don't want to hurt or shame you. I want to free you of all this. I love you and want you to love me and keep all my commandments, so that all will go well with you and your children.

CHAPTER 21

Anger

When I tell anyone that anger is sin, they always say two things. First, they quote scripture that tells us to be angry and sin not, Ephesians 4:26.

The following are a few scriptures that tell us we are to put away ALL anger (Ephesians 4:3). Psalms 37:8 says, “Cease from anger.” Colossians 3:8 says, “Put off all anger.” There is Proverbs 29:22, “An angry man stirs up wrath.” The list continues with James 1:19-21, which says, “The angry man does not achieve the righteousness of God.” Ecclesiastes 7:9 says, “Anger rests in the bosom of fools.” Proverbs 22:24 also says to, “Make no friendship with an angry man.” And Proverbs 14:17, “He that is soon angry does foolishly.

Ephesians 4:26 is telling us if we become angry, get rid of it immediately before satan uses us to hurt or embarrass others. Why would God put all the scriptures in the Bible telling us to put anger away—cease from it, etc., and then give one scripture telling us it is okay? The answer is simple, He wouldn’t.

The other thing they say is that Jesus got angry so it is all right for us. When we become angry, we want to punish the person we have anger toward. Jesus created us. He is the ruler of the universe. He has a right to punish the offenders for their sin. We do not have that right. When our children were small and misbehaved, we did not tell one child to punish another child. We do not have the right or authority to punish others for their sins. When we are angry, we feel that we do have that right. We even make ourselves believe that we do because we desire to hurt and/or embarrass back.

When we are angry, we are not in our right minds. We are in the flesh and not the Holy Spirit. Even our human spirit realizes we were wrong when the anger leaves. The Bible states that if we walk in the Holy Spirit, we will not fulfill the lust of the flesh. When we are angry, we have a desire to hurt someone. Desire is lust. We are lusting to hurt someone.

People have asked me about being angry with a person when they hurt our children. In the past, I would always become angry in those situations. I am sorry to say I even got in physical fights over my brothers and later my children. After turning my life over to Jesus, He taught me that we should focus on showing love and comfort to those who are hurt instead of anger and revenge toward the one who had done the hurting. He told us in the Bible that His ways are above our ways, and His thoughts are above our thoughts.

In Ephesians 4:3, He tells us to be kind and tenderhearted to everyone. One of the fruits of the Spirit is self-control. When I turned my life over to Jesus, I was an angry person. It seemed that I lived in a constant state of anger. I was always ready to express it. The Holy Spirit began to convict me of it. In the past, I always felt or believed I had a right to be angry because people were always doing things I did not want them to do.

I realized I had no control over the anger. It controlled me. I would tell myself when I went to bed at night that I would not get angry the next day. However, the first time someone crossed me, I would go into my tirade. In the Bible, Jesus' family expressed their belief that He was out of His mind by saying He was beside Himself. That is what I seemed to experience. When I would begin the angry words, it seemed that a part of me was watching and listening to the other part of me say the angry words. It seemed the real me would say to the angry me, "Shut up! Shut up! Shut up!" Unfortunately, I just kept on with it. I thank God that He freed me of all that.

It was a long process. I was a very dominating person. I did not realize it back then, but I used anger to try to control people, especially my family. The Holy Spirit taught me that I used anger to defend myself, to fight my battles and to control people. He also taught me that anger is a symptom of fear, selfishness, pride and guilt. So, when we become angry, we should ask ourselves why, not what someone else said or did that made us angry, but what did their actions or words trigger in us.

In the past, I would say someone made me angry, or hurt my feelings, or perhaps embarrassed me. But the Holy Spirit gave me the insight and understanding that those people do not live inside my body. I am the only one living in it. I am the one who decides how I respond. I realized that just because someone wanted me to suffer did not mean I had to. I had the power to make that choice. He taught me that I always reacted to people and circumstances. He taught me to stop and think about it, and then take the appropriate action, not just react without thinking.

He also taught me that I fought situations when I did not like them. Waiting in line, slow drivers, frustration of any kind, I would become angry. He spoke to my spirit one day and told me that I would fight the situation, and, of course, I fought with anger. He told me to quit fighting against them. Rather I should just accept them. "If you can do something about it, do it. If you have no control over it, leave it to Me." I got it! From that time on I accepted things the way they were. In acceptance is peace, not upset and anger.

I have watched people since I learned all of this, and so many people are always on the defensive. They are always ready to defend themselves. That shows a fear of being attacked in some way, usually verbally. We usually defend ourselves by offending the other person. The old saying is the best defense is a strong offense. We will come back at the person with some insult or tell them what a bad person they are or what bad things they have done, so they begin defending themselves as well.

The core of the problem is that we are self-centered. Our mind is usually on our self. What we want others to do, or be, or feel, or show us love and kindness even though we are being self-absorbed and offensive. I learned all of this by experience. I had to be broken by the Holy Spirit. He told me once that if I did not submit, I would be broken. Needless to say, I was broken. It was painful, but I am happy that He did it.

I am so glad He did not leave me in that terrible shape I was in. In the seventh chapter of Romans, Paul explains about how helpless we are in the sinful nature and that is all we are in our flesh.

We are sinful and helpless to change without help. That is why Jesus said, "Without Me you can do nothing." We must recognize anger as sin. Confess it as sin.

Ask God's forgiveness "If we ask anything according to His will, He hears us, and if we know that He hears us, we know that we have the petition that we have asked of Him," 1 John 5:14 and 15.

Ask God to fill you with His Holy Spirit. Luke 11:13, "Your Heavenly Father will give the Holy spirit to those who ask."

Ask God to give you His love for the person or persons you have anger toward. It is God's will that we love them. Matthew 5:44, "Love your enemy." Pray for them to learn and grow spiritually.

I have written elsewhere that anger is a symptom of something else. It covers a multitude of sin. Fear, pride, selfishness, self-centeredness, guilt, shame, embarrassment, hurt, feeling unloved or ignored. These are some of the things we react to with anger. Anger is cruel. With it we hurt, and/or shame others. We cause our families to believe they are not worth being loved. When we use anger to control our children, we are saying, with it, do what I want. They are hearing, I care nothing about you. This causes them to have low self-esteem. Most of them feel they are not as good as others the rest of their lives.

The devil knows all of this. It is part of his plan to destroy our spirit. If parents only knew the damage they do to their children when they deal with them in anger instead of patience and love and discipline. If they taught their children the way they should grow into, they would grow up to be patient, kind, loving people. Instead they grow up trying to solve problems with anger and control just as their parents taught them.

The example we set for our children as they grow, when they are grown, they will not depart from it. That is why in the Bible, God tells us to raise up a child in the way he or she SHOULD go because He knows that they become programmed the way they are taught. It is all programmed into their subconscious mind. That may control them the rest of their lives unless they turn their lives over to Jesus and let Him reprogram their subconscious mind as He wills.

So, when you are hurt or embarrassed, ask yourself these questions. What did I do to deserve this? When did I treat someone badly? Is this how they felt because of my words or actions? Why did I treat them this way?

If anger is not recognized as a sin and repented of, it will eventually express itself hurtfully toward others. We may be angry with one person and take it out on another. We may be angry with our boss or someone we work with, but hold it in and then let it out at our spouse or children.

Held in anger grows and grows the more the think about it. Any strong negative emotion held in turns against the nervous system and begins to destroy it. Anger also destroys our testimony. It causes strife and division among church members. It hurts our loved ones. Our homes become a place of tension and fear instead of peace.

Our attitudes are passed on to our children. The Bible tells us that the sins of the parents are passed on to our children. Anger causes physical consequences. It causes bitterness and resentment. These produce tension, headaches, colitis, ulcers, high blood pressure and more. We teach our children to try to solve life's problems with anger.

Examine yourself. Identify the reason for your anger. Is it from bitterness from a past situation? Pride can produce impatience and then anger. Fear may cause us to use anger as a protection. Anger may be our outlet for grief or pain. When we are very tired, we can become angry at the least provocation. God tells us we can have power to control anger. In Colossians 3:8, as I wrote earlier, we are commanded to put away all anger.

You may have accepted the idea that you just have a bad temper, or that it runs in the family. You must get rid of these false notions and accept the responsibility for your behavior. You must desire victory over this sin. We must be willing to repeatedly humble ourselves if we are to see anger defeated.

Jealousy can cause anger and can even grow into hate. When we are angry with someone, we look for faults in them to justify our wrong feelings for them. God told us to put away all anger.

The first thing is to admit we are wrong for being angry. The Holy Spirit has taught me that anger is the wrong way to deal with anything. We are making decisions by our emotions and not our reasoning power. We are not thinking things out. We are reacting to something with emotions. Once we get rid of the evil spirit or spirits controlling our emotions, we can get the victory over our emotions. Emotions are produced by the thoughts that are given to the brain. Good or bad. The Bible tells us we have the mind of Christ.

The Holy Spirit gives us the thoughts and attitudes of Jesus. The devil tries to give us his. Jesus, through the Holy Spirit, tries to give us His. We choose the ones we will accept. These are the ones the brain works to create the emotions for. We, of course, have our own. That is what we use to make the choice with and for.

As I have written earlier, we must look inside ourselves and ask what is in me that is using anger to deal with situations. Is it fear, pride, selfishness, or something else? We need to know what satan has in us that he controls us with. We need to get rid of the splinter (satan) so the wound (our soul and/or spirit) can heal.

Jesus, can and will, if you let Him, as I did, teach you how to deal with life and its lessons without anger. If we accept people and circumstances instead of fighting against them, we can live in peace. If we accept Jesus' thoughts and attitudes, which are written in the Bible, we learn to deal with them His way. Read over and over the Sermon on the Mount in Matthew 5,6 and 7. There you have his thoughts and attitudes.

As Jesus told us, without Him we can do nothing. We can never achieve this on our own. It is Him and the Holy Spirit who creates His thoughts and attitudes in us. We need to confess our sin, (here it is anger) ask forgiveness and cleansing. He will work to accomplish this in our lives. It may take Him time. That depends on how submissive and obedient we are.

It is His will that we be cleansed and set free of this. The devil and/or his evil spirits will fight against us, but in the name of Jesus, we have the power over them. It is a spiritual battle, not just a battle with self. Remember, any thought or feeling we do not like and do not want; it is not us but the enemy putting it in our mind. Keep a spiritual eye on your mind.

We have to make a choice. Do we really want to give this up? If we find that we do not, then ask Jesus why that is. As I wrote, anger covers many things. We have to get rid of the reason for it first. Then we will not "need" it any more.

I pray that all who read this will understand how destructive anger is, not just to us but also to those around us.

CHAPTER 22

Pride

Pride, the original sin. Pride is the desire to be worshipped, to be in control of others, and to feel superior to everyone else. This was why Lucifer, satan, the devil, was cast out of Heaven and into darkness.

Pride leads to self-will and sell-will leads to rebellion. Rebellion is as bad as witchcraft—worshiping satan.

Proverbs 13:10; "By pride comes nothing but strife." First John 2:16: "For all that is in the world—the lust of flesh, the lust of the eyes and the pride of life—is not of the Father, but is of the world."

Pride centers on self. Humility centers on esteeming others. Pride causes us to feel that we are better than others. Pride causes us to seek our own pleasure and satisfy our own desires. Pride tells us we have a right to hurt and humiliate others. It tells us we should have our own way. We should come first.

Pride causes us to exalt ourselves. We will try to build ourselves up to others.

From my childhood, I never cried in front of anyone. Sometimes I cried while in bed at night so no one would see my weakness. I had been attending church for a short time when one evening my pastor came to visit. He brought a visiting preacher with him. I began telling them how I had changed and what a good Christian I had become. Suddenly, I began to cry! I was mortified. After he left, I asked Jesus why He let that happen. He instantly gave me the scripture Matthew 23:12 which says that if a person exalts themselves, they WILL be humbled, but if they humble themselves, they will be lifted up.

I realized I had been bragging on myself, and exalting myself. I also realized Jesus is with us all the time. He knows everything we say, do, think, and feel.

I also realized that His rules, and consequences to breaking those rules, are written down for our benefit in order to teach us that we WILL be corrected for our disobedience and rewarded for our obedience. There is no getting out of the correction because He loves us and wants us to live in peace.

Even though our pride tells us we are special and God will let us get by with wrong doing, He tells us in His book of instructions that He is no respecter of persons (Acts 10:34), meaning He treats us all according to our thoughts, attitudes, works, feelings or actions. There are natural consequences good or bad. It depends on the choices we make.

His Word is true. We are dealt with according to His Word whether we know it or not or whether we believe it or not. "God rules in the affairs of men." Daniel 4:25. Proverbs 11:2, "When pride comes, then comes shame." Exalt yourself and you will be made to feel shame. Give up the pride and you will not have shame.

PRIDE IS A SIN

Obadiah 3, "Pride of heart deceives." It makes us feel we are important or special. We are deceived into believing we have the right to find fault, criticize, hurt and embarrass others. All of these are sin.

We are born with pride. It is revealed in our words, looks and attitudes. Others can see it, but our ego does not see it unless the Holy Spirit can get through to us and help us see the truth.

The devil knows that he can do things to hurt and humiliate us as long as we hold on to the pride. The Bible is true. If we sin, we suffer. Suffering is allowed in our lives to get our attention on the fact that something is wrong. It is to show us we need to look at self and see where we need to change something.

It could be wrong thoughts or attitudes. It could be wrong actions or words. The suffering of pride is shame. The devil works very hard and long to blind us to pride because he know he has the right to cause situations that bring us shame. He loves to make us suffer.

Remember Proverbs 11:2: "When pride comes, then comes shame; but with the humble is wisdom." We all need to pray for wisdom, understanding and knowledge. Then we will know, understand and use the wisdom God gives us in His instruction book.

We will go through many trials and tribulations in life, but if we think God's thoughts and take His attitudes in and about them, we will get through them in peace because His ways bring peace. He can get us through anything in peace if we keep our focus on Him and His instructions.

He instructs us to shun pride for our sake. It causes us mental and emotional pain when the shame hits us.

One day I took my ten-year-old grandson to the city park. I was sitting on a bench while he played. I saw him walking toward a jungle gym. Suddenly, an expression appeared on his face that if expressed in words would have said, "Boy, am I going to show the people here how very cool I am by jumping up and grabbing the bar and swinging on it."

I knew when I saw that expression he would miss the bar and fall on his bottom. That is exactly what happened. He was exalting himself, so he had one of God's life lessons. James 4:6 says, "God resists the proud but gives grace to the humble."

Pride is one of the reasons our prayers are not granted. God resists the proud. Pride is one of the reasons we cannot make things progress as we wish. God resists the proud. Pride is one of the reasons we cannot convince others to do our will (controlling). God resists the proud.

Proverbs 16:10 says, "Pride goes before destruction and a haughty spirit before a fall." Proverbs 8:13 says, "The fear of the Lord is to hate evil: pride and arrogance."

If we once look at ourselves and see the pride, how destructive to our person, our life and those we love, we will hate it.

None of us have any reason to be proud of ourselves because we in ourselves were born completely and utterly sinful. The only good we may have is what God, through His Holy Spirit, has created in us. We cannot take pride in what He does or we are in trouble.

Many people will be angry at and punish their children when they are just being children and not really doing wrong, because of fear that it will cause someone to think badly of us, the parent. When pride comes, then comes shame (Proverbs 11:2). We will have no peace in our lives as long as we are ruled by pride. It robs us of many, many blessings in life that God wants to give us but cannot because He cannot reward us for sin.

So many people ask, "Why doesn't God answer my prayers? Why did He let this or that happen?" He wants us to look at ourselves for the reason and not (blame) Him. We have the power to make our lives better by asking God to reveal anything in us that is not of Him. Acknowledge it when He does. Ask forgiveness and ask Him to cleanse us of it.

When we look at our sin, acknowledge our sin, confess them to God, and ask for forgiveness, this is the act of humbling ourselves. God resists the proud BUT GIVES GRACE TO THE HUMBLE.

Remember Matthew 23:12? If we exalt ourselves, we will be humbled, BUT if we humble ourselves we will be exalted. By God—not ourselves. The devil wants us to do his will so he can make us suffer. God wants us to do His will so He can make us happy. It is our choice whom we yield our minds to.

Pride is the absence of humility. What is humility? The absence of pride.

God humbles the proud. In Deuteronomy 8:2, "You shall remember that the Lord your God led you all the way these forty years in the wilderness to humble you."

In the book of Daniel, King Nebuchadnezzar glorified himself and claimed credit for himself that he had become king. God gave him a dream that Daniel interpreted.

God was telling the king that he was going to be made to live like and with the beasts of the fields. He would eat grass like the oxen. He would be made wet with the dew at night for seven years until his hair had grown like eagle's feathers and his nails like bird's claws.

After seven years, God brought him back to his right mind and put him back as king. This is what he said, "Now I praise and extol and honor the King of Heaven (instead of himself) all of whose works are truth and His ways justice, and those who walk in PRIDE He is able to put down (or humble)." This is all in the fourth chapter of Daniel.

Again, Proverbs 16:5 says that everyone who is proud in heart is an abomination to the Lord. Though they join forces, they will NOT go unpunished. By holding on to the pride, we cause suffering in our own lives.

With the pride, it is hard to humble ourselves, but the outcome is very worth it. We can never have peace in our life if we won't admit it to ourselves and ask Jesus to forgive and cleanse us of it.

CHAPTER 23

Guilt and Various Subjects

When I started church I really didn't know what was expected of me. What I was supposed to do as a Christian so I listened to the people around me. You should do this; you should do that. You should help clean the church. You should witness to someone every day, and so forth. I did that for a while.

One night in a dream, the Holy Spirit told me that if I didn't quit running around I was going to have a breakdown. When someone asked me to do something I had this feeling of fear at the back of my mind so I would agree to do things against my will.

Finally one morning I had gotten my daughter off to school and was washing the breakfast dishes when I suddenly felt as though someone had pulled a plug at the base of my spine and all my energy drained out. I could hardly make it to the living room to collapse on the couch. I had kept going until I'd had the breakdown the Holy Spirit had warned me of. I could not get up for hours and then I had to struggle to get to the bathroom.

A physical breakdown is of the depletion of physical energy. A nervous breakdown is the inability to cope with too much stress on the nervous system.

The devil was still trying to destroy me. Now that I couldn't get out and go any more, I spent a lot of time reading, studying and meditating. The

Holy Spirit brought to my mind that I feared if I didn't do everything people wanted me to they would hurt me.

I did a lot of studying during this breakdown. It was many years before I began to get some energy back. During that time I had periods of a spurt of energy but would work rapidly to get things done I had let go for a long while. The next day I would be fatigued again.

I had been a fanatical housekeeper but now I had to watch my home be in need of cleaning most of the time. I felt very helpless and depressed because of this.

Depression became my constant state of being. I began to study nutrition trying to eat the foods that would help me have some energy. It was so frustrating not to be able to do the things I wanted.

I couldn't do any work on the outside of myself so I began to look within and work on the inside. I had a lot of anger and fear. So the Holy Spirit began to work with me on these.

Before I turned my life over to Jesus I was aware of myself as a physical being. I wore sexy clothes. I had a nice figure and I dressed to show it off. After I turned my life over to Jesus I became aware of myself inside. Myself, my thoughts, feelings and desires. My main desire now was to serve and obey Jesus.

I loved Him and wanted Him to love me. I realized years later that He had done what the bible stated He would do. He quickened (or had given life to) my human spirit.

My spirit, which was the real me. The part of me that came from God and would go back to Him. When He did this, I began to want to do His will, but the problem was that my sinful soul didn't want to give up the control of the body. So began the battle.

Everything I wanted to do the soul would fight back. The soul would win most of the time. I determined I would not become angry anymore but I couldn't stop myself. I would be angry and say something before I knew I was going to.

I would want to do something for someone or show love and comfort to people who were hurting but fear held me back.

If I wanted to buy something for the house, I would know what I wanted but when I got to the store I would think maybe I'd better buy the more practical thing. Then would begin the battle in my mind. Buy the one you want! No! Buy the practical or the cheaper one! I would become so frustrated I would sometimes go home with nothing or buy the one I didn't want and then be angry with myself. Every decision I wanted to make ended with me having an argument with myself. I was in a constant conflict, which made me more depressed.

I kept at it though. Trying to make myself not sin. Trying to do the right thing. No peace! No joy!

Little by little I began to win a battle. To get over something, to learn something new.

I began to realize that I wasn't just fighting myself but I was fighting satan too. I was trying to fight him but I had no power against him.

I also realized that I was terrified of him. I had never known about evil spirits until I read the Bible. I had seen satan as a child but had pushed that out of my conscious mind. Now I remembered and knew he was real and had evil spirits to control and persecute people. I would have nightmares about it.

For years I tried to fight these battles myself. I had so much tension that I had cramping pains from the back of my head all down my back into my legs and feet. I had to fight myself when I went past the liquor in the grocery store because I knew it would relieve some of the tension. That was one battle I won. I never bought any.

I began to have dreams in which I would say to someone, "I can't do it any more. I can't make it. It is too hard. I just can't do this by myself any more."

I got to the place where I was so depressed that I wanted to die. I woke up in the morning wanting to die. I felt as though I was going to die that I was under so much stress and depression. I had hypoglycemia but I didn't know it. I had hypothyroidism but didn't know that either. I had arthritis, gallstones and allergies. I was still trying to eat right thinking that would bring back my energy and trying to think the right thoughts to get over the depression.

One night I felt I was at the end of my endurance. I knelt by my bed and cried out to God in the Spirit. As I prayed, the Holy Spirit spoke to me and said that satan was trying to destroy me.

I knew I had no power against him so I fervently prayed that God would not let me let go of Him. Even if satan killed me or drove me out of my mind that God would not let me turn away from Him.

I felt inside myself that I was going to die or that my sanity was almost gone. I could feel in my head that if I let go just a little bit I would go insane.

I had a dream a few nights later that Jesus was explaining to me that I couldn't get rid of the depression and the desire to die with psychology. He showed me that satan was distorting my outlook on life and people. I thought the world was a terrible place; that all people were cruel and wanted to hurt and destroy one another. There was no love or happiness in the world. I used to think that earth was the insane asylum of the universe. There was no hope of anything but mental and emotional pain. Why would anyone want to live here?

I went to church one evening and the Lord gave me a message through the pastor. I had not told anyone about what had been going on but the Lord, through the pastor, said, "Because I had prayed to know Him and desired to follow on, He was going to set me free."

I had prayed not to let go of Him even if satan killed me or drove me insane and because of this God was going to set me free.

A few weeks later I was praying. I pictured Jesus in front of me and I asked Him what was wrong. I read my Bible every day. I go to church every week. I witness. I help people. I try to do right. WHAT IS WRONG?

I saw and heard him say, "Let Me do the work." As the days went by and I thought and prayed about this I began to get the understanding that I had been trying to clean myself of sin. I had been trying to change myself. I had been trying to follow all the rules and commandments.

I began to learn that I had done what some of the Jews did in Paul's time when he told them that they had put themselves back under the bondage of the law. I had put myself under the bondage of trying to change myself, of freeing myself of sin.

I would also try to change my husband, children and everyone else close to me. I thought I knew what was best for them and wanted them to do or be that.

I didn't want anyone to suffer because if they did, then I suffered too, so I tried to get everyone to avoid anything that I thought would cause suffering in their lives.

If my children suffered anything I would be in anguish. I would pray for the Lord to take away their suffering. One day I was doing this but this time the Holy Spirit spoke to me about it. He said, "You suffered to learn your lessons, now let them learn theirs."

I remembered the scripture Romans 8:28, "all things work together for our good." He reminded me what He had told me before that everything that happens is for our spiritual growth. We may think it is a catastrophe but it is for our spiritual growth.

Some people have too much pride that they have to live a life of degradation before they will admit that they are no better than their fellow man. None of us are better than anyone else. We are all sinners in need of God.

If we think we can live our lives without God we are living in pride and we will be humbled.

These humbling experiences are for our growth in the fact that as long as we live in pride we will suffer because it is a sin. If we sin, we suffer, so God allows humbling to come so we will see, admit, confess to God, and repent of it so He can then cleanse us of this destructive element in our lives.

It is God's will and goal all the time that we won't have to suffer. Just as I would try to tell my family not to do this or that because I knew if they did they would suffer because of it. I loved them and didn't want them to suffer. God is the same. He loves us. He doesn't want us to suffer the natural consequence of sin.

One of my daughters married a man who would not work. He wanted to be taken care of and have no hardship or upsets in life so my daughter lived a life of abuse and deprivation.

She came to my house one day wanting help. The baby was out of formula. They were out of food and money. She was angry with God that she was in that situation.

I felt God was checking me to not help her but I did it anyway. I took her to the grocery store and bought her some groceries, a case of baby formula and gave her money to buy herself a pair of shoes, which she badly needed. On my way home I was worried she would turn away from God. I prayed to Him, "Oh God, please don't let her turn away from You. Please let her turn to You."

He said to me loud and clear, "Why should she? She has you." So many people become dependent on their parents and the parents keep them there by solving the children's problems for them. This then causes the children to go through more suffering because they take the easy way out and turn to the parents or others to help them out of their problems instead of turning to the Lord and letting Him help them grow up. Others have such a hard life they feel helpless and inadequate to work out their problems.

I went through that myself. I would try to find an easy way out of every problem instead of facing it and working through it myself. I'd try to get someone else to do it for me.

The Lord finally showed me this and told me that as long as I tried to take the easy way out, I would just make life harder for myself.

If we will give our lives to Him, He will help us become the responsible, confident and capable adults we should be.

He taught me if our parents make all of our decisions for us as we grow up, we would not develop a confidence in our ability to make a right decision. My mother's verbal abuse was why I feared making a decision.

Some people withdraw within themselves and live in quiet frustration never telling the other person how they feel, but doing things to show them or in anger they get even. Maybe the wife will burn the toast or forget to run an errand the husband asked her to or ruin his favorite shirt or pants. We will manifest some way the things going on the inside of us. The husband may cut down the wife's flowers when he mows the grass or forget what she asks him to pick up at the grocery.

We have lost the confidence in taking responsibility for ourselves. We then look for someone to take responsibility for us. A lot of times we will turn to one after another trying to find someone to solve our problems for us, take care of us, take the blame when we make a mistake. We don't want the pain of guilt.

When my husband died I was forty-eight years old. After being controlled all those years, I was almost helpless or felt that way.

Now Rob was five years old and he had seen his helplessness and in deep fear had a very strong desire to be in control. In my fear and helplessness, I let him control me too. All through these years I did not want to be controlled. I would become very angry but I didn't know how else to cope with it. The anger was with me almost all the time.

When my husband died, Rob and I both had the same problem. We both felt helpless. We were both full of fear. We both wanted to control the other and we both tried to control with anger.

Rob would not obey one thing I said. He did everything I told him not do and would do nothing I told him. We were angry at one another at times.

There were times I thought I would have a nervous breakdown. I had dreams about having one and about the ego being broken. I was afraid I wasn't going to make it. I felt trapped in the house and had no way out. I couldn't take him any place because he wouldn't obey me.

One day the Holy Spirit told me that satan made Robbie act the way he did because he wanted me to yell at Robbie and hurt him mentally and emotionally. The devil's main objective was to destroy us both, using one against the other.

A lot of us never learn to deal with life's circumstances in a healthy way; consequently we never have peace.

One day I was crying and praying about it. The Lord told me that He had sent Rob to help me. He said I would fight battles for Rob. I would not fight for myself. I had let myself be controlled all those years and I had tried to control others to keep myself safe from hurt but it hadn't work. Now I was in anguish because I knew I was hurting Rob with my anger and control.

People who need to control will automatically take the opposite view as the other person. We have to be the one who is in control. The one who has the final word.

The Lord showed me this and told me, “Do not control Rob and don’t let him control you.” I had both problems, which most people do. If not our actions we let people control our emotions.

If someone says or does something to hurt us we feel hurt. If they want to make us angry, we get angry. If they want us to feel guilty or embarrassed we feel that too.

The Lord showed me that I had to quit trying to control others (because we reap what we sow) and He would help me take back the control of myself.

The Holy Spirit also taught me that this was what Jesus meant when He talked in Revelations about he who overcomes. He said that it is God’s will for us to live in peace no matter what is happening on the outside of us. We do God’s will, not others, unless theirs is one with His. No matter what other people say or do, He wants us to obey His word. Do His will. Follow the instruction book and we will live in peace.

He helped me understand that when things are going bad for us. Or not the way we want them to. We get upset. Our emotions and thoughts are down in the negative. If they are going well, the way we want, our emotions are up, and so we are letting circumstances control our emotions. They go up and down depending on outward circumstances, but we live inside.

We let other people control how we feel. I did this all my life and didn’t realize it until the Holy Spirit gave me the understanding. I knew then I didn’t have to suffer just because someone wanted me to.

I was the one who lived in this body and I was the one to determine what happened on the inside of it. I didn’t just make that decision and then do it. It took a lot of practice but gradually I got more and more control of myself. I realized that I had let people control me like this all of my life. As for as I could see, everyone around me did too.

I learned that satan also controlled my thoughts and emotions. He would give me an upsetting thought and my mind would react by having some emotion that fit the thought. He would put a thought in my mind of something in the past that he knew I would feel guilty for, and sure enough, I would feel guilty or he would put a fear thought in it and I would have the feeling of fear. Once he got it started, he would keep it going as long as he could.

For years I thought I was thinking those thoughts. I thought they belonged to me. I would try not to think them or feel guilty or angry with myself for thinking them. I would try to fight them but to no avail.

I then said, "Okay, Jesus. This is a work of satan in my life so you take over and fight satan for me. If I can't fight him in my power and win, then you fight him with your power."

In a minute they were gone. The devil had been waking me up and tormenting me for years like this, but after that night, every time he would start that I would say, "Here he is again, Jesus. You take over and fight him for me." I would go back to sleep in peace because Jesus fought the battle for me and I could go to sleep in peace.

The devil kept trying that for a while but I had learned one of his wiles (tricks) and been taught what to do about it so he finally quit that one.

I had a problem with thinking critical thoughts of others. The Holy Spirit helped me see that I was doing that and helped me understand that as long as I was critical of others I would have something others could criticize me for.

I was overweight and felt that when people looked at me they were being critical of me. He helped me see that I would find something wrong in others so I could feel superior to them so I wouldn't have to feel inferior.

I asked His forgiveness and asked Him to cleanse me of this. He not only cleansed me of this but He got me over the inferiority, which satan had put into my mind also.

I was learning the difference of satan putting thoughts into my mind and my thoughts. I wanted only the kind of thoughts it spoke of in Philippians 4:8. True, honest, just, pure, and lovely, of good report, virtues or praise worthy. I began to be more aware of what went on in my mind.

All day, everyday our minds are working. We think thoughts all day. I began to spy on my own mind to find what kind of thoughts I allowed. If they weren't the kind I wanted, I would rebuke them in the name of Jesus.

Our mind has been trained to react the way satan wants us to react. For instance, if someone does or says something to hurt us, satan will put into our mind to feel sorry for ourselves and be angry at or hate the person who did the deed that hurt us.

He will then take it further and try to get us to do something to hurt the person for hurting us. If we can't hurt them back, we will desire over and over to hurt them. The devil knows that we reap what we sow. He knows that if we hurt someone else or even desire that they suffer, he is free to cause us hurt and/or suffering. He knows if he can keep us doing wrong then he has a right to attack us so he (or his evil forces) works to train our subconscious to do and be what he wants. If we walk or live in the flesh we will live out what satan has trained us to do and be.

Anytime someone said or did anything that hurt my feelings, I reacted with anger. The strange part was that I didn't allow myself to feel the hurt. Some how my mind denied and protected me from the hurt. It went directly to the anger. The Holy Spirit taught me this by an experience one day when I talked to a counselor. He told me he didn't like me because I refused to do some things he told me to do.

When he said he didn't like me, it seemed as though my mind quit functioning. I just shut down for a couple of minutes. I couldn't think. I couldn't speak. He didn't speak either for a few minutes but finally he asked me what had happened to me. My mind began working again to try to answer his question but I didn't know what had happened.

My time with him was up in a couple of minutes so I left. I walked to my car and got in but I couldn't start it. Suddenly I began to cry. I sat in the car and cried for about fifteen minutes. I was finally able to drive so I went to my friend's house. I told her what had happened and cried all the time I was there. I had always been this tough person who never let anyone see me cry. I was trying to explain why I was crying but didn't really understand why myself.

The next morning as I awoke the Holy Spirit told me what had happened. He said that I had been hurt very deeply in the past but didn't know how to deal with hurt so I denied it. I put it somewhere inside my mind where I could not see or feel it.

Hurt creates stress and stress not dealt with causes pressure in the nervous system. Hurt causes a lot of this pressure and needs to have a pressure outlet. My outlet was anger. I've seen many, many people who have the same one. Instead of seeing and dealing with the hurt, they bury it.

Years ago I knew a woman who had seizures. She had one at my house one day. As she fell to the ground, she held out one of her arms to me and pleaded for me to help her.

At that time I didn't know about evil spirits. I was helpless. I did not know how to help her.

Later the Holy Spirit gave me the understanding that she had a spirit of guilt that oppressed her from the past concerning sex. He told me that she kept this all inside. At times the guilt would build up in her until it put so much pressure on the nervous system that the nervous system would have a seizure to release some of the pressure.

After I learned this I happened to attend a church meeting where they were praying for the sick and afflicted. I had in the meantime learned much about satan and evil spirits. This lady came forward to be prayed for. I went to her, cast out the evil spirits of guilt and shame. I prayed for Jesus to clean out all the guilt and shame that they had put in her subconscious mind. Then I prayed for Him to replace that with peace.

He did! She never had another seizure. I had only prayed this from my human spirit. I did not say it out loud, but the evil spirits received it spiritually and in the name of Jesus, had to leave.

Jesus always knows what goes on inside us. He heard my prayer even though I did not speak it verbally. He granted my plea for her.

There was a young man who attended a church I attended. He would just fall down unconscious. One evening he collapsed. Some of us prayed for him. The Holy Spirit told me later the same thing about him, but his was caused because he felt guilty for hating his mother and hurting her.

I had not yet begun to cast our spirits. I knew about them but not my power in the name of Jesus. Alas, the young man had a seizure in a pond and drowned.

One time before all of this, I had an episode that I began feeling a pressure inside that became stronger and stronger. One day a little insignificant problem arose.

I sat down and began screaming. As I screamed, I thought, "Oh, God! I'm having a nervous breakdown." The Holy Spirit said to me, "No you are not, just scream until you don't feel like it any more." So I did that. For weeks

I felt very peaceful. Then the pressure began to build again. Again I had what I called a screaming fit. That night I dreamed I was talking to my pastor. He told me I had a guilt complex. That I felt guilty all the time. When anything bad or sad happened to anyone I cared about I would find some reason in my mind I had said or done something to cause it and feel guilty.

He then told me that I had felt guilt from childhood because Dad was abusive to Mom and my older brother, John. The devil had put into my mind, and I believed him, that because Dad didn't abuse me, but tried to defend me from Mom, that I had somehow robbed them of Dad's love so it was my fault he abused them.

The message so set in my subconscious mind that a spirit of guilt would control me. The pastor in my dream told me that he, representing Jesus in my dream, was freeing me of it immediately. I never had the pressure nor a screaming fit again.

It is very important for us, no matter how painful, to look inside ourselves and dig out the things about which we feel guilt, shame, fear or negative thoughts or emotions and let Jesus help us deal with it so He can free us of it. The devil wants us to hide things because he knows the damage he can cause us with them.

The Bible tells us to confess our faults to one another and pray for one another so we can be healed.

Hiding things only makes them grow like a cancer in our soul and spirit. We can confess anything to God. He already knows and accepts and loves us anyway.

Guilt is self-punishment and a tool of satan to torment God's children. God does not give guilt. The Holy Spirit will convict us of sin, but when we repent, the conviction leaves. Guilt goes on and on until we acknowledge it, get rid of the spirit and let the Holy Spirit free us of it.

Held-in emotions eventually cause damage to parts of our body. We cause a lot of illness to the body because of held-in negative emotions. It doesn't happen instantly but gradually does a little damage here and a little there.

The Holy Spirit told me one time that a nervous breakdown is a blessing because the person can no longer hold those things in. They have to come out for the person to deal with and get rid of them. A lot of us never learn to deal with life's circumstances in a healthy way; consequently we never have peace.

People bury emotions because they feel guilty for feeling what they don't want to feel. The Holy Spirit taught me that it is like a splinter. We need to get it out immediately so the wound will heal. If we leave it in the wound, it will become infected and cause trouble until it is taken out. We need to look at the hurt and ask ourselves why it hurts us.

What is in me that I was hurt by what someone else did or said? Why did I allow myself to be hurt? Did I say or do something that hurt someone else? Did I earn this hurt or embarrassment?

We do earn these by treating others badly. When we hurt or embarrass someone we have just created a situation in the future for ourselves to be hurt or embarrassed. This is true even if it is our family members.

The Bible states that God is no respecter of persons. Just because we are doing the hurting doesn't mean we can get away with it. We can justify or excuse ourselves all we want but we still must face the consequences of our actions.

I have been hurt very deeply at times and became very angry at the person but when I asked the Lord why He allowed it and was told it was because I had done something hurtful to someone else, my anger at the other person faded away.

Most people will not be honest with themselves. We are either too proud or we are afraid to look and see the bad because we will not like ourselves. We all have good and bad qualities. Some of us won't let ourselves see the good. All we see is the bad and we hate ourselves for it.

When I turned my life over to Jesus, I hated myself. I was ashamed of myself but I tried to keep that out of my mind because it caused much pain when I let it out so I could feel it.

I tried never to look at anything bad in myself because I would feel ashamed and be depressed for days. I finally got to being depressed all of the time. I saw nothing good in myself at all. Finally I let myself see that I was a good driver and swimmer.

It was very difficult to admit that to others because I thought they would think I was bragging about myself but I made myself do it and it reinforced the knowledge in my mind.

I began to understand that Jesus wanted me to confess (bring out and look at) the good as well as the bad. I would confess the bad and be ashamed for a while. I would fight the shame and it would gradually go away then bring out something else I was ashamed of and get over that. I finally realized that God forgave me for these. All I had to do was confess it, ask His forgiveness and he forgave me instantly. As I understood this I began to forgive myself. Some things took longer and were harder for me to forgive myself for but gradually I forgave myself sooner and easier.

I understood that by denying these things and burying them in my mind that the shame stayed there too. If I brought them out, looked at them, asked for forgiveness, received the forgiveness, then the shame left.

It was a cleansing process. As I got rid of the bad things the self-hate became less and less. The Holy Spirit began to help me remember some of the good qualities I had as a child. I remembered that I had loved people. I wanted to be helpful. I was protective of others. I could see that I still was that person. That was the real me, the spiritual me. I began to understand that I needed to look inward. To ask the Holy Spirit to help me find and be the real me.

I saw a little vision in my mind one day of a diamond buried in the earth. Someone was digging out the earth to get the diamond. I understood that the diamond was the real me, and the Holy Spirit would get rid of the dirt that covered it.

CHAPTER 24

Money

Matthew 6:24 says, "No man can serve two masters; for either he will hate the one and love the other; or else he will hold to the one and despise the other." You cannot serve God and money.

I knew a man who attended a poker party once a week. It was the highlight of his week. He would win money at times. He also got to spend time with his friends. I began telling him about Jesus. I had just turned my life over to Jesus. I knew I had found the reason for life and the wonderful privilege of serving a wonderful, loving Christ. I had found the joy of belonging to Jesus. I wanted everyone to know what life was all about. I began telling others so they could have what I now had.

I witnessed to this certain man a number of times. He eventually went to church with me and went to the altar and asked for salvation. His family eventually did too, but he still attended the poker games. His wife told me one day that he had dreamed he was supposed to read Matthew 6:24. After that he quit church and clung to the poker games. He did not want to hear anything about God or Jesus from then on. His life went downhill from there. His wife did not love him anymore. His health went bad. He became disabled.

He lived the rest of his life in much pain. The last few months of his life he was almost helpless to do for himself. He died alone. He made the choice that satan wanted him to because satan knew he could prevent him from following Jesus. We must be very careful to make the choice for God and not against His word and will. I pray you always choose God's Will and be rewarded, not against Him and suffer.

Money, money, money! We all need money. I worked at RCA when I gave my life to Jesus. Some Fridays I would borrow money for my lunch from my mother who worked there, too. One morning as I was getting ready for work, the word "Malachi" popped into my mind. All day long it would often pop in. It was as though someone would say the word inside my head.

I rode to work with my mother, as did four other people. One man went to church, so when we got into the car to go home, I asked him if there was something in the Bible about Malachi. He told me that it was the last book in the Old Testament. That evening I read it. I found that God really gave the Jews heck for not paying their tithes. I got the message. I began paying tithes and after that I would loan lunch money on Fridays.

When I paid my tithes, my finances went well, but once in a while, I would tell myself it was all right not to. After all, that was the Old Testament. It really was not necessary to give a whole ten percent, so I would give a few dollars. When I would do this, my finances would get messed up again. I finally realized the pattern and always gave the ten percent.

We all have our own thoughts and attitudes about money. I would go shopping and see something I wanted, but I would not buy it even though I had the money with me.

God teaches, or tries to teach us, about the wrong thoughts and attitudes we have. He finally gave me a dream about some of mine. I dreamed I was riding with an old farmer on a horse-pulled wagon. It was very full of hay. I told him I was like one of my brothers. I told him we were very poor and underprivileged growing up, and when we got a dollar, we did not want to let go of it. I thought about that the next day and realized the Lord was telling me (by the very full wagon of hay) that He has plenty. I did not have to be afraid to spend the money because He would supply more.

After that, when I shopped, if I had money to spare, I bought things more often. I went a little too far sometimes, and spent more than I should have, then be angry with myself. He taught me that when I felt depressed, shopping gave me pleasure, so I would go shopping to feel better. The problem was the better feeling went away when I got home, and I realized I had spent too much again.

I quit that after He gave me the understanding. My next lesson was on trying to save a lot of money. Of course, I could only save a few dollars at a time. I would get a little saved then someone would borrow it. They would pay me back a little at a time, if at all. I would spend that little bit before I got to the bank. I finally asked the Lord why I could not save any money. He gave me the understanding that I felt safer if I had some money saved.

I also had to have some extra in my purse all the time. I did not want to be without it. He showed me that money was my security. I did not trust Him to keep me safe. He kept me struggling with and/or about money so I would see my wrong thoughts and attitudes about it.

When our adopted grandson, Rob, was five years old, my husband died. We had no savings because my husband was the opposite of me. He spent every penny he made and then some. He had been in debt almost all of the twenty-four years we had been married.

Because we had adopted Rob, I was able to receive Social Security. I managed to stay out of debt until Rob became a teenager. I never went too far with it though. After Rob left home, I borrowed some money in my name for a close relative to help them buy a home. The scripture went through my mind that stated a person is a fool to take on another person's debt. Being the fool I was, I did it anyway.

Of course I was left paying the whole twelve thousand dollars myself. It is written in Romans 8:28 that all things work together for our good. I learned that is true. During the six years it took me to pay off that loan, I would sometimes have maybe one hundred and fifty dollars to last me the whole month after all my bills were paid. I never went hungry or never missed paying one of my bills.

When things went wrong, I had a repair bill or needed some extra money, the Lord would supply it. Oh yes, I never missed paying my tithes during these years. One time I needed one hundred dollars. I got a letter from the IRS saying they had redone my taxes and I had one hundred dollars coming back, and a check for a hundred dollars was enclosed.

One time I needed two hundred dollars. I asked the Lord for it, but if He would give me three hundred, I could do this other thing, and if He would give me four hundred, I could get these little things I had been wanting. The next week a lady called me out of the blue and asked if I would house and dog sit for four weeks at one hundred dollars a week, paid in advance!

Another time I was down to three dollars to last a whole week. This was during the time I had been making numerous trips to take my mother to Indianapolis thirty-five miles away during her cancer treatments and to Bloomington, Indiana, for surgery on her eye. My youngest brother, Mike, came by. He handed me sixty dollars. He said he and my other two brothers, Jim and John, had chipped in because I took Mom to all of her doctor appointments.

One time I needed two hundred dollars, so I asked the Lord for it. I had a fender bender accident. The insurance agent said my car was totaled. He asked me if I wanted to keep it and I said yes, so he paid me what he thought it was worth. I took the money, had my car repaired, and had two hundred and thirty dollars left over.

All through the years of paying the loan, if I needed money, someone would ask me to work for them. Something always came up. God even gave me six hundred dollars to have my furnace repaired. It was a gift from one of my brothers. I did not ask for it from him. He just gave it to me. Romans 8:28. The good that came from that was I learned the great and wonderful lesson that I have nothing to fear, because God will supply all of my needs. He is now my security. He has plenty of money. He can supply my needs.

He has taught me that people who have problems about money usually have the wrong thoughts and attitudes about it. Some think the more they have the more important they are. Some think it makes them better than less fortunate souls. Some use it to have power over others, i.e., children, spouses, employees, etc.

These people usually fall into hard times. They may lose everything. Sometimes they are cheated or robbed. People can go to church for years, but still have financial problems because they have the wrong thoughts and attitudes about money.

My husband has been gone for thirty years now. In all those years, the Lord has never let me down. When I needed money, He supplied it one way or another. Someone would ask me to house and dog sit, clean house or some other odd job.

When I borrowed the $12,000 for a relative, a lady at church asked me if I would fill in for a while at the real estate office where she worked until they found someone to take the lady's place that had quit. As it turned out, that job lasted six years until the $12,000 loan was paid off. During that time, when I needed extra money, the lady who worked all week would ask me to take her place while she had to be off or for vacation. It always came at the very time I needed money, and the pay always covered what I needed.

Some people believe we do not have to pay tithes because that was a law of the Old Testament. I have learned through the years that the rule still applies to our time, also, just as the Ten Commandments do. We do not have to follow all the sacrifices they were told to do because Jesus became the sacrifice for all sins, and all of our sins, but we still are supposed to obey His instructions if we want to live peaceful lives.

One reason we are instructed to give is to show we love God more than we love money. Another reason is to help us give up some of our selfishness. Still another reason is to learn to help others in need, and to help the church keep going to win people to Jesus and teach them God's ways.

People who love money will do many evil things for it. Many use money to do evil things. Money is just money, and we can use it for good or for bad. God's word is true. When it says we reap what we sow, it is true whether we sow good or bad. If we use our money for good, we will be rewarded for that. If we use it for bad, we will reap bad consequences for that. If we sin, we suffer. If we obey, we are rewarded. Simple, isn't it?

Scripture tells us that God loves a cheerful giver. One time I needed a lawn mower, but I did not have the money to buy one. One evening I went to church and was told someone needed something important. They took up a collection for the person. I gave what I could which was $10.00. I was very happy that I had been able to give something, even if it was just $10.00. The next week a friend bought me a brand new mower. In the Bible there is a scripture about some will reap 10 fold (Matthew 25). That is what happened to me because I was a cheerful giver. I was given a mower that cost $100.00

If we can only realize that God's rules apply to our everyday lives. Scripture tells us that God rules in the affairs of men (Daniel 4:17). God loves us and wants us to be happy to live peaceful lives. That is why He gave us the instruction book, to teach us how. Oh, if only everyone would read it and obey, our existence on this planet would be so much better.

First Timothy 6:10: The love of money is the root of all evil. For years I could not understand how that could be. Then one day I read that verse again for about the hundredth time and asked the question, how?

The Holy Spirit opened my spiritual understanding and showed me how. The next line in first Timothy explained it. When someone falls into the devil's trap of loving money, they will put the love of money before the love of God.

They stray away from living for God and begin living for self. The Bible tells us that the heart of man is deceitful above all things and desperately wicked. Jeremiah 17:9.

When we turn away from God to serve self we are capable of committing any sin. So we see the love of money turns us to following the wicked desires of our sinful heart, and that it is true that the love of money IS the root of all evil. We have strayed from our faith in all greediness. First Timothy 6:10 again. So we must examine very carefully our attitude toward money and be sure we do not put it before our Heavenly Father, who will supply all of our needs if we follow and serve Him.

Matthew 6:33 again. Seek FIRST the Kingdom of God and HIS RIGHTEOUSNESS and He will supply all of your needs.

Money is to be used for good, not to be desired above God.

He not only supplies our needs, but it tells us in Hebrews 11:6 that He is a rewarder of those who diligently seek Him.

CHAPTER 25

Husbands and Wives

First we will deal with the wives. I've been one and known many and have discussed husbands many, many times.

These are some of the rules I have learned: Wives, respect your husbands. Some marry for love, some security, some because of loneliness, some because they are afraid to be responsible for themselves, some because they fear if they don't marry the first one who asks them, they may never get another chance. Some are forced into marriage, some for other reasons.

I believe they all hope for happiness. They hope they will be loved and cared for. But when the husband shows selfishness or other faults the wife had not known about, they usually begin trying to change him.

He does not want to be changed (controlled). So he rebels. This brings on feelings of helplessness and fear and "he doesn't love me" thoughts." This causes hurt, shame, guilt, anger and revenge.

When she sees he is not the man she thought he was, she begins to feel superior to him. This is the beginning of a down hill slippery slope.

Here are some more rules: No superiority, no contempt, no fault-finding, no put downs, no deceptions, no controlling, no using sex as punishment, no running him down in front of others, no trying to control, no raising the voice.

We are to obey the Word of God. It tells us to be kind and tenderhearted to everyone. We use all kinds of tactics to change our husbands but this is the instruction I received concerning trying to change someone.

The Holy Spirit said to me, very emphatically, "You just love him and let the Holy Spirit convict him of his sins." We try to do the Holy Spirit's work, but do it the devil's way. This only causes destruction of the relationship.

The Holy Spirit showed me in a dream that men have the same emotions that women have. They get hurt, shamed, embarrassed, fearful and so forth. Wives sometimes (I was one) think men have no feelings except selfishness, sexual desires, and anger. We need to pray for God to help us understand (remember understanding is more valuable than gold or silver) and we are to pray for that. Then pray for wisdom, to know how to use the knowledge and understanding He gave us for our husbands and the other people we encounter.

Love covers a multitude of sins. When we really unselfishly love someone, we overlook his or her faults. We are centered on making them happy.

When we are centered on self, we are seeking for ourselves, what we refuse to give them. The Golden Rule, treat others as you want to be treated, because, since we reap what we sow, we will be treated as we treat others.

Loving and overlooking our husband's faults brings forth a happier marriage. He will be grateful for the kindness shown him. But controlling and finding fault does not make us happy.

The devil has his evil spirits there all the time to influence us to do his will, which is to destroy. Submit to God. Resist the devil and he will flee from you. All harsh words come from the devil.

Anytime we have used harsh words, we hurt and embarrass someone. James 3 tells us the tongue needs to be controlled. Read that whole chapter and see what a great need that is.

So to conclude, wives, let the hidden person of the heart with incorruptible beauty of a gentle and quiet spirit, which is very precious in the sight of God. Be ruler of your thoughts, emotions, words and actions. Walk in the Spirit and not the flesh and your marriage shall bring forth many blessings.

God's Will is the only thing that will make you happy.

Trust God to keep you safe. Don't try to do it yourself by trying to control others. IT NEVER WORKS!

It is sin to try to control others. We are not to rule over our husband or wife but we may and can rule over the evil spirit that is controlling them.

If they are being verbally or physically abusive we can bind the power of the spirit controlling them and command them to leave. ALWAYS do this in the name of Jesus and ALWAYS bind their power in Jesus' name.

Husbands, these rules apply to you also. No superiority, no faultfinding, no put-downs, no contempt and so forth.

First Peter 3:7, "Husbands, dwell with your wife with understanding, giving honor to the wife as to the weaker vessel and being heirs together of the grace of life so your PRAYERS MAY NOT BE HINDERED.

First Peter 3:10-12, "He who wants to love life and see good days let him refrain his tongue from speaking evil, and his lips from speaking deceit. Let him turn away from evil and DO GOOD. Let him seek peace and pursue it. For the eyes of God are on the righteous, and His ears are open to their prayers; but the face of God is against those who do evil." Hurting others is evil.

Ephesians 5:25, "Husbands, love your wife just as Christ also loved the church and gave Himself for her (Husbands, give your life for your wife, put her first before self) that He might sanctify and cleanse her with the washing of water by the Word.

Verse 28: So husbands ought to love their own wives as their own bodies; He who loves his wife loves himself.

Verse 33: Let each one of you in particular so love his own wife and see that the wife respects her husband.

When a woman has a good husband and feels that he loves and will protect her, she will not fear. She will feel secure and therefore will have no reason to try to change or control him.

Fear causes the desire to control. The men who are insecure fear that their wives may betray them and will become controlling. Some will even try to beat their wives into submission.

If the wife leaves, he feels he has lost complete control. This may cause him to lose complete control of himself and kill his wife. The devil has destroyed two people, plus the children they may have had, by programming them to destruction.

God's way is to love, be kind, tenderhearted, unselfish. To be centered on the wife and not on self. If he helps her feel happy and safe, he will have a more peaceful life. We all need to read God's Instructions, obey them, live by them, and reap the rewards of obeying God.

If we sin, we suffer. If we obey, we are rewarded.

Women and/or men who have contempt for their spouse usually lose their sexual desire for them.

Remember, if you make someone feel good about themselves, they will want to spend time with you. If you make them feel bad about themselves, they will want to be somewhere else.

Read the Bible and strive to obey. Trust and obey. There is no other way to be happy in Jesus but to trust and obey.

CHAPTER 26

The Tribulation Period in a Nutshell

As you read this chapter, it is very important that you focus on the following promises of God.

Matthew 6:33: Seek FIRST the kingdom of God and HIS RIGHTEOUSNESS, and He will supply all of your needs.

Psalms 91 tells us that if we dwell in the secret place of the Most High, we shall live under His protection.

He will protect us from fatal epidemics, destructive happenings, or wars. It states that a thousand may fall at our side but it won't come near us.

Ten thousand may fall at our right hand, but the only effect it will have on those who are abiding in God is that they will see it with their eyes. It won't affect them.

Read and study all of Psalms 91. It is very encouraging.

Isaiah 41:10: Fear not, for I am with you. Be not dismayed, (look to the future with fear) for I am your God. I will strengthen you. Yes, I will help you. I will uphold you with the right hand of My righteousness.

Isaiah 41:1-3: Fear not, for I have redeemed you. I have called you by name; you are Mine. When you pass through the waters, I will be with you; and through the rivers, they shall not overflow you.

When you walk through the fire you shall not be burned, nor shall the flame scorch you. For I am the Lord your God, the Holy One of Israel, your Savior.

I had something like that in a small way, happen one time. I was cleaning a paint can and brushes out with gas. I was at my sink, which was close to my cooking stove. I heard a voice say to me, three times, "Take that outside." I don't know whether it was my guardian angel or the Holy Spirit. Whoever it was I did not obey. Then suddenly the whole area in front of me burst into flames. I had gas on my hands and part way up my forearms. They, and the front of my blouse, were on fire. Covered with flames. I ran from one end of my house to the other, to the phone to call the fire department. When I reached for the phone, I thought, "I won't call them. Maybe I can put it out myself." So I ran back to the kitchen, my hands still covered in flames.

When I got back to the kitchen, the fire had gone out because it was the fumes from the gas that had burst into flames.

I was relieved, but wondered how to put out the fire on my hands and the front of my blouse.

Without really thinking, (I believe my guardian angel or the Holy Spirit took over), I suddenly crossed my arms over my chest and put my hands on the opposite side, under my arms and across where my blouse was burning. Every bit of the flames instantly went out.

The amazing thing to me was, that in all the time I was on fire, I never felt any heat. My hands were fine. Nowhere on my face was burned by the flames from the front of my blouse shooting up, although I did have a small scorched place on my blouse. By experience I know God can protect us from the effects of fire. I understood then of Daniel in the fiery furnace and I sure thanked the Lord for protecting me in my disobedience and stupidity.

My point in giving the promises God gave us of His protection is for your peace of mind after reading the rest of this chapter.

I had a conversation recently about the time of the tribulation period. I had my own ideas about it but never really studied it. After the conversation, however, it kept coming to my mind. For years I have read the New Testament all the way through, then began reading it again. Wouldn't you know that the time for me to read the book of the Revelation came up during my time of wanting to know the truth about the tribulation period?

This time when I read it, I asked the Holy Spirit to help me understand it. As I read, more and more questions came to my mind. This chapter will be of what I believe the Holy Spirit told and/or gave me the understanding.

The first thing I'll write is that the mark of the beast will not be a stamp put ON our forehead or ON our right hand. It will be put IN them.

It will be some kind of very small chip that carries information. It will be read by computers at the checkout in businesses. The time will come when we will not be able to buy or sell without this chip. These little chips are already being put into people's pets and I heard on TV that they are putting them into babies born to welfare people to keep track of foster children.

My next big question was would the followers of Jesus have to go through the tribulation period? I believe, from reading Matthew 24 that we are in the beginning of sorrows now. Matthew 24:8. Read the whole chapter of Matthew 24. The time of the tribulation period will be right after the time of sorrows. The time of sorrows is to show people how helpless we are in this world. It is also for people to see how destructive the love of money and possessions is to our spiritual growth.

To see how unimportant they are compared to helping people in need. It is to learn to put our hearts to caring for, and helping others, rather than just focusing on our own comfort and pleasure.

In other words, it is to help us see our helplessness; turn to Jesus, if we haven't already, and to help us grow spiritually. Everything is for our spiritual growth.

Now comes the big question. Will saved people go through the tribulations? The Holy Spirit led me to study this. I finally put down the Bible and asked Him, "Will saved people go through the tribulation period?"

He told me that those who are alive at this time would go through it. He said the whole world would be tested. Revelation 3:10: God said He let the Israelites go through the wilderness for forty years to humble and test them. The saved will be tempted to renounce Jesus. This will be their time of testing. The days of tribulation will be shortened because of those who refuse to renounce Him. They are the elect.

In Luke 3:16 it tells us that Jesus will baptize us with the Holy Ghost and with FIRE. We will be tested (tried) as by FIRE. (First Peter 1:7) during this period.

Those who take the mark of the beast will suffer the wrath of God. They will suffer torment forever.

Now at the time the tribulation period ends, is when the catching away occurs. We will not have to experience any of the wrath of God. Jesus catches us away before it begins.

Even during the wrath of God, men will still refuse to repent of their sins. They will curse God. They will be cast into the lake of fire and be tormented forever and ever.

Those who die for Christ will get to live forever in Heaven. The rest will live on the new Earth.

After the wrath of God has gone on until God wants it stopped, Jesus will come back and take over the rule of the Earth. He will rule for a thousand years. He will rule with a rod of iron. No more grace period if we sin. We will be punished immediately.

There is much more in the book of Revelation but my reason for this chapter is to write what I believe the Holy Spirit gave me about the tribulation period.

Revelation 20: 4 & 5 tells us that only the ones who were beheaded for their witness for Jesus and for the word of God who had not worshipped the beast or his image and had not received his mark in their foreheads or in their hands and they lived and reigned with Christ for a thousand years. But the rest of the dead did not live again until the one thousand years was finished.

I hope we all realize how important it will be to choose death in and for Jesus, than to choose the mark of the beast and live through the wrath of God and then torment in the lake of fire forever.

To die for Christ is gain.

Psalms 34:17 says, "The Lord hears His people when they call to Him for help. He rescues them from all their troubles. The Lord is close to the BROKEN HEARTED; he rescues those whose spirits are crushed.

CHAPTER 27

Perfection

This subject is one I have gotten more opposition on than any other. Even though it tells us to be, and explains what it is, and how to become perfect in God's instructions. Here are some of the scriptures God gave us about it.

Colossians 3:14, "And above all these things put on love, which is the bond of perfectness." Colossians 4:12, "Epaphras who is one of you, a bond-servant of Christ greets you, always laboring for you in prayers that you may stand perfect and complete in all the will of God."

Second Corinthians 13:11, "Be perfect, be of good comfort, be of one mind, live in peace; and the God of love and peace shall be with you." Ephesians 4:13, "Until all come in the unity of the faith, and the knowledge of the Son of God, unto a perfect man, unto the measure of the stature of the fullness of Christ."

Colossians 1:28, "Whom we preach, warning everyone and teaching everyone in all wisdom, that we may present everyone perfect in Christ Jesus." Hebrews 6:1, "Therefore leaving the principles of the doctrine of Christ, let us go on unto perfection." James 1:4, "Let patience have her perfect work that you may be perfect and complete (mature).

In Matthew 5:43-48 God explains what perfection is. "Love your enemies, bless those who curse you, do good to those who hate you and pray for those who spitefully use and persecute you." That is a perfect and mature Christian.

To be mature, we must grow from birth. When we ask Jesus to save us from the power of satan and sin, we become newborn babes in Christ. He begins the work of growing, teaching, healing, and cleansing. Some people grow faster than others. Some never grow because they refuse to let Jesus or the Holy Spirit have control of their lives.

Jesus will not force us to be under His control. He tries to get us to yield to Him. He will not force us into submission. Those who refuse to yield and grow prevent many, many gifts and blessings from being manifest in their lives. They go on year after year struggling against life. They never are at peace, which is one of the blessings we prevent in our life because we refuse to obey. They may become angry with God or discouraged and quit trying because they have made life so hard for themselves, but they blame God.

They are like children in school who refuse to do their lessons, and then blame the teacher for giving them low grades. Hebrews 2:10 tells us that Jesus became perfect through suffering. He did not give up on or become angry with His father. He endured because of His love for us. If we want to become a perfect and mature Christian, we must endure what suffering it may take to reach that goal.

Never give up; examine yourself to find what it is that is causing you to suffer. A TV personality in years past would say "The devil made me do it!" Well, the devil puts pressure on us to do his will, but we must have some sin that he can use to influence us. We need to find what that sin is.

What is in our lives that prevent us from loving our enemy? What is there that prevents us from blessing those who curse us, or doing good to those who hate us, or praying for those who spitefully use us, and persecute us. It is sin in our lives! We should humble ourselves and, miracle of miracles, admit that we are wrong sometimes.

The book of Hebrews tells us that there is a rest in God we can obtain. We can live in peace and rest from our working and let God do the work for us. God's word is TRUE. HE KEEPS HIS PROMISES. But we need to meet some requirements. We must read the instruction book everyday, pray for His cleansing and help us endure it.

Hebrews 10:22, "Let us draw near with a true heart in full assurance of faith and having our hearts sprinkled from an evil conscience and our bodies washed with pure water." Verse 23, "Let us hold fast the confession of our hope without wavering, for He who promised is faithful." Verse 24, "And let us consider one another in order to stir up love and good works."

We are not saved by good works. We are saved to do good works. When we come to Christ, our righteousness is as filthy rags. We will suffer many things to bring us to the perfection Jesus told about. We will be chastised for the sins we commit after salvation. We are chastised by God for the same reasons we are chastised by our earthly fathers, which is to correct and bring us into the kind of person we should be. FOR OUR GOOD.

Matthew 22:37-40 is where Jesus told us to love God with all our heart, mind, soul and strength, and our neighbor as ourselves. This is perfection. These are the greatest COMMANDMENTS. Of course none of us can do this on our own. We must yield to the Holy Spirit and He will create this love in us as He cleanses us of the sin that has prevented it in the past. IT IS POSSIBLE or God would not have commanded us to do it.

The first fruit that we are told that the Holy Spirit produces in us is love (Galatians 5:22). Some people think being perfect is never making a mistake, never forgetting anything, never losing anything, and so forth. It is simply Matthew 5:44.

That should be our first desire (Matthew 6:33) to seek God's kingdom and His qualities, FIRST, above everything else. Second Peter 1:3&4, "His divine power has given to us all things that pertain to life and Godliness through the knowledge of Him who called us to glory and virtue." Verse 4: "By which was given to us exceedingly great and precious promises, that through these you may be partakers of the divine nature (Jesus' nature).

This divine nature can be created in us by God's power through the Holy Spirit. We must confess and repent of sin and yield ourselves to Him. Matthew 5:48, "Be ye perfect as your Father in Heaven is perfect."

About the Author

Esther Suter was born into what she calls a dysfunctional, dysfunctional family. Consequently, this greatly and negatively affected her three brothers and her.

She grew up feeling inferior and unloved and she became a dysfunctional person. She struggled through life until she finally turned her life over to Jesus.

After this, she felt cleansed and healed and was compelled by what He was teaching her. She learned about and grew in spirit and in her life. The Lord eventually instucted her to start a teaching program on a local TV station and she was on television for five years. Her ministry was teaching the way to liberation.

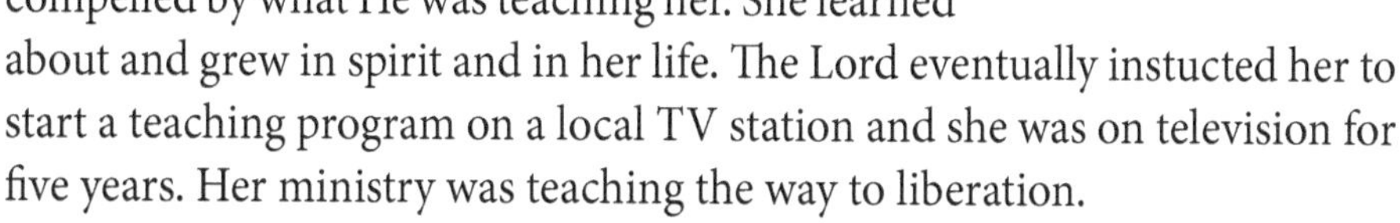

God has used her to win souls, heal the sick, and teach people about His kingdom to free them from satan's oppression.

She believes that all who accept Jesus as their Savior have the power to do what He wants them to do.

She has been a widow for many years and calls herself an "everyday" person who heard God's instruction and wrote a book aimed at teaching people that we are all in a spiritual battle, but all who know Jesus have His power to gain the victory.

www.ingramcontent.com/pod-product-compliance
Lightning Source LLC
Chambersburg PA
CBHW071722120626
46550CB00001B/351
9781962402224